TEACHING FOR TRANSFER
Fostering Generalization in Learning

TEACHING FOR TRANSFER
Fostering Generalization in Learning

Edited by

Anne McKeough
Judy Lupart
Anthony Marini
University of Calgary

LEA LAWRENCE ERLBAUM ASSOCIATES, PUBLISHERS
1995   Mahwah, New Jersey   Hove, UK

Lawrence Erlbaum Associates, Inc., Publishers
10 Industrial Avenue
Mahwah, New Jersey 07430

Cover design by Jan Melchior

Library of Congress Cataloging-in-Publication Data

Teaching for transfer : fostering generalization in learning / edited
by Anne McKeough, Judy Lupart, Anthony Marini.
    p.   cm.
Includes bibliographical references and index.
ISBN 0-8058-1309-8 (alk. paper)
1. Transfer of training. 2. Stimulus generalization.
3. Learning, Psychology of. I. McKeough, Anne. II. Lupart, Judy
Lee. III. Marini, Anthony.
LB1059.T42 1995
370.15—dc20   94-41465
                                                          CIP

Books published by Lawrence Erlbaum Associates are printed on acid-free
paper, and their bindings are chosen for strength and durability.

Printed in the United States of America
10 9 8 7 6 5 4 3 2

Contents

Preface

Transfer of learning is universally accepted as the ultimate aim of teaching. However, achieving this goal is one of teaching's most formidable problems. Researchers have been more successful in showing how people fail to transfer learning than they have been in producing it, and teachers and employers alike bemoan students' inability to use what they have learned. And yet we see evidence of transfer every day—when students read a new book, when a competent tennis player rapidly masters the game of squash, or when a 2-year-old refers to a strange dog by the name of the family pet. Such examples of successful transfer, considered alongside numerous misses or near misses, highlight two educationally relevant points: Learning generalizes and transfer is not under our control.

Given the obvious importance of learning transfer, it is perhaps surprising that the field has not made more rapid progress toward understanding and facilitating it. However, recent advances in cognitive science have moved us toward the possibility of a deeper understanding of learning transfer, and several researchers who work within this tradition have developed approaches to teaching that aim for varying degrees of knowledge generalization. The relative success of these programs led us to invite several of these individuals to present at our Fall Lecture Series at The University of Calgary—a lecture series designed to bring our local educational community into direct contact with innovative conceptualizations of the teaching and learning process. Invited were Carl Bereiter, Joe Campione, Robbie Case, Don Dansereau, Mark K. Singley, and Mike Pressley.[1] We asked

[1]Videotapes of the lectures are available through ComMedia, The University of Calgary, Calgary, Alberta, Canada, T2N 1N4.

each to prepare a chapter, outlining his view of transfer, what we can reasonably expect, and how we can best achieve it. These comprise the present volume. Additionally, we have included an introductory chapter that frames the contents by tracing the historical development of the concept of transfer, highlighting current problems and concerns, and providing a brief overview of each chapter, as well as a chapter that examines the transfer literature in light of its applicability to exceptional learners and a chapter that examines learning transfer in the narrative domain.

Although the claims made by the authors for the method, type, and degree of transfer differ considerably, we see this as indicative of the complexity of the phenomenon. More than highlighting the unanswered questions and unsolved problems, we believe this diversity reflects a rich area of research, with multiple potential pathways. Taken as a group, then, the chapters convey a promising beginning in our efforts to achieve transfer of learning. Finally, we see a book that describes instructional methodologies that successfully foster transfer as long overdue and are optimistic that, from these investigations of transfer of learning, educators will glean ways to improve curriculum design and teaching.

ACKNOWLEDGMENTS

As with any project of this sort, the contributions of many brought it to fruition. We are very grateful for the financial support provided by the local school districts and The University of Calgary that made it possible to bring the presenters to Calgary. Specifically, we thank Bill Dever (Calgary Catholic Board of Education), Bill Dickson (Calgary Board of Education), Jim Brandon (Foothills School Division), Doug Courtice (Rocky View School Division), Brian Callaghan (Mount Rundle School Division), Bart Cant (County of Mountain View), Garry McKinnon (County of Wheatland), Alana Gowdy (Learning Skills Centre, Mount Royal College), Frank Oliva (Faculty of Education, The University of Calgary), and Lorna Cammaert (The University of Calgary Endowment Fund). We are also deeply indebted to M. J. Samuelson and Lorraine Templeton for their considerable assistance with all organizational aspects of the lecture series, Beth Sparks for her work on the video production, and to Chrystina Dolyniuk for her preparation of the indices. Finally, without the interest and commitment of our students and colleagues in the field this series would not have been possible. We gratefully acknowledge their participation.

Anne McKeough
Judy Lupart
Anthony Marini

The Challenge of Teaching
for Transfer

Anthony Marini
Randy Genereux
University of Calgary

Transfer of learning is widely considered to be a fundamental goal of education. When students cannot perform tasks only slightly different from those learned in class, or when they fail to appropriately apply their classroom learning in settings outside of school, then education is deemed to have failed. Accordingly, educators have for many years been concerned with how best to teach for transfer of learning.

Unfortunately, achieving significant transfer of learning has proven to be a difficult chore. Dating back to the beginning of this century, the research literature on transfer is replete with reports of failure. Thorndike and Woodworth (1901) found little evidence for general transfer of training on estimation and perceptual tasks. Thorndike (1924) discovered, contrary to the popular doctrine of formal discipline, that studying difficult subjects such as Latin and mathematics did not generalize to better performance on other memory and reasoning tasks. Reed, Ernst, and Banerji (1974) observed little transfer of learning from one form of river-crossing problem to another, as did Hayes and Simon (1977) from one version of the tower of Hanoi puzzle to another. Other studies of analogical problem solving have confirmed that students often fail to spontaneously transfer what they have learned about one problem to a structurally similar problem. This is so even when the transfer problem is presented immediately after the training problem (Gick & Holyoak, 1983), even when the solution strategy is clearly explained to students during training (Gick & Holyoak, 1983), and especially when the training and transfer problems differ in surface features (Holyoak & Koh, 1987). Research on classroom learning has similarly found that students typically show little ability to flexibly apply what they have learned in school to the solution of novel tasks (Nickerson, Perkins, & Smith, 1985).

Lest we present a distorted picture of the transfer literature, amidst the notorious reports of transfer failure have been some notable successes. These include Judd's (1908) early report of children transferring their learning of the principal of refraction to hitting submerged targets with darts, Katona's (1940) success at demonstrating transfer of strategies for solving card-trick and match-stick problems, and Palincsar and Brown's (1984) use of reciprocal teaching to foster transfer of comprehension strategies across a variety of tasks and settings.

The lesson to be learned from the many reported transfer failures is thus not that transfer is impossible. The failures certainly indicate, however, that transfer is not as easy to attain as we would hope, and that transfer does not occur in many cases where we might readily expect it. In short, we cannot take transfer of learning for granted. To ensure that transfer occurs we must come to understand clearly its nature and design our instruction carefully so as to facilitate it. The purpose of this book is to explore several promising contemporary attempts to do just that.

The challenge of understanding and effectively teaching for transfer has been taken up by the contributors to this book, each in his or her own way, and each with considerable success. As becomes apparent, the perspectives on transfer represented here are diverse. Although echoing some common themes, the perspectives reflect fundamental differences in theoretical orientation and considerable differences in opinion regarding the essence of transfer and how best to achieve it. To provide a framework for conceptualizing the essential differences and similarities among the perspectives presented here, we present a brief overview in this chapter of the transfer process and discuss several controversial transfer issues. We then preview the chapters to come by summarizing each author's contribution.

OVERVIEW OF TRANSFER

Broadly defined, *transfer* involves prior learning affecting new learning or performance. The new learning or performance can differ from original learning in terms of the tasks involved (as when students apply what they have learned on practice problems to solving a new problem), and/or the context involved (as when students apply their classroom learning to performing tasks at home or work). The basic elements involved in transfer are thus the learner, the instructional tasks (including learning materials and practice problems), the instructional context (the physical and social setting, including the instruction and support provided by the teacher, the behavior of other students, and the norms and expectations inherent in the setting), the transfer task, and the transfer context.

The learner comes to the initial learning situation with a set of personal resources and constraints including declarative knowledge, procedural knowledge, dispositions, and processing capacity. To succeed on a targeted transfer task, the learner must possess the knowledge, strategies, dispositions, and processing capacity required for that particular task. If the learner emerges from initial learning without the necessary resources, successful transfer will not be possible. The challenge for educators is thus to design instructional contexts and tasks so that learners do emerge with the necessary resources to succeed on transfer tasks. This requires, among other things, clear understanding of students' initial characteristics and of the requirements of each targeted transfer task.

The challenge of teaching for transfer does not end there, however. Successful transfer also depends on the learner's ability to readily access required resources when a transfer opportunity presents itself (Prawat, 1989), the ability to recognize (automatically or consciously) appropriate transfer situations (Prawat, 1989), and the motivation to take advantage of transfer opportunities (Pea, 1987). Even if a learner has acquired all the resources necessary for a particular transfer task, if he or she cannot easily access those resources, does not recognize the relevance of prior learning to the task at hand (e.g., because the task is presented in a very different context from original learning), or has no desire to take up recognized transfer opportunities, then transfer will not occur. Furthermore, learners should ideally be able to adapt and flexibly apply what they have learned to a variety of transfer situations (Perkins, Jay, & Tishman, 1993; Prawat, 1989).

The challenge of teaching for transfer is thus a demanding, multidimensional one; we must try to ensure that students acquire, can easily access, and can flexibly adapt the resources necessary for each transfer task, and that students can recognize suitable transfer situations and be motivated to transfer when the opportunity arises. Given the complexity of this challenge, it is not surprising that diverse views exist on how best to achieve transfer. Depending on their general theoretical perspective, different authors have emphasized different aspects of transfer and arrived at different conclusions about how to achieve it. Furthermore, even the question of how best to conduct research on transfer of learning is an open one. In the rest of this chapter, we discuss five crucial transfer issues and differences in opinion about each one. The issues are as follows: Should we focus on tasks, learners, or contexts in teaching for transfer? What extent of transfer can we reasonably expect to achieve? What should we teach in order to enhance transfer? How should we teach in order to enhance transfer? What research paradigms should we use to learn more about teaching for transfer?

KEY ISSUES IN TEACHING FOR TRANSFER

Should We Focus on Tasks, Learners, or Contexts?

As just noted, the basic elements involved in transfer are the learner, the training and transfer tasks, and the training and transfer contexts. Researchers from different theoretical perspectives have tended to focus on different combinations of these elements. Stimulus–response (S–R) psychologists, with their belief in external stimuli as the primary source of knowledge and their rejection of the study of unobservable internal processes, have, not surprisingly, emphasized the role of task stimuli in the transfer process. Thorndike's (1913; Thorndike & Woodworth, 1901) well-known identical elements theory of transfer, for example, is essentially a theory of task features—the higher the proportion of identical elements between two tasks, the greater the likelihood of transfer from one task to the other. Similarly, traditional verbal learning theorists focused on the match between encoding cues inherent in the initial learning task and retrieval cues available in the transfer situation (Cormier, 1987).

Theorists from other perspectives have paid more attention to the role of the learner in the transfer process. Gestalt psychologists such as Katona (1940), with their theoretical focus on perception and subjective experiences such as insight, have emphasized how transfer is influenced by the learner's perception and understanding of tasks and their solutions. This emphasis on internal processing of tasks has also been a trademark of information-processing theorists. For example, Gick and Holyoak (1987) concluded that the key determinant of transfer from one task to another is not actual similarity of the tasks, as Thorndike had maintained, but rather *perceived* similarity of the tasks from the viewpoint of the learner. Other information-processing theorists have focused on the processing strategies that learners use and how they can be improved to enhance transfer of learning (Pressley, Snyder, & Cariglia-Bull, 1987; Sternberg, 1986).

A different kind of emphasis on the learner has come from developmental theorists. These theorists focus on the child's level of cognitive development and how it interacts with instruction. Case and his colleagues (Case, 1992; Griffin, Case, & Capodilupo, chapter 6, this volume; McKeough, chapter 7, this volume) are among those who have stressed that we must take into account the existing knowledge structures and processing capacity limitations of children when developing curricula and designing instruction.

The other major element of transfer, context, has traditionally received the least attention from North American theorists (Pea, 1987). With the recent emergence of the sociocultural perspective in North America, however, there has been a surge of interest in the role of context in learning and development (e.g., Broughton, 1987; Cole, 1986; Kessen, 1979; Rogoff, 1990; Wertsch & Kanner, 1992). Building largely on the seminal work of Russian psychologist Lev Vygotsky (1962, 1978), many contemporary authors have come to view social contexts, rather than individual learners or tasks, as the most important element of learning and transfer. For example, Rogoff (1990) argued that most of what children learn about how to think and act in various settings comes not from formal schooling but from informal apprenticeships in everyday settings, settings characterized by rich social interaction with parents, siblings, and peers. Rogoff and others (e.g., Collins, Brown, & Newman, 1989) accordingly proposed that we should transform formal educational contexts into contexts of cognitive apprenticeship. In a similar vein, Pea (1987) argued that to enhance transfer of learning we must take into account and design thoughtfully the sociocultural contexts of formal education.

In summary, at one time or another the importance of each basic element of transfer—task, learner, and context—has been emphasized by educational theorists. Given that each element plays a key role in the transfer process, taking all three into account when designing instruction is most advisable. A trend in this direction, toward a more wholistic approach to achieving transfer, is apparent in many of the chapters in this book.

What Extent of Transfer Can We Reasonably Expect to Achieve?

In designing instruction for transfer of learning, a key issue is the extent of transfer we can expect. Can we expect students to transfer their classroom learning to very different tasks and contexts, or is transfer to relatively similar tasks and contexts all we can reasonably hope to achieve?

Unfortunately, it is difficult to provide a clear-cut answer to this question of how extensive transfer can be. One reason is that empirical tests of instructional programs designed to achieve extensive transfer have been lacking (Larkin, 1989). Another reason is that cases of transfer failure are inconclusive, in that failures may reflect inappropriate teaching rather than inherent limits to the transfer of learning.

Perhaps most importantly, there is considerable conceptual confusion concerning extent of transfer. Various phrases are used freely to characterize degree of transfer, including "near versus far," "specific versus general," "within-domain versus cross-domain," and "cross-task versus cross-domain." Rarely, however, are these terms consistently defined. One fundamental difficulty is that little agreement exists on how to define *task* and *domain* and no standard classification scheme exists for splitting up tasks into domains (e.g., Ennis, 1990; McPeck, 1990). One researcher may thus identify two tasks as belonging to the same domain, whereas another describes the tasks as belonging to different domains. As a result, what some researchers describe as cross-domain, far transfer, others may define as cross-task, within-domain, near transfer.

Although it is beyond the scope of this chapter to attempt to redress this state of affairs, a few points of clarification do seem in order. First, it is important to consider both task and context variables when determining extent of transfer. Ideally, each case of transfer would be clearly described in terms of extent of both cross-task transfer (the degree of difference between the training and transfer tasks) and cross-context transfer (the degree of difference between the training and transfer contexts).

Second, it is important to clearly distinguish between the distance and the generality of transfer. Distance of transfer can be defined as the degree of difference between the training and transfer tasks or contexts. Using cross-task transfer as an example, the more similar the tasks (e.g., two almost identical math problems), the nearer the transfer, and the more different the tasks (e.g., a language arts and a math problem), the farther the transfer. The generality of transfer, on the other hand, is a measure of the breadth of transfer, that is, the number of different tasks or contexts to which original learning is successfully applied. An example of general transfer across contexts would be applying a memory strategy learned in one class to aiding one's memory in several other contexts, including other classes, at home, at work, and at different social events. Specific transfer in this case would be applying the memory strategy in only one of these other contexts and not the others.

To summarize, a clear and complete description of extent of transfer would specify the amount of cross-task and cross-context transfer in terms of both the distance and generality of transfer. Given this framework, extent of transfer can conceivably range from near, specific, one-dimensional transfer (involving one task or context only slightly different from original learning), to the opposite extreme of far, general, multidimensional transfer (encompassing a wide variety of tasks and contexts very different from original learning). Returning to the substantive issue at hand, where within this range can we reasonably expect to find the results of effective teaching for transfer? That is, what extent of transfer can we realistically expect to attain?

As noted at the outset of this chapter, this issue has been vigorously debated since the beginning of this century. Contemporary views of the potential extent of transfer continue to reflect an extremely broad range of opinion. At the identical elements end of the spectrum are those who, in direct opposition to the notion of powerful general heuristics, argue that a multitude of subareas of expertise exist, each with its own unique set of required knowledge and strategies, and each stored as a compartmentalized microstructure in memory (e.g., Chi, 1988). These authors believe that only near transfer (i.e., within each limited subarea) can be reasonably expected. A similar view is held by proponents of situated learning (e.g., Brown, Collins, & Duguid, 1989), who claim that knowledge is tied to the particular sociocultural context in which it is acquired (e.g., school) and tends not to be activated in other settings interpreted as distinct (e.g., everyday life).

At the opposite end of the spectrum are those who maintain that there are some generally transferable items that can be fruitfully taught, including learning skills, metacognitive strategies, general dispositions, communication skills, and idea generation techniques (Bereiter, chapter 2, this volume; Campione, Shapiro, & Brown, chapter 3, this volume; Perfetti, 1989; Pressley, chapter 8, this volume; Perkins, Jay, & Tishman, 1993; Sternberg, 1985). For example, Weber and Perkins (1989) proposed that although the effective evaluation of ideas depends on functions and criteria that tend to be highly domain specific, the generation of new ideas can be accomplished by applying relatively powerful heuristics that cut across domains. In the middle of the debate are those who believe in transferability of strategies of moderate but not universal generality (e.g., Larkin, 1989; Singley, chapter 4, this volume) and those who propose that extensive transfer can occur within each major knowledge domain (e.g., numerical, spatial, or social domain) but not across domains (e.g., Case, 1992; Dansereau, chapter 5, this volume; Griffin et al., chapter 6, this volume; McKeough, chapter 7, this volume).

The issue of the potential extent of transfer is clearly one that will be actively debated for some time to come. Although the contributors to the present volume all believe in at least a moderate degree of potential transfer, the essence of this debate readily emerges from the diversity of opinions reflected in the chapters to come.

What Should We Teach in Order to Optimize Transfer?

Another challenge in teaching for transfer is deciding what should be taught. As already noted, the requirements of any transfer task include content/conceptual knowledge, procedural/strategic knowledge, and appropriate dispositions. Each of these major task requirements is a potential candidate for what should be taught in order to facilitate transfer. Adding to the complexity of the decision is the multiplicity of subcomponents from which to choose. Content knowledge can take the form of basic facts, core concepts, schematic relationships among concepts, and so on. Types of procedural knowledge include knowledge of the steps involved in performing tasks, performance strategies for completing task components, and metacognitive strategies for directing, monitoring, and evaluating one's own thinking and learning. Many different dispositions are conceivably relevant to transfer, including perseverance, openness to new experiences, willingness to take risks, self-confidence, and desire to perform optimally.

Of course, we need not exclude any of the above when teaching for transfer. Most transfer theorists would undoubtedly agree that it is not only possible but also desirable to teach a combination of various types of content knowledge, procedural knowledge, and dispositions. Nonetheless, many theorists have tended to emphasize the teaching of one of these over the others.

For example, teaching of strategies has been emphasized by information-processing theorists such as Sternberg (1986) and Pressley (Pressley et al., 1987; Pressley, chapter 8, this volume), by Palincsar and Brown (1984) in their program of reciprocal teaching, and by many proponents of the teaching of thinking and learning skills (e.g., Beyer, 1988; Lupart, chapter 9, this volume). Indeed, entire courses and programs dedicated to strategy instruction have been developed and implemented. A common argument for emphasizing strategies is that if one can identify and teach very general strategies applicable to a broad range of tasks (e.g., metacognitive strategies or generic problem-solving strategies), then very general transfer of learning can presumably be achieved.

Teaching of content knowledge instead of strategies has been vigorously promoted by other theorists, particularly those who have studied the development of expertise in particular domains. Their emphasis on content is based largely on the discovery that once having mastered the content knowledge of a particular domain, experts spontaneously display sophisticated use of effective strategies, including ones never explicitly taught (e.g., Chi, 1988). These theorists also maintain that without requisite domain-specific knowledge, general strategies have only a weak effect on enhancing performance of most tasks. Other theorists have promoted the teaching of conceptual knowledge in conjunction with procedural knowledge, believing that both are essential to the transfer process (e.g., Case, 1992).

Still others have argued that the crucial ingredient in transfer of learning is a set of positive dispositions toward learning and thinking. For example, Langer (1989, 1993) and Salomon and Globerson (1987) stressed that we should help students develop a mindful (attentive, nonautomatic, and volitional) disposition to learning and thinking.

The contributors to the present volume represent a broad cross-section of views on the general issue of what to teach to enhance transfer. Some place most emphasis on strategies (Campione, Shapiro, & Brown; Lupart; Pressley; Singley), others on conceptual knowledge (Dansereau; Griffin et al.; McKeough), and still others on dispositions (Bereiter). They also reflect interesting differences in terms of which particular type of knowledge, strategy, or disposition should be taught. As one example, among those who emphasize conceptual knowledge, Dansereau tends to focus on detailed schematic knowledge of quite limited domains, whereas Griffin et al. and McKeough emphasize the "central conceptual structures" of much broader domains.

An additional dimension to the issue of what to teach involves the selection of the model to be emulated in terms of appropriate knowledge, strategies, and dispositions. Two main approaches to this problem can be identified. One is the novice–expert approach that strives to turn novices into experts, and therefore targets the characteristics of domain experts as what should be taught. The other is a developmentally oriented approach that seeks to move children up to the next level of cognitive development, and thus targets the characteristics of children at the next developmental level as what should be taught. The former approach requires extensive analysis of the nature of expertise in each domain of interest. The latter approach requires careful mapping out of the course of development in each domain. In this volume, both perspectives are represented, the novice–expert approach most notably by Campione et al., Singley, Pressley, and Dansereau, the developmental approach by Griffin et al. and by McKeough.

How Should We Teach in Order to Facilitate Transfer?

Determining *how* we should teach to optimize transfer involves a number of subissues, including the following. Should we teach for automatic transfer or transfer based on conscious and effortful processing? How explicitly should we teach students when and how to transfer what they have learned? Which instructional modes, learning activities, and knowledge representation formats are best for enhancing transfer?

As with the other transfer issues discussed here, various theorists have provided different answers to these important questions. For example, in terms of automatic versus effortful transfer, Salomon and Perkins (1989) identified two alternate routes that can be taken to transfer: the "low-road," based on extensive practice and automatization on training tasks; and the "high-road," based on deep and explicit understanding of training tasks. Echoing Katona's (1940) conclusion from many years ago, Salomon and Perkins argued against those who promote transfer via automatization of learning. They claim that although low-road learning can result in fast attainment of transfer, the resulting transfer tends to be very limited in scope and flexibility. In contrast, high-road learning results in slower attainment of transfer, but the transfer attained is much more extensive and adaptive in nature.

Regarding the explicit versus implicit issue, several contributors to this book, particularly those promoting strategy instruction (e.g., Pressley, Singley, and Campione et al.), believe it is crucial to not only teach relevant resources, but to also explicitly teach students when and how to use those resources. Otherwise, suitable transfer opportunities will go unrecognized and acquired resources will remain "inert." On the other hand, others including Bereiter, Griffin et al., and McKeough apparently believe that as long as new learning occurs at a deep enough level, then it will become so ingrained that transfer will automatically occur, without the need for explicit instruction on when and how to transfer.

In terms of instructional modes, learning activities, and representational formats, a variety of intriguing options for promoting transfer are recommended by the contributors to this book. The following provides an overview of the chapters in this volume and demonstrates the diversity that characterizes current thinking in the field of transfer.

OVERVIEW OF THE VOLUME'S CONTENT

In chapter 2, Bereiter presents a unique perspective on the issue of transfer by conceptualizing it as a disposition rather than as a mental ability or cognitive skill. In this sense, transfer is "no longer thought of as skill training or strategy instruction but something like character training." As an example of how one might begin to think of transfer in such a manner, Bereiter presents the Kolbergian dilemma of a poor man who must decide whether to steal medicine in order to save his wife's life. In discussing the issues, students generally come to the recognition of respect for human life as an important moral principle. What would constitute evidence of transfer in this situation? Bereiter argues that there are two distinct issues that must be addressed. First, is there transfer of the principle, that is, will students recognize new cases in which respect for human life is embedded? Second, will understanding the principle result in dealing in a reflective and principled way when the situation occurs in life? This question addresses not the issue of transfer of principle but of transfer of disposition.

In a second example, Bereiter describes a group of children discussing the notion that the world is round. As in the previous example, a principle emerges that in this instance can be identified as the gravitational principle and the realization that down refers to the direction of gravitational pull. In this case, the author argues that transfer of disposition refers to the act of thinking scientifically, which it is hoped, will transfer to other issues in the science class and to everyday events and situations. This may be a challenging task given that scientific thinking frequently is eclipsed by uncritical belief or superficial explanation. Bereiter underscores the importance of both transfer of principle and transfer of disposition, by suggesting that a "concept or principle is only achieved when it is incorporated so thoroughly in to the cognitive system that it becomes like a part of one's personality."

If, as Bereiter suggests, the challenge to educators is in the teaching of transferable dispositions, what prospects exist for success in this venture? From the traditional perspective of transfer across situations the prospects do not look promising. As the author points out, efforts to demonstrate transfer of character education and social skills training have proven disappointing. A more promising perspective involves transfer not across situations but of situations. For example, "learning to participate in thoughtful, critical and imaginative discourse in the classroom may not instill children with dispositions to think that way in general, but it may dispose them to seek out companions and situations for the same kind of discourse." As an example of how transfer of situations can actually occur in the classroom context, Bereiter reports on his work with the Computer Supported Learning Environments (CSILE). The example provides a very clear illustration of the manner in which transfer of situations might occur and the significant benefits such an act offers a learning community.

In chapter 3, Campione, Shapiro, and Brown emphasize the importance of the classroom setting in understanding transfer. Although acknowledging the contribution of the laboratory approach in our understanding of transfer, they argue that such an approach has been limited by conceptualizing learning and transfer as distinct processes occurring at different points in time. Moreover, the brief "training" phase in the majority of laboratory studies minimizes the possibility for "the development of any true understanding that would mediate transfer."

In the classroom setting the search for transfer, while potentially richer is much more complex and not likely to be constrained by the brief time frame used by laboratory studies. As the authors state "the understandings that lead to transfer (in the classroom) are typically built up over extended periods and learners may show evidence of transfer in a variety of ways." Within this context, the authors define *transfer* as "understanding" or the ability of learners to explain the resources they are acquiring and to make flexible use of them.

A critical driving force in the authors' work is the design of classroom practices that encourage students, teachers, and researchers to rethink the philosophy of learning that underlie those practices. Emerging out of this reflection is the design of the Fostering Communities of Learners program, which in the context of transfer includes: (a) metacognitive factors: students are made aware of the central importance of understanding and transfer to their learning, (b) an emphasis on discourse, (c) students' explaining to others what they are learning, (d) supporting the content being studied through extended analysis, and (e) practicing activities in the context of their intended use. The principal vehicles that guide both student and teacher activities are reciprocal teaching (a method of enhancing reading comprehension) and the jigsaw method (a cooperative learning activity that assigns each student a subtopic of the area under study), both of which provide the structure that underlies a collaborative learning environment. Through the use of such strategies the authors are able to demonstrate that there are many manifestations of transfer, ranging from the understanding of domain-specific concepts to the use of domain-general reading and argumentation. Moreover, they provide compelling findings that students exposed to a Community-of-Learners environment, containing the elements described earlier, demonstrate significantly higher degrees of transfer than students in control group settings. A valuable addition to the chapter is the inclusion of student responses and the wide range and complexity of academic content for which the authors successfully demonstrate transfer.

In chapter 4, Mark Singley argues for adopting the "new realism in transfer research," which is rooted in the situated learning movement. This orientation is in part a response to almost a century of research that has produced disappointing evidence for general transfer. The new realism movement adopts a more realistic view of what kinds of transfer are possible. Evidence is beginning to build that at least moderate levels of transfer are feasible using this framework.

Singley identifies three factors that contribute to the success of such studies and make them different from previous efforts. First, there is a recognition for the importance of an explicit task analysis as a necessary precondition in teaching for transfer. Second, there is a greater appreciation for the computational demands of applying abstract knowledge across domains resulting in a more modest expectation for the kinds of transfer possible. Finally, an enhanced role for the teacher is emphasized in which the teachers play a more active role in presenting the strategy to the student.

Against the backdrop described earlier, the chapter reports on attempts to teach abstract problem-solving strategies in the domains of mathematics and programming. The method of instruction involves a computerized model-tracing intelligent tutoring system. In such a system, problem-solving strategies are specified in the form of running cognitive simulations of ideal student performance. These simulations serve as the benchmark against which actual student performance is judged. A central characteristic of the model-tracing tutor is its facility to provide instruction as the student is in the act of solving the problem. Moreover, the system provides individualized feedback related to actual performance, not simply outcome. These features result in specific feedback and are effective in helping the student with learning impasses they might experience. Finally, as students solve problems with the model-tracing tutor, the underlying abstract goals or strategies can be reified, that is, made concrete as graphical objects in the user interface. As a result, the student is offered a mechanism for making explicit the goals and strategies that organize the actions taken. Making these components explicit forms the basis for possible transfer across problems.

By way of a more specific illustration, Singley presents an example of the model-tracing approach designed to teach algebra word problems. Consistent with the approach just advocated, Singley presents a cognitive task analysis and subsequent codification of abstract strategies for algebra word problem solving. The method of instructing students in three distinct strategies is presented and the effectiveness of these strategies is examined. Overall, the chapter presents a detailed analysis of how model tracing serves to promote learning and transfer and underscores the complexity and amount of effort necessary to construct learning situations likely to lead to transfer.

In chapter 5, Dansereau examines the derivation and the learning and communication value of derived structural schema. As a starting point, the author distinguishes the more familiar natural schema from the derived schema. According to Dansereau, natural schema are described as "relatively abstract categories or placeholders and their interrelations." Examples of such schema are face and building schema, which Dansereau argues are used without much awareness and typically in an unsystematic fashion. In contrast, derived schemas are best understood as consciously derived and labeled by experts. An example of such a schema is the DICEOX (i.e., *D*escription, *I*nventor and history, *Con*sequences, *E*vidence, *O*ther theories and *X*-tra information) theory schema that was developed by Brooks and Dansereau (1983) to help students in studying and recalling elements of scientific theory. In their study, half the students were trained to use DICEOX, whereas the remaining students received training in such skills as time management. Both groups were asked to study a theory passage related to plate tectonics and later were assessed on a recall measure. The results clearly indicated that students using the derived schema had better recall of the main ideas of the passage than did the control group. Dansereau includes the work of other researchers investigating the efficacy of derived schemas and concludes that the findings all converge to demonstrate the potential of derived schemas for enhancing learning and promoting transfer. The chapter concludes with guidelines for deriving structural schema and demonstrates the value of schema experts and content experts working cooperatively.

In chapter 6, Griffin et al. address the declining mathematical performance of North American students. As the authors point out, too many children are not acquiring the mathematical concepts and skills needed to function in our technological society. Moreover, the problems in mathematical learning are particularly evident in children from lower socioeconomic groups who enter formal schooling disadvantaged in this area and experience a slower rate of success compared to their more advantaged peers. Borrowing from the work of Ginsburg and Russel (1981), Griffin et al. suggest that the difficulties children experience in mathematical learning may be related to the increasing separation between their intuitive, informal understanding of mathematics and the algorithms required to succeed in formal mathematical instruction.

To address this issue, the authors have developed Rightstart, an instructional intervention program to help first graders understand the conceptual basis of addition and subtraction. The theoretical framework for the Rightstart program is linked to Resnick's (1983) suggestion that children represent the conceptual underpinnings of arithmetic strategies through the use of something like a mental number line. According to this view, such strategies as counting on one's fingers is essentially a means by which children transverse a mental number line to arrive at their answers. Poor mathematical ability in some children may then in part be attributable to the lack of a mental number line representation or, as the authors suggest, an organizing schema referred to as a central conceptual structure. More specifically, the authors argue that a "central dimensional structure" will transfer to a range of tasks that have different surface features but that share this underlying concept (i.e., a structure in which properties such as weight are represented as quantitative dimensions with two poles and a continuum of values in between might mediate children's performance on a wide range of quantitative tasks).

To address the question of whether such knowledge can be taught, the authors conducted two intervention studies using a math "readiness" curriculum that was designed to help students conceptualize the world in terms of quantitative dimensions. Two control conditions, one reflecting a traditional mathematical curriculum and one a reading readiness unit, were also used in the study. For Study 1, the sample involved children from three kindergarten classes of families recently immigrated from rural Portugal to Toronto. All children in the study were administered the number knowledge test designed to measure predimensional, dimensional, and bidimensional numerical understanding. Assignment to the treatment group (Rightstart program) or either of the two control groups (i.e., traditional math or reading readiness) was done using a ranked-ordering procedure with the lowest scoring students being assigned to the Rightstart program, the second lowest group to the traditional math, and finally the highest scoring group to the reading readiness intervention. The Rightstart group received training in all the components of the number line, whereas the traditional math group received some components of the Rightstart module but not those that were unique to the treatment intervention and critical to the development of a mental number line conceptual structure. Control Group 2 received instruction in a reading readiness module with no number training. In addition, five transfer tests, thought to assess the centrality of the Dimensional structure were administered to students. First-grade level instructional units in addition, subtraction, and musical sight-reading, along with tests to assess the effects of the reading readiness training, were also designed. In Study 2, the sample population was primarily from three inner-city schools in central Massachusetts. The procedures for Study 2 were similar to those employed in Study 1. The findings from both studies converged to indicate that children in the Rightstart program performed significantly better than those in the control groups on virtually all of the measures designed to assess skill attainment and transfer. Taken together the data supports the hypothesis that the Rightstart program gives children a central conceptual structure that enhances their ability to profit from instruction in formal arithmetic instruction.

In chapter 7, McKeough adopts Case's theoretical framework to explore the presence of a central conceptual structure in the domain of narrative. The chapter poses two questions. First, is there empirical evidence for a central narrative structure and second, can an instructional program be designed to facilitate the development of story composition and its transfer to social context outside the classroom?

In arguing for the emerging role of narrative within psychology, McKeough cites Bruner, who conceptualizes the narrative mode of thought upon temporal and causal ordering of events, those that take place in the physical world (i.e., "on the landscape of action") and those that take place in the mental life of the characters (i.e., "on the landscape of consciousness"). As she points out, children as young as 4 years of age possess at least limited narrative schema such as scripts for going to a birthday party. These stories use an action/event schema that maps onto states and events in the physical world but does not typically utilize the children's knowledge of mental states. By the age of 6, most children demonstrate the ability to coordinate both knowledge structures with the result that action sequences often contain reference to the mental states that underlie them thereby producing a simple version of Bruner's dual-landscape narrative. McKeough refers to the structure used by the 6-year-old as intentional narrative because the intentions of the characters motivate the action.

Following Case, she argues that the ability of 6-year-olds to coordinate both structures is thought to be related to a maturationally based increase in processing speed and exposure to an environment rich in children's literature. In order to test this position, McKeough undertakes two instructional studies designed to develop the intentional narrative structure. In the first, average-functioning 4-year-olds were provided instruction involving the use of a conceptual mnemonic to address the limited processing capacity issue thought to underlie the inability for these children to coordinate the two knowledge structures (i.e., action/event and mental state). In the second study, McKeough worked with academically at-risk children from lower socioeconomic neighborhoods who were thought to have the necessary processing capacity but who lacked the experiential base. For both studies, the explicit goal was to teach the intentional narrative structure and to produce transfer to conceptually related tasks.

The results of these two studies indicate a strong training effect for the target groups compared to control participants. Children involved in the instructional training showed a marked improvement over the period of instruction on the story measure as well as significantly stronger performance on measures of transfer to everyday social reasoning tasks. Taken together, the work of McKeough and her colleagues (Griffin et al., chapter 6, this volume) offer a promising direction in recognizing the value of central conceptual structures and their role in promoting transfer generalization.

In chapter 8, Michael Pressley and his colleagues provide an instructive and revealing example of how researchers and practitioners can collaborate to enhance instructional effects. For Pressley, it is a journey in which an empiricist rooted in the world of quantification confronts the limitations of that orientation and turns to the possibilities offered by qualitative methodologies. This metamorphosis, by no means absolute, is cast against the backdrop of Dickens' "A Christmas Carol," in which Pressley works through the frustrations of strategy research past, the promising emergence of strategy research present, and his great hope for transactional strategies instruction future.

At the core of the chapter is Pressley's new perspective on strategies designed to help readers extract meaning from text. This perspective, which Pressley refers to as "transactional instruction of comprehension strategies," involves teachers and students interpreting text with both substantially contributing to the actual course of the interaction. The roots of this new perspective emerged while Pressley was working on a chapter on reading comprehension strategies during Christmas of 1986. Pressley's review of the literature revealed that many of the studies focused on single strategies taught out of context by experimenters under artificially contrived conditions over brief periods of time. As he suggests, these characteristics fail to capture the complex interactive nature of a real classroom and are unlikely to inform either teachers or students engaged in developing reading comprehension strategies. In an attempt to uncover information that would be more useful to educators, Pressley set out to observe strategy instruction in several exemplary classroom settings. From these visitations a number of research collaborations emerged. Most notable were the programs at Benchmark school in Media, Pennsylvania and Montgomery County Schools. Pressley offers a detailed description of the teacher–student interactions at both these schools along with the philosophical and theoretical underpinnings of the strategy programs found in these settings. The observations and interpretations offered are made even more convincing as Pressley carefully guides the reader through the qualitative methodology he employs to understand the teaching of comprehension strategies within the natural setting of the classroom.

The findings of Pressley and his collaborators across both school settings indicate that effective reading comprehension strategy instruction involves long-term teaching with only a few new strategies introduced each year. Instruction typically took place in small group settings with teachers providing extensive guidance and modeling. Moreover, the value of each strategy in the development of skilled reading was emphasized. For both school settings, the strategies of prediction, visualization, question generation, clarification, and summary were central to the programs. The chapter is enhanced by the inclusion of a critical review of both the strengths and limitations of each strategy instruction approach. In addition to serving as a summary of effective strategy instruction programs, the chapter serves as a very useful blueprint for any researcher considering a transition from quantitative to qualitative research methodologies.

The development of self-regulation in atypical learners is examined in chapter 9 by Lupart. As the author states, studies on transfer have consistently shown that a student's self-regulation of cognitive and metacognitive strategies is an essential factor in facilitating learning and transfer. The features of self-regulation include the purposeful use of strategies and a self-oriented feedback loop to determine their effectiveness. Currently, researchers have focused their efforts on describing the mechanisms and motivation related to learner self-regulation. In addition, considerable interest has arisen related to factors contributing to a student's failure to self-regulate during a learning experience. Given the importance of self-regulation for all students, Lupart suggests that the study of self-regulation would benefit from a focus on atypical learners who have consistently demonstrated difficulty (i.e., students with learning disabilities or mental handicaps) or proficiency (students identified as gifted) in self-regulation.

Lupart addresses the issue of self-regulation through the presentation of four perspectives. As a starting point, she argues for adopting a dynamic versus static view of learners. In this context, dynamic learners are seen as active self-regulating and intrinsically motivated in contrast to a static view of learners, which casts students in the role of passive recipients of knowledge, skills, and strategies. A second fundamental perspective reflects Lupart's view that all students, including atypical learners, can and need to learn to self-regulate. The author builds on this view with the presentation of the studies of transfer with learners with mental handicaps, students with learning disabilities, and gifted students. In each case, unique learner characteristics and the impact of these characteristics on instructional strategies and ultimately transfer are considered. Finally, the increasingly recognized role of motivation and student attitudes are examined in terms of their impact on fostering self-regulated learning.

Taken together, the chapters in this volume reflect the complexity associated with the issue of transfer. A greater sensitivity to this complexity has given rise to ways of understanding and perusing transfer in a more focused and systematic method than has traditionally been the case. Perhaps now more than ever, teaching for transfer is crucial. Given the tremendous variety of tasks and settings that comprise our rapidly changing world, it is clearly impossible to directly teach each particular task in each particular setting that students will encounter in their everyday lives. Instead we must strive, as the contributors to this volume have done, to find effective ways to promote the generalization of learning.

Despite the diversity of the approaches presented here, each has achieved considerable success. Each one therefore represents a promising path to meet the difficult challenge of teaching for transfer. Collectively, the contributors of this volume offer a wealth of theoretical insight and practical guidance that should prove invaluable to educators seeking to enhance transfer of learning.

REFERENCES

Beyer, B. K. (1988). *Developing a thinking skills program.* Boston: Allyn & Bacon.

Brooks, L. W., & Dansereau, D. F. (1983). Effects of structural schema training and text organization on expository prose processing. *Journal of Educational Psychology, 75,* 811–820.

Broughton, J. M. (1987). An introduction to critical developmental psychology. In J. M. Broughton (Ed.), *Critical theories of psychological development* (pp. 1–30). New York: Plenum.

Brown, J. S., Collins, J. S., & Duguid, P. (1989). Situated cognition and the culture of learning. *Educational Researcher, 18,* 32–42.

Case, R. (1992). *The mind's staircase: Exploring the conceptual underpinnings of children's thought and knowledge.* Hillsdale, NJ: Lawrence Erlbaum Associates.

Chi, M. T. H. (1988). Children's lack of access and knowledge reorganization: An example from the concept of animism. In M. Perlmutter & F. E. Weinert (Eds.), *Memory development: Universal changes and individual differences* (pp. 169–194). Hillsdale, NJ: Lawrence Erlbaum Associates.

Cole, M. (1986). Society, mind, and development. In A. Siegel (Ed.), *The child as a cultural invention* (pp. 89–114). New York: Ablex.

Collins, A., Brown, J. S., & Newman, S. E. (1989). Cognitive apprenticeship: Teaching the crafts of reading, writing, and mathematics. In L. B. Resnick (Ed.), *Knowing, learning and instruction: Essays in honor of Robert Glaser* (pp. 453–494). Hillsdale, NJ: Lawrence Erlbaum Associates.

Cormier, S. M. (1987). The structural processes underlying transfer of training. In S. M. Cormier & J. D. Hagman (Eds.), *Transfer of learning: Contemporary research and applications* (pp. 152–182). New York: Academic Press.

Ennis, R. H. (1990). The extent to which critical thinking is subject-specific: Further clarification. *Educational Researcher, 19*(4), 13–16.

Gick, M. L., & Holyoak, K. J. (1983). Schema induction and analogical transfer. *Cognitive Psychology, 15,* 1–38.

Gick, M. L., & Holyoak, K. J. (1987). The cognitive basis of knowledge transfer. In S. M. Cormier & J. D. Hagman (Eds.), *Transfer of learning: Contemporary research and applications* (pp. 9–47). New York: Academic Press.

Ginsberg, H. P., & Russell, R. C. (1981). Social class and racial factors on early mathematical thinking. *Monograph of the SRCD, 46,* Serial No. 193.

Hayes, J. R., & Simon, H. A. (1977). Psychological differences among problem isomorphs. In N. J. Castellan, D. B. Pisoni, & G. R. Potts (Eds.), *Cognitive theory* (Vol. 2, pp. 21–41). Hillsdale, NJ: Lawrence Erlbaum Associates.

Holyoak, K. J., & Koh, K. (1987). Surface and structural similarity in analogical transfer. *Memory and Cognition, 15,* 332–340.

Judd, C. H. (1908). The relation of special training to general intelligence. *Educational Review, 36,* 28–42.

Katona, G. (1940). *Organizing and memorizing.* New York: Columbia University Press.

Kessen, W. (1979). The American child and other cultural inventions. *American Psychologist, 34*(10), 815–820.

Langer, E. J. (1989). *Mindfulness.* Reading, MA: Addison-Wesley.

Langer, E. J. (1993). A mindful education. *Educational Psychologist, 28*(1), 43–50.

Larkin, J. H. (1989). What kind of knowledge transfers? In L. B. Resnick (Ed.), *Knowing, learning and instruction: Essays in honor of Robert Glaser* (pp. 284–306). Hillsdale, NJ: Lawrence Erlbaum Associates.

McPeck, J. E. (1990). Critical thinking and subject specificity: A reply to Ennis. *Educational Researcher, 19*(4), 10–22.

Nickerson, R. S., Perkins, D. N., & Smith, E. E. (1985). *The teaching of thinking.* Hillsdale, NJ: Lawrence Erlbaum Associates.

Palincsar, A. S., & Brown, A. L. (1984). Reciprocal teaching of comprehension-monitoring activities. *Cognition and Instruction, 1,* 117–175.

Pea, R. D. (1987). Socializing the knowledge transfer problem. *International Journal of Educational Research, 11,* 639–663.

Perfetti, C. A. (1989). There are generalized abilities and one of them is reading. In L. B. Resnick (Ed.), *Knowing, learning and instruction: Essays in honor of Robert Glaser* (pp. 307–336). Hillsdale, NJ: Lawrence Erlbaum Associates.

Perkins, D., Jay, E., & Tishman, S. (1993). New conceptions of thinking: From ontology to education. *Educational Psychologist, 28*(1), 67–85.

Piaget, J. (1970). Piaget's theory. In P. H. Mussen (Ed.), *Carmichael's manual of child psychology* (Vol. 1, pp. 703–732). New York: Wiley.

Prawat, R. S. (1989). Promoting access to knowledge, strategy, and disposition in students: A research synthesis. *Review of Educational Research, 59*(1), 1–41.

Pressley, M., Snyder, B. L., & Cariglia-Bull, T. (1987). How can good strategy use be taught to children? Evaluation of six alternative approaches. In S. M. Cormier & J. D. Hagman (Eds.), *Transfer of learning: Contemporary research and applications* (pp. 81–120). New York: Academic Press.

Reed, S. K., Ernst, G. W., & Banerji, R. (1974). The role of analogy in transfer between similar problem states. *Cognitive Psychology, 6,* 436–450.

Resnick, L. B. (1983). A developmental theory of understanding. In H. P. Ginsburg (Ed.), *The development of mathematical understanding* (pp. 110–151). New York: Academic Press.

Rogoff, B. (1990). *Apprenticeship in learning: Cognitive development in social context.* Oxford: Oxford University Press.

Salomon, G., & Globerson, T. (1987). Skill may not be enough: The role of mindfulness in learning and transfer. *International Journal of Educational Research, 11,* 623–637.

Salomon, G., & Perkins, D. N. (1989). Rocky roads to transfer: Rethinking mechanisms of a neglected phenomenon. *Educational Psychologist, 18,* 42–50.

Sternberg, R. J. (1985). *Beyond IQ: A triarchic theory of human intelligence.* New York: Cambridge University Press.

Sternberg, R. J. (1986). *Intelligence applied.* New York: Harcourt Brace Jovanovich.

Thorndike, E. L. (1913). *Educational psychology* (Vol. 2). New York: Teachers College, Columbia University.

Thorndike, E. L. (1924). Mental discipline in high school studies. *Journal of Educational Psychology, 15,* 1–22.

Thorndike, E. L., & Woodworth, R. S. (1901). The influence of improvement in one mental function upon the efficiency of other functions. *Psychological Review, 8,* 247–261, 384–395, 553–564.

Vygotsky, L. S. (1962). *Thought and language* (E. Hanfmann & G. Vaker, Trans.). Cambridge, MA: MIT Press.

Vygotsky, L. S. (1978). *Mind in society: The development of higher psychological processes.* Cambridge, MA: Harvard University Press.

Weber, R. J., & Perkins, D. N. (1989). How to invent artifacts and ideas. *New Ideas in Psychology,* *7*(1), 49–72.

Wertsch, J. V., & Kanner, B. G. (1992). A sociocultural approach to intellectual development. In R. J. Sternberg & C. A. Berg (Eds.), *Intellectual development* (pp. 328–349). Cambridge, MA: Cambridge University Press.

A Dispositional View of Transfer

Carl Bereiter
Ontario Institute for Studies in Education

There seems to be a trend toward reinterpreting what are usually thought of as mental abilities or cognitive skills and treating them instead as dispositions. Schrag (1988) and Brell (1990) both argued for reinterpreting critical thinking in this way—treating it as a virtue, like honesty and kindness, rather than as a mental skill like deductive reasoning and problem solving. Perkins (1991) made a similar proposal regarding creativity, offering what he called a *dispositional view*—in which creative accomplishment is seen as depending on a combination of personal characteristics, such as persistence and willingness to take risks, which thus *dispose* a person to do creative work. I offer a dispositional view of transfer. This is a somewhat different matter from the previous ones, because transfer is not usually thought of as an ability but rather as an event, and the potential for transfer is not usually thought of as residing in the learner but rather in whatever has been learned.

A consequence of this emerging dispositional view is that teaching for critical thinking or creativity or, in the present case, transfer is no longer thought of as skill training or strategy instruction but as something more like character education. To show that this is not altogether a crank notion, I start by examining two vignettes, one from moral education and one from science education, to show how similar problems of transfer arise.

> *A moral education vignette*: A Grade 5 class is discussing the famous moral dilemma in which a poor man must decide whether to steal medicine in order to save his wife's life. In a lively discussion, opinions fly thick and fast, but with little principled

argument. However, by use of Socratic questioning, the teacher gradually induces the students to examine the principles behind their opinions, and out of this emerges a recognition of *respect for human life* as an important moral principle. The class ends with a discussion of other situations in which that principle is relevant.

Most educators, I imagine, would count this a successful lesson. But of course its actual educational value would have to be measured by transfer. The students are unlikely ever to find themselves in the situation of deciding whether to steal medicine to save a life, and so if the lesson is to have any value, it must be through transfer to other kinds of situations. Two distinct issues of transfer are relevant here. The first is *transfer of the principle*: Will students recognize new cases as ones in which respect for human life is an issue? The second is *transfer of the disposition*: One hopes that, through guided discussion of moral dilemmas, students will acquire a disposition to deal with moral issues in a reflective and principled way. But will this disposition transfer to the street?

Although both of these are legitimate transfer issues, I want to argue that only the second poses problems of *teaching* for transfer, which is the concern of this essay. Research on conceptual-change teaching provides good reason to believe that transfer of principles depends preeminently on how thoroughly and deeply the principles are understood. When the teacher ends the lesson with a discussion of other situations in which the principle of respect for human life is relevant, this discussion will be effective insofar as it helps students understand the principle better. If they don't grasp the principle, they will not appreciate what the examples have in common, and the discussion is likely only to confuse them. In short, when it comes to transfer of principles, the teacher is better off forgetting about transfer and concentrating on teaching for understanding.

It is a different problem, however, with transfer of dispositions. No matter how well a principle like respect for human life is understood, there is still a question of whether it will function in situations of crisis or mass emotion or when group pressures militate against moral reasoning. History gives us plenty of examples where people who must surely have held such a principle during their better moments failed to act according to it. Transfer of dispositions, thus, is what character education is supposed to be about, as well as its more clinical derivative, social skills training. Both are renowned for failures to achieve transfer: Whatever is learned about moral conduct and self-control tends to vanish outside the classroom or clinical situation in which it was learned. My point is that the same fundamental problem exists in transfer of subject-matter learning in science, social studies, and the like. The following vignette shows how this is so:

A science education vignette: On another occasion, the same Grade 5 class is discussing the notion that the world is round. Again there is a flood of opinions, with students voicing many of the common children's misconceptions: that the earth is shaped like a saucer, round but flat; that we live on a flat surface *inside* a round earth; that people in Australia are upside down. Again, through Socratic questioning and some explanation, the teacher succeeds in getting the students to recognize that many of their problems come from assuming that *down* is an absolute direction. By the end of the period, many students have begun to grasp the gravitational principle and to realize that *down* refers to the direction of gravitational pull.

The same two issues of transfer arise as in the moral dilemma lesson. Will the gravitational principle transfer to other situations? Even more strongly than before, it can be argued that transfer of the principle will depend on how well the principle is understood, and that instead of being concerned about transfer the teacher ought to be concerned about understanding. If the students understand gravity only as "what holds us on the earth," the concept will not be much good for explaining anything else, whereas if they actually grasp the notion that it is an attractive force between any two bodies in the universe, it has broad potential for making sense of the world (Bereiter, 1992). But what does transfer of disposition mean in the science learning case? The students described in the vignette were not simply receiving a lesson about gravity. They were engaged in a group effort at sense-making that the teacher guided in a scientific direction. They were led to question common sense assumptions and everyday meanings of terms like *down*. They were led to strive for explanations that provided coherent accounts of all the facts, which philosophers of science take to be the hallmark of scientific thinking (Thagard, 1989). So it is this disposition to think scientifically that we might hope would transfer to other situations. In other words, we do not want students to think scientifically only in science class, but to do so in their daily lives, when there are puzzling facts to be accounted for. Will they think scientifically when there is no teacher to guide them, and when the surrounding milieu may encourage uncritical belief or superficial explanation? There clearly is a problem of teaching for transfer here, and it is analogous to the problem of teaching for transfer in character education.

Table 2.1 summarizes the parallels between the two kinds of transfer in the two domains of moral education and science education. It seems reasonable to extend these parallels to academic learning in general: In any academic activity or lesson there is some idea or principle that we hope will transfer outside the school context and some disposition, some way of approaching things, that we hope will carry over into other situations. In some cases the principle will be more important than the disposition, in other cases it will be the reverse; but in most cases both will be worthy of attention. In saying that teachers do not need to be worried about teaching for transfer with respect to concepts, I do not at all mean to diminish the importance of conceptual transfer. I am only arguing that it is best served by aiming for the deepest and most thorough understanding—that doing something else in the interests of transfer is likely to defeat the purpose. To summarize the main pedagogical points: (a) transfer of *principle* depends on depth of understanding, and (b) transfer of *disposition* depends on incorporation into character.

It might seem that the second statement goes too far. Does a disposition to think scientifically, for instance, need to be incorporated into character? I would

TABLE 2.1
Comparison of Transfer of Learning in Moral and Scientific Spheres

Transfer of Principles	Transfer of Disposition
Moral Sphere	
Recognizes new cases where *respect for human life* is an issue.	Ethical principles prevail in times of crisis, riot, rage, etc.
Scientific Sphere	
Recognizes new cases where gravitational principle explains phenomena.	Quest for deeper explanations is carried over into new situations, beyond teacher guidance.

rather admit that the first statement does not go far enough. There is a sense in which a principle like gravitation, in order to become fully effective, needs to be incorporated into the way we perceive the world and comprehend communications. An adult in the modern world should not have to *remember* that the world is round. The roundness of the earth should figure automatically and unconsciously in any thinking we do about long-distance travel and communications and in any reading that we do about space travel, the ozone layer, theories of dinosaur extinction (where, for instance, it is relevant to the spread of effects from a meteorite striking the earth), and on and on into areas where it would not occur to us that the concept was relevant if we had to think about it. Thus it could be said that full transfer of a concept or principle is only achieved when it is incorporated so thoroughly into the cognitive system that it becomes like a part of one's personality.

Similarly, a well-educated person should not need to remember to think scientifically when trying to explain a natural phenomenon. That should be a natural, spontaneous way for the person to think—thus, a part of personality. Some people, of course, may carry scientific thinking to excess, to the point where it gets in the way of feelings. But that too is a character issue. The solution is not to teach rules for when to use scientific thinking and when not. That would never work. The solution is to develop a well-rounded personality and intellect, well attuned to the variety of life's situations; but that well-rounded personality would include, among other dispositions, a disposition toward scientific thinking.

THE QUESTION OF BROAD TRANSFER

Perhaps the oldest issue concerning transfer has to do with mental discipline: Is it possible through exercise on mental tasks to strengthen abilities of memory, reasoning, concentration, and the like in ways that will generalize to the full range of other activities that call on these abilities? Although we have probably all been taught that this notion was laid to rest many years ago by psychologists like Woodworth and Thorndike, the notion refuses to die and keeps resurfacing in new guises. Once it was believed that Latin had this amazing power to strengthen the mind. Now similar hopes are being invested in Logo and in Instrumental Enrichment. I hasten to acknowledge that the originators of these contemporary approaches provide much more sophisticated rationales than that of exercising the faculties (Feuerstein, 1980; Papert, 1980). What they share with the faculty psychologists of old, however, is a belief that activities extremely remote from ordinary subject-matter learning or practical life can produce cognitive benefits that will transfer across a very broad range.

I do not attempt to summarize the results of research on the transfer effects of Logo and Instrumental Enrichment (see Keller, 1990, for review of evaluative research on Logo; Bachor, 1988; Savell, Twohig, & Rachford, 1986, for Instrumental Enrichment). It is clear that they are variable, but it does seem in both cases that there are enough positive results to indicate that remote transfer effects are obtained in some cases. Modern cognitive research does not make it at all apparent how such effects are possible—how, for instance, learning to solve matrix and dot pattern problems could enhance people's performance in the armed forces (Feuerstein, 1980) or how writing computer programs that generate graphics could improve performance on conditional reasoning tasks (Seidman, 1981). A more typical finding, from research that looks closely at transfer of learning, is that learning how to solve a certain kind of mathematical word problem does not transfer to problems that are even slightly different (e.g., Reed, Dempster, & Ettinger, 1985).

The two notions discussed earlier provide at least the beginnings of an explanation for such paradoxical results. The first notion is advances in conceptual understanding. As Papert (1980) eloquently argued, Logo does involve important mathematical concepts, such as the concept of function. Logo activities of the usual kind may not be sufficient to instill that concept in students, but in combination with other experiences it might make a vital contribution. Instrumental Enrichment involves explicit work on concepts such as time and number, and so it too may achieve generalizable effects through teaching concepts and principles of very wide generality. In these respects, Logo and Instrumental Enrichment may produce advances in what Griffin, Case, and Capodilupo (chapter 6, this volume) call "central conceptual structures," and which he shows do have broad transfer value.

And then there is the matter of dispositions. Feuerstein has been quite explicit about this, that an important aspect of Instrumental Enrichment is getting students to believe in themselves as learners and thinkers. It is not at all an overstatement to call what goes on in many Instrumental Enrichment programs character development. This aspect of Logo is not so explicit, but there is certainly a kind of religious fervor in many Logo teachers, which could well carry over into character education—developing in students a general disposition to treat all problems as solvable and to have great confidence in their own powers of thought.

WHERE TRANSFER IS AND IS NOT A PROBLEM

Most research on transfer has been bad news for educators. It gives the impression that transfer usually doesn't happen, and that when it does it is limited to tasks and situations quite similar to those in which the learning occurred. This is discouraging for educators, because, schools being the isolated environments that they are, if learning does not produce positive transfer beyond the school walls there is not much point to it.

Accordingly, it is worth noting that there are vast areas in which transfer is not a problem at all and where it is so straightforward that no one bothers to do research on it. Reading is a highly transferable skill. Whether you will understand what you read depends on a number of factors, especially how much you already know of what the text is about. But in any sort of encounter with text, there is simply no question that, other things being equal, the skillful reader has an enormous edge over the unskillful reader or the nonreader. The same is true of writing and also of arithmetic. In the case of arithmetic, educators often torment themselves over the fact that training in arithmetic computation does not ensure success in solving realistic problems. They regard this as a failure of transfer, but that is quite wrong. Computational skills typically transfer perfectly. Consider the following problem:

> Jane has 15 guppies. She has 8 more than Sharon. How many guppies does Sharon have?

Many students will give 23 as an answer. That suggests they have done a perfect job of adding 15 and 8. The fact that they should have subtracted 8 from 15 instead of adding is another matter, perhaps having to do with constructing a mental representation of the problem. But transfer of computation skill was working just fine. If a student's answer was 158 or 13, then we might have reason to question the student's arithmetic skills; but even then, it is likely that the student's faulty addition skills were being transferred perfectly.

It might seem that this point is trivial or facetious, but in reality it has important educational consequences. The basic academic skills—the traditional and frequently scoffed-at three Rs—show highly reliable transfer to situations extremely remote from the school context. By the same token, deficiencies in these skills have widespread deleterious effects. Students with reading disabilities, regardless of origin, tend to have deficiencies in word recognition that handicap them despite other strengths they may possess (Stanovich & Cunningham, 1991). Students with mathematical disabilities similarly have as their common unifying characteristic weakness in mastery of addition and multiplication facts, and this impedes their dealing with quantitative problems, despite whatever strengths they may have in problem-solving strategies (Russell & Ginsburg, 1984). Where transfer is problematic is in the higher level skills of reading comprehension, written composition, and mathematical problem solving. Much remains to be found out about how to achieve effective transfer at these levels, but that should not deter us from doing whatever we can to ensure that students acquire those basic skills that we know do transfer very reliably and very broadly.[1]

There is another kind of transfer that is so obvious people tend to ignore it: *transfer of conceptual understanding to further conceptual learning.* The vast research literature that shows the importance of prior knowledge for comprehension (Voss, 1984) is a literature showing the enormous power and range of transfer of conceptual knowledge. Understanding evolution, for instance, makes you better able to understand texts that deal with the subject, to participate in conversations dealing with evolution, and so on, thus extending your knowledge and acquiring additional concepts that empower you for still further learning. A theory currently under discussion among evolutionists is the "radiator theory" (Falk, 1990). It proposes that the large human brain did not evolve because of the special benefits it afforded *homo sapiens* but because the evolution of an efficient vascular cooling system made large brains viable. Having a basic understanding of natural selection is no guarantee that you will be able to grasp this new theory. Grasping it may additionally require considerable thought—what Salomon and Globerson (1987) called "mindful transfer." What can be fairly well guaranteed, however, is that if you do not have a basic understanding of natural selection, you will not be able to grasp the radiator theory. If, for instance, you have the typical school student's belief that evolution occurs through small changes that occur within the lifespans of individuals in response to their adaptational needs, you will be unlikely to see that there is any problem in explaining brain size to begin with: People needed to think, and so they developed larger brains to do it. From this viewpoint, misconceptions are serious insofar as they interfere with comprehension, and valid concepts are useful in giving you access to discourse that further advances your knowledge.

If basic academic skills and conceptual knowledge—which between them account for a large part of the school curriculum—transfer so readily and so reliably, what is the source of the general feeling that school learning does not transfer well to real life? I can suggest two answers to this question. One answer has to do with the increasingly well-documented finding that most subject-matter instruction in schools does not produce conceptual understanding but only a

---

[1]Here is an example of just how far basic skills can transfer. A 15-year-old Mexican boy of very limited mental abilities had had 2 years of schooling, both at the first-grade level. As a result, he could read Spanish aloud quite fluently, although often with poor comprehension. Although he knew no English at the time, it was possible with about 20 minutes of instruction to teach him to read English text aloud. Half of that time went into teaching the silent "e" convention. After that he could read English text so well that strangers were convinced he was fluent in English. Of course, he didn't understand what he was reading, but his English-speaking listeners did. This may seem like rather limited competence, but it is worth noting that, according to typical estimates of reading disability prevalence, something on the order of 15% of native English-speaking 15-year-olds in North America cannot do as well.

restricted ability to answer certain kinds of content-related questions (cf. Anderson & Roth, 1989). There is not space to discuss this issue farther here (see, however, Bereiter, 1992). Suffice it to say that what is typically viewed as a failure of knowledge to transfer is actually a failure to teach the conceptual knowledge in the first place.

The second explanation of the widespread pessimism about transfer is that *what typically fails to transfer from one situation to another is learned intelligent behavior.* In a typical transfer study, people learn the solution to a problem such as Duncker's famous problem of how to destroy a tumor using x-rays without destroying the surrounding tissue. In a limited sense, they have learned to act more intelligently in this problem situation. Then they are given an analogous problem—that is, a problem in a different setting that can be solved in essentially the same way. The typical finding is that, unless they are prompted in some way, people do not make use of what they learned in the first situation when tackling the problem in the second situation. They do not act any smarter as a result of having learned to behave intelligently in the first situation. It is the same story with failures of transfer from teaching general problem-solving strategies, reading comprehension strategies, and social behavior strategies. There is some measure of success in getting students to behave more intelligently within the instructional situation, but there is little transfer. Furthermore, transfer is usually poorest with students who need it most—with learning disabled students in the case of reading strategies, students with behavior problems in the case of social skills and self-control strategies. What all this adds up to is a sense that you cannot really teach people to act more intelligently, except in particular situations on particular tasks. This is a conclusion that, quite understandably, acts as a wet blanket on smoldering hopes for improving the human condition through education.

TRANSFER BETWEEN SITUATIONS
VERSUS TRANSFER OF SITUATIONS

Perhaps we human beings are simply not built in such a way that we can readily transfer learned intelligent behavior from one situation to another. Creative problem solvers do it, but we call them creative because what they do is uncommon and seems to draw on abilities not shared by all members of the species. Perhaps what our brains are really good for is learning to act intelligently in particular situations within which we live out significant parts of our lives. The need to adapt to novel situations and to act intelligently in them from the beginning may be a circumstance of modern times and not one that evolution could have equipped us for.

These musings are consistent with, and in fact inspired by, a recently emerged school of thought called "situated cognition" (Brown, Collins, & Duguid, 1989; Rogoff, 1990; Suchman, 1987). According to the "situated" view, which comes out of a lot of insightful investigation of people working and learning in real-life situations, the natural way of human learning is quite at variance with the way learning is conceived of in schools. People learn by entering ongoing "communities of practice"—a building crew, a taxicab group, a scientific discipline, a nuclear family—and gradually working their way into full participation. In the process they acquire the concepts and skills needed to participate effectively and intelligently. Apprenticeship is a formalization of this normal process (Collins, Brown, & Newman, 1989).

The knowledge and the intelligent behavior acquired in these communities of practice tends to be quite situation specific. For instance, both loaders of dairy trucks and Third-World street vendors develop highly effective quantitative skills, but they are specifically adapted to the tasks and the material conditions of the situations in which the skills are used and are thus quite different from one another as well as from the mathematical skills taught in schools (Saxe, 1988; Scribner, 1984). At a very basic level the skills are related, in that they all involve additive combinations of whole numbers, and so it is to be expected, as we have already noted, that basic numerical skills should transfer across these situations. But what makes the quantitative behavior *intelligent* in the various situations is not the same and could not be expected to transfer. In the case of the dairy truck loaders, the intelligence lies in taking advantage of the standardized quantities and arrangements of products in crates. By using these as the basis for calculation, the workers not only achieve more efficient calculations but they also save their backs by minimizing the number of crates they have to move about. In comparison to student summer employees, who rely on school-learned mathematical procedures, the experienced loaders act much more intelligently and effectively. But none of that could be expected to transfer to other situations.

Suppose that for the sake of argument we accept this as a hard fact: Learned intelligent behavior does not transfer to novel situations. Where would that leave schooling? The view of the situated learning theorists seems to be that it pretty much thoroughly discredits schooling of the typical sort. Where possible, students should be taken out of school and allowed to do their learning within relevant communities of practice. What remains of formal schooling should itself become a "cognitive apprenticeship" (Collins et al., 1989), in which students enter the communities of practice of the various scientific and scholarly disciplines. The latter proposal, however, has been rightly criticized as "romantic," inasmuch as teachers are seldom practitioners of the disciplines they teach (A. Brown et al., in press).

In view of the preceding discussion, we could claim several valuable functions for schools, even if it is accepted that intelligent behavior learned in school situations is unlikely to transfer. There are the basic skills of numerical and script literacy, as well as other lesser skills such as map-reading, that have wide transfer value simply because their use pervades the culture. There is also the value of conceptual understanding, which schools ought to be in a good position to foster.

And then there is the possibility of *transfer of dispositions*, with which we began this analysis of transfer. Although the intelligent behavior of the dairy truck loader cannot be expected to transfer to, let us say, behaving intelligently as a restaurant waiter, it may be that there are certain dispositions of mindfulness and willingness to learn that will assist one in learning to act intelligently in any situation. If schooling could inculcate those transferable dispositions, it would justify the higher hopes that have been invested in it, hopes that have seemed to be demolished by the research on transfer and on the situatedness of cognitive skills.

But can schools be expected to teach transferable dispositions? If we are to judge by efforts to do so in character education and social skills training, the answer would have to be no. The results have been so uniformly disappointing that educators seem for the most part to have given up on character education, and social skills training continues to be pursued largely out of desperation. Lack of transfer across situations is the reason. The original Hartshorne and May (1928) studies on moral behavior showed this, and there has been little since to suggest a more optimistic picture. The review of moral and values education in the most recent *Handbook of Research on Teaching* (Oser, 1986) does not even mention character education and suggests rather that moral educators have quit thinking about transfer altogether and are treating moral discourse as an end in itself.

Character education and social skills training may be thought of as efforts to produce learned intelligent behavior in the interpersonal realm. Modern educators are also concerned with learned intelligent behavior in other realms such as science, literature and the arts, history, health, citizenship, and career development. Research on transfer would suggest that there is nothing special about character education and social skills training, that transfer of learned intelligent behavior is problematic across the board. It is just that in some areas failures of transfer are easier to ignore.

In all areas we have tended to think of transfer in essentially the same way. We think of it as something inside the head of the individual that is carried from one situation to another. When transfer fails we assume it is because the thing in the head didn't get turned on or else failed for some reason to work in the new situation. Having, for instance, gotten children to act reflectively in certain situations of classroom discourse, we imagine that they now have a little reflectiveness module planted in their heads and we vainly hope that it will get turned on from time to time in other situations.

I call this the *heroic* view of transfer. For the hero is someone who sustains a purpose or value, despite adversity and lack of social support. Hercules, Don Quixote, and Madame Curie are varied examples. Heroic transfer undoubtedly does exist. There are people who credit some teacher with having instilled in them a disposition or aspiration that stayed with them and influenced their behavior throughout life. But this is too chancy a business to serve as a basis for educational practice; it probably depends on just the right input in just the right emotional context, at just the crucial moment in a person's development. For the most part, the advocates of situated learning are surely right. We learn to act intelligently in specific situations. The intelligence of the behavior, in fact, consists of its fine attunement to the constraints and possibilities inherent in the situation. There is not some module of intelligence planted in the head that can be expected to fire off intelligent behavior in new situations. On this view, the prospects for heroic transfer are slim indeed, not because of weaknesses of the human spirit but because of the very nature of learning.

There is, however, another view of transfer that offers more hope and that is more in accord with the situatedness of learning. This is transfer of situations, rather than transfer *across* situations. In favorable social environments, human beings have considerable freedom to select and even create the situations within which they function. (One of the saddest facts about children growing up poor in U.S. inner cities is that this freedom is so severely limited.) It may be too much to expect that moral education, whether through school, church, or family, will imbue children with virtues that they will sustain against adversity. But a good upbringing may dispose them to prefer the company of virtuous people. Similarly, learning to participate in thoughtful, critical, and imaginative discourse in the classroom may not imbue children with dispositions to think that way in general, but it may dispose them to seek out companions and situations for that same kind of discourse. What is required for this is not the development of heroic virtues or iron-hard habits of thought but the more modest acquisition of tastes and preferences. The looked-for result is a disposition to seek out and to create situations similar to those in which reflective discourse was experienced initially.

Is there any reason to suppose that transfer of situations can actually occur? I can report one instance, which may at least serve as a prototype for the concept. In work that we have been doing with a software environment called Computer Supported Learning Environments (CSILE), elementary school teachers working with us have been fairly successful at creating situations in which students work collaboratively on knowledge problems (Scardamalia & Bereiter, 1991, in press). An important medium of communication is commenting on one another's notes, which are all entered into a communal database. Teachers have emphasized and coached students in making supportive, helpful comments; and visitors often remark on the unusually high level of civility shown in the students' comments to one another. When a new site was established in a nearby secondary school, a quite different sort of commenting prevailed—largely negative, often accompanied by sarcastic put-downs. There were, however, some clusters of notes and comments that stood out as exceptions, where the same friendly, supportive spirit of collaborative inquiry seemed to exist as in the elementary school. Examination revealed that they were the work of a group of students one of whom was a graduate of the elementary school CSILE class. When interviewed, she revealed that she was quite aware of the discrepancy and that she had deliberately, by means of commenting, recruited a circle of friends who carried on the sort of cooperative discourse she was accustomed to from elementary school days.

One could say that this student had transferred the disposition toward constructive commenting, but it seems there was more than that: She had worked to recreate in the high school the kind of situation that had sustained constructive commenting in the elementary school. If she had not succeeded, it is questionable how long she would have kept up constructive commenting herself instead of conforming to the prevailing negative style. If she did keep going on her own, it would be an instance of heroic transfer. But by recreating a cooperative situation, in which her friends came to look for support from one another's comments and were willing to reciprocate, she no longer needed heroic dedication.

Thomas Rohlen is an anthropologist who has studied socialization and education in Japan from childhood to adulthood. He observed that from kindergarten on up, children work in small cooperative groups where the group is expected to regulate the behavior of its members. If some child is misbehaving, the teacher poses it as a problem for that child's group to handle, and then provides such guidance as the group may need—which may be a great deal at the kindergarten level, tapering off as the children grow into their roles as responsible group members. Rohlen (1989) remarked that it is not surprising that quality control circles work so well in Japanese factories: They are essentially the same kinds of groups that Japanese people have been accustomed to since kindergarten. Again, it is not simply a matter of people acquiring social skills that transfer to new situations. If that were it, we would expect partial or unreliable transfer. What seems to have happened, rather, is that a kind of situation that has worked well in schools is transferred to the workplace, with the result that people who have been through Japanese schools already know how to function in this situation.

For years, radical critics have said that North American schools are like factories and that schooling serves the industrial state by conditioning students to docile acceptance of authoritarian management and meaningless work. This too is best understood as a claim about transfer of situations—in this case, transfer that is achieved by making the school resemble the factory rather than by making the factory resemble the school.[2]

Possibilities for transfer of situations from schools to other areas of life are naturally limited. In schools as we know them now, the most likely situations for transfer are of the kinds already discussed—situations of reflective discourse of various kinds, and situations where informal, leaderless groups collaborate in achieving goals and dealing with internal problems. Even these situations are often not structured in ways that would make them transferable. They depend

---

[2]As this example suggests, transfer of situations is not necessarily beneficial. Much of neurotic behavior could be interpreted as people striving (sometimes successfully) to recreate in later life situations of their childhood.

too much on the teacher's direction, so that students are unlikely to be able to recreate similar situations by themselves.

If education were seriously to aim at transfer of dispositions and to invest in the possibilities of transfer of situations rather than relying on heroic transfer, teaching would have to shift to a different level. It would not be sufficient for teachers to create situations in which desirable kinds of thinking and cooperative effort go on. Teachers would need to work progressively toward enabling students to create those situations for themselves, with different participants, and with different constraints. Then there might be reason to expect that intelligent behavior acquired in school situations would—let us not say *transfer* to other situations, but rather, *reappear* as people recreate similar situations later.

REFERENCES

Anderson, C. W., & Roth, K. J. (1989). Teaching for meaningful and self-regulated learning of science. In J. Brophy (Ed.), *Advances in research on teaching* (Vol. 1, pp. 265–309). Greenwich, CT: JAI.

Bachor, D. G. (1988). Do mentally handicapped adults transfer cognitive skills from the instrumental enrichment classroom to other situations or settings? *The Mental Retardation and Learning Disability Bulletin, 16*(2), 14–28.

Bereiter, C. (1992). Referent-centred and problem-centred knowledge: Elements of an educational epistemology. *Interchange, 23*(4), 337–361.

Brell, C. D. (1990). Critical thinking as transfer: The reconstructive integration of otherwise discrete interpretations of experience. *Educational Theory, 40*(1), 53–68.

Brown, A. L., Ash, D., Rutherford, M., Nakagawa, K., Gordon, A., & Campione, J. C. (in press). Distributed expertise in the classroom. In G. Salomon (Ed.), *Distributed cognitions.* New York: Cambridge University Press.

Brown, J. S., Collins, A., & Duguid, P. (1989). Situated cognition and the culture of learning. *Educational Researcher, 18*(1), 32–42.

Collins, A., Brown, J. S., & Newman, S. E. (1989). Cognitive apprenticeship: Teaching the crafts of reading, writing, and mathematics. In L. B. Resnick (Ed.), *Knowing, learning, and instruction: Essays in honor of Robert Glaser* (pp. 453–494). Hillsdale, NJ: Lawrence Erlbaum Associates.

Falk, D. (1990). Brain evolution in *Homo*: The "radiator" theory. *Behavioral and Brain Sciences, 13*(2), 333–381.

Feuerstein, R. (1980). *Instrumental enrichment: An intervention program for cognitive modifiability.* Baltimore, MD: University Park Press.

Hartshorne, H., & May, M. A. (1928). *Studies in the nature of character: Vol. 1. Studies in deceit.* New York: Macmillan.

Keller, J. K. (1990). Characteristics of Logo instruction promoting transfer of learning: A research review. *Journal of Research on Computing in Education, 23*(1), 55–71.

Oser, F. K. (1986). Moral education and values education: The discourse perspective. In M. C. Wittrock (Ed.), *Handbook of research on teaching* (3rd ed., pp. 917–941). New York: Macmillan.

Papert, S. (1980). *Mindstorms: Children, computers, and powerful ideas.* New York: Basic Books.

Perkins, D. (1991, November). *Creativity and its development: A dispositional view.* Paper presented at the first international conference on Psychology and Education, Madrid.

Reed, S. K., Dempster, A., & Ettinger, M. (1985). Usefulness of analogous solutions for solving algebra word problems. *Journal of Experimental Psychology: Learning, Memory, and Cognition, 11*(1), 106–125.

Rogoff, B. (1990). *Apprenticeship in thinking: Cognitive development in social context.* Oxford: Oxford University Press.

Rohlen, T. (1989). Order in Japanese society: Attachment, authority, and routine. *Journal of Japanese Studies, 15,* 5–40.

Russell, R. L., & Ginsburg, H. P. (1984). Cognitive analysis of children's mathematics difficulties. *Cognition and Instruction, 1*(2), 217–244.

Salomon, G., & Globerson, T. (1987). Skill may not be enough: The role of mindfulness in learning and transfer. *International Journal of Educational Research, 11*(6), 623–637.

Savell, J. M., Twohig, P. T., & Rachford, D. L. (1986). Empirical status of Feuerstein's "instrumental enrichment" (FIE) technique as a method of teaching thinking skills. *Review of Educational Research, 56,* 381–409.

Saxe, G. B. (1988). Candy selling and math learning. *Educational Researcher, 17*(6), 14–21.

Scardamalia, M., & Bereiter, C. (1991). Higher levels of agency for children in knowledge building: A challenge for the design of new knowledge media. *The Journal of the Learning Sciences, 1*(1), 37–68.

Scardamalia, M., & Bereiter, C. (in press). Schools as knowledge-building communities. In S. Strauss (Ed.), *Human development: The Tel Aviv annual workshop: Vol. 7. Development and learning environments.* Norwood, NJ: Ablex.

Schrag, F. (1988). *Thinking in school and society.* London: Routledge.

Scribner, S. (1984). Studying working intelligence. In B. Rogoff & J. Lave (Eds.), *Everyday cognition: Its development in social context* (pp. 9–40). Cambridge, MA: Harvard University Press.

Seidman, R. H. (1981, April). *The effects of learning a computer programming language on the logical reasoning of schoolchildren.* Paper presented at the meeting of the American Educational Research Association, Los Angeles, CA.

Stanovich, K. E., & Cunningham, A. E. (1991). Reading as constrained reasoning. In R. J. Sternberg & P. A. Frensch (Eds.), *Complex problem solving: Principles and mechanisms* (pp. 3–60). Hillsdale, NJ: Lawrence Erlbaum Associates.

Suchman, L. A. (1987). *Plans and situated actions: The problem of human-machine communication.* Cambridge: Cambridge University Press.

Thagard, P. (1989). Explanatory coherence. *Behavioral and Brain Sciences, 12*(3), 435–502.

Voss, J. F. (1984). On learning and learning from text. In H. Mandl, N. L. Stein, & T. Trabasso (Eds.), *Learning and comprehension of text* (pp. 193–212). Hillsdale, NJ: Lawrence Erlbaum Associates.

CHAPTER 3

Forms of Transfer in a Community of Learners: Flexible Learning and Understanding

Joseph C. Campione
University of California, Berkeley

Amy M. Shapiro
University of Massachusetts, Dartmouth

Ann L. Brown
University of California, Berkeley

The theme of this volume is teaching for transfer. This seems a reasonable topic for us to address. After all, we have been concerned with this topic one way or another for all our professional lives (Brown, 1974, 1978, 1989; Brown & Campione, 1981, 1984; Campione & Beaton, 1973; Campione & Brown, 1974, 1978; Campione, Brown, & Ferrara, 1982). Currently, our research program is to reconceptualize and redesign classrooms, with the aim of Fostering Communities of Learners (FCL; Brown & Campione, 1990, 1994). The goal is for students to come to grips with the major agendas of schooling. Certainly, transfer must be a major issue. However, in the context of extended classroom interventions, it is not easy to know how to look for, or conceptualize, transfer. *Transfer* is most centrally a theoretical term, and it is not always obvious what its referents are. Nor is it clear that a single theory could exist to cover the range of phenomena to which the term might be, and has been, applied.

LABORATORY STUDIES OF TRANSFER

Historically, many investigators working in laboratory settings appeared to be clear on the concept of transfer and on the relevant procedures for detecting it. In the main there has been an agreed-upon methodology. Experimenters brought participants into the laboratory and presented them with a sequence of two tasks, typically back-to-back. On the first task, the participants were taught something—a response, rule, or principle, depending on the guiding theoretical orientation.

They were then observed performing on one of a potential array of tasks presumed to share some features in common with the task on which the instruction had taken place. If performance on the "transfer" tasks was influenced in some way by the "original learning," it was concluded that transfer had taken place. It was also possible to modify the conditions of original learning—increase the amount of training, situate the training in multiple contexts, explain the significance of the activities being learned, emphasize the generality of what was being learned, and so on—in an attempt to identify the variables that influenced transfer. Within this approach, there were two quite distinct lines of inquiry, one emphasizing identical elements, the other, guiding principles.

Identical Elements

One line of inquiry, which dominated research for the first two-thirds of the century, was stimulated by the "identical elements" theory of Thorndike and his colleagues (e.g., Thorndike, 1913; Thorndike & Woodworth, 1901). There are three prominent features of this body of research: (a) transfer was expected only between tasks that shared common stimulus elements, typically defined in physical terms; (b) the learner was viewed as a passive recipient of information; and (c) transfer was investigated following the acquisition of arbitrary associations (e.g., red is correct). The force of this research was to limit the extent to which transfer might be expected. Further, given the focus on general—context-, species-, and age-independent—laws of learning it was uninformative about mechanisms that would explain individual differences in transfer. Why might some, but not others, manifest transfer in a given situation (Campione et al., 1982)?

To use the work of one of the authors as an example, Campione (1973; Campione & Brown, 1973, 1974) carried out a series of experiments investigating transfer between two physically dissimilar tasks used to study concept identification—simultaneous and successive discrimination formats.[1] Transfer was obtained when the training and transfer tasks were of the same type, but not otherwise. Indeed, this pattern was obtained with groups of participants ranging from preschoolers through university undergraduates. This limited transfer was, however, not without benefit. When participants, again ranging widely in age, were taught potentially conflicting responses in the two formats, they did not become confused. Rather, their responses on transfer tasks were predictable on the basis of what they had learned initially in the format on which testing took place and were uninfluenced by what they had learned in the contrasting setting.

---

[1]The apparatus contained three horizontally aligned windows. In the simultaneous version, stimuli differing in color and shape appeared in the two outside windows. One attribute along one dimension, for example, red, represented the target concept. The learner's task was to press the window containing that attribute. In the successive version, a single object was presented in the center window, and again the particular concept was defined in terms of a single attribute. If the object contained the attribute, the correct response was to press the left window; if it did not, the correct response was to press the right window. During the original learning phase, for half the participants, the target attribute was a particular color, for the others a particular shape.

They had learned two different responses in two different contexts and kept this learning separate.

In situations involving problems with arbitrary solutions, transfer is determined primarily by physical similarity, which includes contextual elements. If problem settings appear the same to the learner, transfer is likely to be obtained; if they appear different, transfer is not likely to occur. This selective transfer is quite adaptive, for if humans were to attempt to transfer willy-nilly from numerous settings, there would be more interference than guidance. These effects appear across a wide range of age and ability.

Guiding Principles

Contemporaries of Thorndike did consider alternative positions on transfer: specifically, that one cannot expect transfer if there is nothing meaningful to transfer. When learning can be organized around a guiding principle, however, transfer is determined by the extent to which the learner understands that principle. Judd (1908) argued persuasively that transfer is determined by the extent to which the learner discerns the common underlying causal structure that two situations share. Consider one example of what Judd actually did. Twelve-year-old boys were asked to throw darts at an underwater target, a skill that requires considering the deflection that the light suffers through refraction. Half the boys were instructed in the principle of refraction, the remainder were not. Both groups did equally well at first; all needed time to practice the skill. But when the amount of water was reduced, thereby altering the degree of deflection of the light, the boys without the principle became confused; practice with one setting did not transfer to the other. In contrast, the boys with the principle adapted readily. The same pattern recurred when the target was changed again, with the principle group adjusting more rapidly, and the no-principle group less rapidly.

In this approach, it is possible to expect students to transfer what they have learned across tasks that share no physical similarity. It is also possible to deal with the fact that some individuals may demonstrate transfer, whereas others may not. If someone understands the principle involved, transfer is likely. If, however, the principle or the causal structure relating the situations is not understood, the participant is essentially placed in the position of having learned an arbitrary response, and transfer effects are likely to depend on superficial physical cues. Indeed, although a minority of participants did succeed in many studies of this kind, many, whether young children or college students (e.g., Gick & Holyoak, 1980), failed to show transfer.

The Training Study

Switching to particular methodological tools, of special interest to those interested in instruction, the 1970s generated a spate of "training studies" involving young or academically delayed children working on a number of memory tasks (e.g.,

Brown, 1974, 1978; Campione & Brown, 1977, 1978; Flavell, 1970). These studies fit into the Judd mold in that it was possible for the learners to understand why the particular strategy being taught would work, that is, the chosen strategy was a logical solution to the memory problem being posed. Nonetheless, the most frequent finding was that training led to impressive improvements on a variety of memory tasks, but when challenged to apply what they had learned to novel tasks, participants acted as though the training problem had never existed.

One interpretation of these data is through a stagelike theory: The developmentally young do not manifest transfer across dissimilar tasks because of some maturational limitation. Lacking some of the cognitive resources necessary for reasoning by analogy, or for inferring causal structure, they are forced to rely on physical or perceptual features to mediate transfer. However, another interpretation is that, independent of age, being shown a solution to a problem, or being told how to remember a set of items, does not guarantee that the participants will understand the problem solution. And in most cases, the training portions of the experiments with children involved what have been called "blind instruction" (Brown et al., 1983; Campione et al., 1982). Children were told exactly how to go about remembering something, precisely how to structure and carry out a rehearsal strategy, told in detail how to organize incoming information, and so on. But they were not told why they were to do that, or how the activity related to the structure of the memory problem. Not surprisingly, at least in retrospect, they showed no transfer following such instruction.

The interesting question is, then, what are the factors that increase the likelihood that learners will come to understand novel principles in ways that will result in their flexible use? And do these change with the age of the participants? We now know a considerable amount about these factors. And we know that by taking them into consideration, it is possible to induce even very young children to transfer across task boundaries. By way of illustration, consider a series of studies reported by Brown and her colleagues (Brown & Kane, 1988; Brown, Kane, & Echols, 1986; Brown, Kane, & Long, 1989). Working in a variety of task domains, they were able to show that 3- to 5-year-old children would show evidence of analogical transfer if they were either: (a) given experience and practice with a series of pairs of analogous problems; (b) directed to attend to the goal structure of the original problem; (c) asked to reflect on similarities between pairs of problems; or (d) required to teach what they had learned to others. Findings of these kinds have played an important role in decisions regarding the classroom environments we design.

Although this laboratory approach is neat enough, and has provided important data, it does have several limitations. A conceptual problem is that, within this approach, learning and transfer are somehow seen as distinct processes, occurring at different points in time. Methodologically, the "training" phase in the majority of laboratory studies is very brief, allowing little opportunity for the development of any true understanding that would mediate transfer. Still another is that transfer must be demonstrated by the participant in a specific way and at the whim of the experimenter: transfer now, or forever be seen as a nontransferrer. We believe that this leads to an underestimation of the transfer or understanding capabilities of all, but particularly of young children.

TRANSFER IN CLASSROOM SETTINGS

In the classroom environments in which we now conduct research, and attempt to build theory, a straightforward extension of the laboratory protocol is close to impossible. Such neat slices of life—Problem A followed immediately by Problem B—are not that often apparent. In these naturalistic settings, any distinction between learning and transfer is ephemeral. The understandings that lead to transfer are typically built up over extended periods. And learners may show evidence of transfer in a variety of ways and at somewhat unpredictable times. This allows a richer picture of emerging competence, but poses methodological problems of no small proportions. As one example, if transfer can occur on somewhat random occasions, it takes constant vigilance, and a bit of luck, to capture the phenomenon. Also, if the classroom environments involve multiple changes from the norm, it is difficult to see how to arrange for appropriate control groups. Although we can, as researchers, build mini-experiments—with their attendant strengths and risks—into the classroom milieu, in the main the classroom consists of continuous and overlapping streams of activity where teachers and students, or students and students, work together on an array of different activities. Further, neither all individuals nor all groups necessarily work on the same agendas at any given time (Brown, 1992).

In such a situation, what is it that we mean by transfer? Stated most simply, in our work, we mean understanding; and understanding is indexed by the ability of learners to *explain* the resources (knowledge and processes) they are acquiring and to make flexible use of them. In previous papers (Brown et al., 1983; Campione et al., 1982), the terms identified with *reflective* and *multiple access* were borrowed from Pylyshyn (1978). Basically, we want students to come to understand a variety of domain-specific concepts and the more general processes that they can use in the service of new and continued learning. If they understand them, they can talk knowingly about them (reflective access) and use them flexibly (multiple access).

How do we organize classrooms to accomplish this? Operationally, we begin by setting students the task of mastering a rich domain of knowledge. We structure their activities in such ways that they are led to use what they are learning as a bridge to new knowledge within that domain. And, as they are doing this, we include instruction and modeling designed to help them acquire some of the critical thinking and reflection activities that can guide their learning as they enter new areas. They are taught to read for the purposes of learning and answering questions of interest to them. They see writing as a tool that serves both communicative and knowledge-building functions. And, finally, they spend a considerable amount of time explaining to others (and themselves) the features and limitations of what they are learning, and the reasons they are engaging in the activities currently occupying their attention. If this all sounds suspiciously like metacognition, it is not accidental.

FORMS OF TRANSFER

In designing the program, we had in mind a number of forms of transfer, or understanding, we wished students to demonstrate:

1. Tools of Wide Applicability: A major goal of the program is that students learn to read and write in ways that will guide their learning across areas. Specifically, they should come to regard reading as an avenue for answering questions and doing research. We would like them, over time, to improve their ability to extract and coordinate main ideas from multiple texts, and to identify gaps in their evolving knowledge.

We want students to change their conceptions of writing from knowledge telling to knowledge building (Scardamalia & Bereiter, 1991) and communication. Ideally, writing becomes a tool for reflecting on and evaluating one's own state of understanding.

Another aim is for students to become knowledgeable users of technology, and to come to know ways in which it can aid their learning.

2. Understanding Within Domains: The FCL program has so far been established within the context of environmental science/biology. Students are introduced to "big ideas" in biology as early as second grade, and the program has been extended as far as eighth grade. From the beginning, the aim is not to have students acquire isolated facts about, for instance, animals or their habitats; rather, the goal is an understanding of the interdependence among form and function as animals become adapted to their environments, and the consequences of changes in those environments. The concepts they work with are intended to be generative and to provide a basis for future learning.

3. Reasoning Strategies: As students are immersed in learning about significant issues, we are able to foster a variety of knowledge-extending and -monitoring strategies. One major role of the teacher is to model these learning strategies, and to show how she uses them herself whenever she is presented with a query for which she does not have an immediate answer. In this way, students are taught to reason on the basis of incomplete information, to generate possible worlds, to make recourse to analogy, to engage in self-explanation, and so forth. In this category, we look for increases in the use of analogy and explanation in

their discussions and written work, and for increasing local and global coherence in the arguments they present.

4. Reflection and Other-Explanation: The program is heavily dialogic: A lot of discussion takes place. The discussion formats serve multiple functions. One is simply that they provide many chances for students to practice and refine their oral presentation skills. We can thus chart the ways in which student fluency develops across time, and the ways in which students organize and present their material. Of more importance, much of what students understand, or do not understand, is revealed through these presentations. A frequent way of evaluating students' understanding is to have them describe what they are doing, and why they are doing it, to a variety of expert visitors. They engage in exhibitions of the sort emphasized by the Coalition of Essential Schools, but with the addition that they expand upon both process and content.

Our goal in the remainder of the paper is to lay out the features of the learning environments we are designing, emphasizing the principles upon which they are built, and then illustrate some of the ways in which we search for evidence of transfer.

ENGINEERING A COMMUNITY OF LEARNERS

Since the late 1980s, we have focused on the design of innovative classroom practices that encourage students, teachers, and researchers to rethink the philosophy of learning that underlies those practices. In this section of the chapter, we describe the philosophy upon which the program is built, illustrate the basic classroom activity structures, then describe how we foster the classroom ethos that leads to understanding and transfer. In the next section, we discuss data from a number of different implementations of the program. In general the students are second through seventh graders from inner-city schools, the majority of whom can be described as academically at-risk based on standardized scores.

The Underlying Philosophy

The FCL program is built on a set of principles regarding the nature of learning and instruction. Across different exemplars of the program, many surface details change, but there is constancy at the level of these organizing principles, which are summarized in Table 3.1. There are two major classes of principles: "original principles," derived from laboratory and classroom research on children's learning and transfer, that influenced the original design of the program; and "emergent principles," those that resulted from observations and reflections on effective features of earlier versions of the program. Because of the emergent principles, the overall set has changed over successive reinventions of the program, and will continue to do so. We have no space here to describe and justify the principles

TABLE 3.1
Steps Toward First Principles of Learning

Active, Strategic Nature of Learning
Metacognition
   Awareness and understanding
   Intentional learning, self-selection, and direction
   Self-monitoring and other-monitoring
   Reflective practice
Multiple Zones of Proximal Development
   Multiple expertise, multiple roles, multiple resources
   Mutual appropriation
   Guided practice, guided participation
Dialogic Base
   Shared discourse, common knowledge
   Negotiated meaning and defining
   Seeding, migration, and appropriation of ideas
Legitimization of Differences
   Diversity, identity, and respect
   Creation of community and individual identity
   Multiple access, multiple ways in
   peripheral to full participation
Community of Practice
   Communities of practice with multiple roles
   Sense of community with shared values
   Volunteers establish curriculum
   Elements of ownership and choice
   Community beyond the classroom wall
Contextualized and Situated
   Purpose for activity, nothing without a purpose
   Theory and practice in action
   Repeatable participant structures
   Fantasy and sociodramatic play (being a researcher, being a teacher)
   Link between current practice and expert practice transparent
Intellectually Honest Curriculum
Responsive, Transparent Assessment

Note: From Brown and Campione (1994).

in any detail, and the reader is referred to Brown and Campione (1994) for a fuller treatment.

In the context of transfer, central aspects of the learning environment include: (a) metacognitive factors: Students are made aware that understanding and transfer is the name of the game, as they are explicitly and frequently reminded that the concepts and processes to which they are introduced are intended to be generative and useful across many settings; (b) an emphasis on discourse: There is continual talk involving students, teachers, and outside experts about context and process, allowing multiple interpretations and perspectives; (c) a continuing role for students in explaining what they are learning to others; (d) the content being studied supports extended analysis; and (e) all activities are practiced in the context of their intended use.

Main Features of the Classroom

Two forms of collaborative learning serve as repetitive structures in the classroom: reciprocal teaching (Palincsar & Brown, 1984) and the jigsaw method (Aronson, 1978).

Reciprocal teaching is a method of enhancing reading comprehension (Brown & Palincsar, 1989). The procedure was designed to encourage the externalization of simple comprehension-monitoring activities and to provide a repetitive structure to bolster student discourse. An adult teacher and a group of students take turns leading a discussion, the leader beginning by asking a question and ending by summarizing the gist of what has been read. The group rereads and discusses possible problems of interpretation when necessary. Questioning provides the impetus to get the discussion going. Summarizing at the end of a period of discussion helps students establish where they are in preparation for tackling a new segment of text. Attempts to clarify any comprehension problems that might arise occur opportunistically, and the leader asks for predictions about future content. These four activities—questioning, clarifying, summarizing, and predicting—were selected to bolster the discussion because they are excellent comprehension-monitoring devices. The strategies also provide the repeatable structure necessary to get a discussion going, a structure that can be faded out when students are experienced in the discourse mode (Brown & Palincsar, 1989).

A major feature of reciprocal reading groups is that students with varying levels of skill and expertise can participate to the extent they are able and benefit from the variety of expertise displayed by other members of the group. Reciprocal teaching was deliberately designed to evoke zones of proximal development (Vygotsky, 1978) within which novices could take on increasing responsibility for more expert roles. The group cooperation ensures that mature performance is maintained, even if individual members of the group are not yet capable of full participation.

As with all activities within the FCL, the authenticity of the target task (text comprehension) is maintained throughout; components are handled in the context of an activity, reading for meaning; skills are practiced in context. The aim of understanding the texts remains as undisturbed as possible, and the novice's role is made easier by the provision of expert scaffolding and a supportive social context that does a great deal of the cognitive work until the novice can take over more and more of the responsibility. The task, however, remains the same, the goal the same, the desired outcome the same. There is little room for confusion about the point of the activity.

The jigsaw method of cooperative learning was adapted from Aronson (1978). Students are assigned part of a classroom topic to learn and subsequently to teach to others via reciprocal teaching. Students are partially responsible for designing their own curriculum. They are assigned curriculum themes (e.g., animal defense mechanisms, changing populations, food chains, etc.) depending on grade and amount of experience in the program. Each theme is divided into five subtopics (e.g., changing populations: extinct, endangered, artificial, assisted, and urbanized; food chains: producing, consuming, recycling, distributing, and energy exchange). Students form five or so research groups, each assigned responsibility for one of the five subtopics. The research groups prepare teaching materials using modern but inexpensive computer technology (Campione, Brown, & Jay, 1992). Then, using the jigsaw method, the students regroup into learning groups in which each student is expert in one subtopic, holding one-fifth of the information. Each fifth needs to be combined with the remaining fifths to make a whole unit, hence "jigsaw." It is the expert on each subtopic who is responsible for guiding reciprocal teaching learning seminars in his or her area. Thus, the choice of a learning leader is based on expertise rather than random selection, as was the case in the original reciprocal teaching work. All children in a learning group are expert on one part of the material, teach it to others, and prepare questions for the test that all will take on the complete unit.

The Research Cycle. The modal research cycle lasts approximately 10 weeks, but with considerable variation. It begins with the classroom teacher or a visiting expert introducing a unit with a whole class discussion, in which she elicits what the students already know about the topic and what they would like to find out. She also stresses the "big picture," the underlying theme of that unit and how the interrelated subtopics form a jigsaw; the complete story can be told only if each research group plays its part. Subsequent benchmark lessons are held opportunistically to stress the main theme and interconnectedness of the activities and to lead the students to higher levels of thinking. The teacher highlights connections across groups, emphasizes recurring themes, lays the basis for transfer, and models the kinds of thinking and reasoning skills necessary to supplement the incomplete pictures that are a necessary feature of standard science texts. The students see that their studies are connected to larger global issues. Gradually, distributed expertise in the varying groups of students is recognized. Students turn to a particular group for clarification of information that is seen to be within their domain. Faced with questions and information from nonexperts, the research teams upgrade, revise, and refine their research agendas.

The majority of time is spent in the research and teach part of the cycle. Here the students generate sets of questions to be addressed, a process that is under continual revision. They plan their research activities and gather information using books, videos, and their own field notes. Students also have access, via electronic mail, to experts in a wider community of learners, including biologists, computer experts, and staff at zoos, museums, and other research institutes (see Campione et al., 1992).

At intervals during the research cycle, reciprocal teaching sessions are scheduled opportunistically by the students themselves when a research group decides that a particular article is crucial for their argument and is difficult to understand.

Reciprocal teaching thus becomes a form of self-initiated comprehension monitoring to attempt to teach their evolving material to their peers. Throughout the research cycle, the students and teacher engage in a variety of activities that enable students in the different research groups to share their progress with the other groups, whose members ask questions, make suggestions, and share common findings. Fueled by questions from their peers that they cannot answer, they redirect their research and undertake revisions of a booklet covering their part of the information.

The culminating event of the unit is the final jigsaw, where the students use reciprocal teaching to teach their material to each other. After this experience, the students revise their booklets and combine them into a single whole class book on the entire unit, including the separate sections of the five research teams and an overall introduction and discussion concentrating on the common theme and big picture to which all subunits contributed. This research cycle is then repeated with the next unit.

The Classroom Culture. In order for these classrooms to be successful, it is imperative that a certain culture be established early and maintained throughout. The classroom climate that can foster a community of learners harbors four main qualities. First is an atmosphere of individual responsibility coupled with communal sharing. Students and teachers each have "ownership" of certain forms of expertise but no one has it all. Responsible members of the community share the expertise they have or take responsibility for finding out about needed knowledge. Through a variety of interactive formats, the group uncovers and delineates aspects of knowledge "possessed" by no one individual. The atmosphere of joint responsibility is critical for this enterprise.

Coupled with joint responsibility comes respect, between students, between students and school staff, and between all members of the extended community. Students' questions are taken seriously. Experts, be they children or adults, do not always know the answers. Respect is earned by responsible participation in a genuine knowledge-building community (Scardamalia & Bereiter, 1991). When an atmosphere of respect and responsibility is operating in the classroom, it is manifested in several ways. One excellent example is turn-taking. Compared with many excerpts of classroom dialogue, we see relatively little overlapping discourse. Students listen to each other.

This brings us to the third critical aspect of the classroom: A community of discourse (Fish, 1980) is established early in which constructive discussion, questioning, and criticism are the mode rather than the exception. Meaning is negotiated and renegotiated as members of the community develop and share expertise. The group comes to construct new understandings, together developing a common mind and common voice (Wertsch, 1991).

The final aspect of these classrooms is that of ritual. Participation frameworks (Goodwin, 1987) are few and are practiced repeatedly so that students, and indeed observers, can tell immediately what format the class is operating under at any one period of time. One common classroom organization is for the students to be divided into three groups, one composing on the computers, one conducting research via a variety of media, with the remaining children interacting with the classroom teacher in some way: editing manuscripts, discussing progress, or receiving some other form of teacher attention. Another activity has the classroom teacher, or an outside expert, conducting a benchmark lesson, introducing new items, stressing higher order relationships, or encouraging the class to pool its expertise in a novel conceptualization of the topic.

The repetitive, indeed, ritualistic nature of these activities is an essential aspect of the classroom, for it enables children to make the transition from one participant structure (Erickson & Shultz, 1977) to another quickly and effortlessly. As soon as students recognize a participant structure, they understand the role expected of them. Thus, although there is room for discovery in these classrooms, they are highly structured to permit students and teachers to navigate between repetitive activities with as little effort as possible.

EVIDENCE OF TRANSFER

In this section, we review the kinds of data that have been collected to evaluate transfer. The data come from different schools and from different years. Because it is impossible to collect in-depth data on all activities each year, the research strategy has been to focus on different features of the data on separate occasions. Hence, in one year the focus might be on reading and content acquisition in sixth grade; in another, on reasoning strategies in second and sixth grade; in still another, on computer use.

We do not intend to provide an overall evaluation of the FCL program; that would be well beyond the scope of this chapter. Rather, our goal is to illustrate some of the ways in which transfer has been evaluated, along with some approaches that have been taken to the methodological problems posed by working in the noisy context of elementary school classrooms.

Tools of Wide Applicability

Reading. We begin with two examples of sixth graders' performance on tests of reading comprehension. The first involved both between- and within-subjects analyses of improvements in comprehension following a year-long program. The analysis involved four groups of sixth graders, each of whom studied three main units during the course of the year. One group, the Research group, got the full FCL treatment throughout (in fact, there were two such classes, but their data were combined in most analyses). A second group, the Partial Control (PCont) group, was treated exactly the same as the Research group during the first unit; for the second and third units, the science teacher used his own approach but with access to the materials, computer supports, and so on, used by the Research group. A third group (Reciprocal Teaching Control—RTC) studied the main texts for each of the units using reciprocal teaching procedures. The final group (ROC) served as a read-only control, reading all of the texts, but as individual assignments.

The data were derived from criterion-referenced tests designed to evaluate the extent to which students would not only recall information from a passage, but would also be able to use that information in novel ways. At the beginning and end of the year, students read expository passages unrelated to the curriculum and answered a set of questions from memory. The overall data are shown in the top half of Fig. 3.1, where it can be seen that students in the Research classroom outperformed the various control groups. Of most interest, they outperformed the RTC group, which actually received a more intensive dose of reading instruction.

A more detailed analysis was undertaken to determine the locus of the improvements in the Research group. On each passage students were asked four fact and four inferential questions, together with a gist question requiring them to summarize the main theme of the entire passage, and an analogy question on which they were asked to solve a problem analogous to one featured in the target passage.

In the bottom half of Fig. 3.1, we show the differential improvement according to question type. The tests included some simple fact-based questions intended to guarantee that all students would achieve some success. Indeed, all students did score well on those questions with the result that there was no improvement on factual questions. On inferential, gist, and analogy questions, however, there were significant improvements. In particular, regular practice greatly improved the students' ability to use analogous information to solve problems; that is, practice created a mind set to reason by analogy (Brown & Kane, 1988). Initially students failed to solve the analogy problems, but with practice they were able to solve the majority of the analogies by reference to the prior passages.

The second example stemmed from a dissatisfaction with the method employed in the previous study to evaluate reading to learn. Students in the FCL program seldom read single passages, rather they are forced by the nature of their research to skim a number of selections, identify which of those are most relevant to their specific research purposes, and then collate information from those sources to generate new understandings. A group of our colleagues working on the project[2] joined us in the design of a new instrument that would look more directly at these skills.

At the same time, the 1993–1994 school year presented us with an unusual (and extremely fortunate) situation in which to assess student progress. The fifth-

---

[2]They included Doris Ash, Cathy O'Connor, Stella Kennedy, and Marty Rutherford.

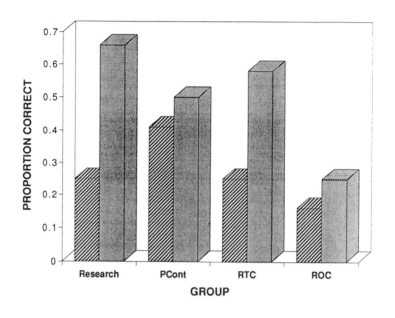

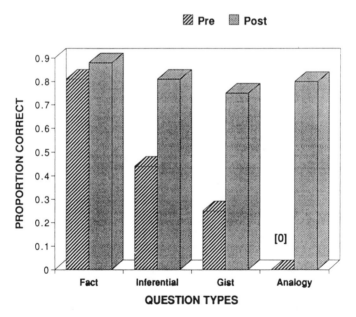

FIG. 3.1. Proportion of correct responses on pre- and posttests for the Research and Control Groups (top panel) and across Question Types for the Research Group (bottom panel).

grade students who had been part of the FCL during the 1992–1993 school year were actually part of a combined fifth- and sixth-grade classroom. Classes during the 1993–1994 school year, however, were partitioned into their respective grade levels. The result was a single Grade 6 class, half of whom were returning FCL students. The remaining students had attended a non-FCL combined Grade 5 and 6 class in the same school. In short, we were presented with a test group and a natural control population in the same classroom, allowing us to assess formally the ability of the former FCL students to transfer their skills to a new setting in a new domain.

In the first study, students were taught a 1-week anthropology unit, a domain unfamiliar to all students, during the first month of the 1993–1994 school year. The unit dealt with a group called the Tasaday, a group of people discovered in the Mindanao Forest of the Philippines in 1971. The Tasaday were thought to be the last surviving Stone Age culture on Earth. A controversy soon erupted, however, about whether this society was genuine or an elaborate hoax concocted by an ambitious government official. There is strong evidence on both sides of the argument, stemming from linguistic analyses, studies of their tool use, ethnobotanical data, and more. In fact, no definitive evidence has yet been found to end the controversy. The class was given an introduction to the topic and, over the course of a week, read articles and viewed videotapes about the Tasaday. During that period, they spent time working alone and meeting in groups to discuss the issues, summarized articles and presented them to their classmates, and participated in whole class discussions led by the teacher.

Two written assessments were taken by the children during the week. The assessment items were designed to probe for evidence of transfer of reading, writing, and comprehension skills. As the students worked, they were allowed to refer to their source material and ask questions of the teacher. Analyses are not yet complete, but here we present some of the initial findings.

> Example 1: The authors of the articles you read wrote about some of the same information, but they disagreed about what the information meant. In the space provided below, please do the following: (a) give an example of some information that two authors disagreed about, (b) briefly explain both sides of the argument, and (c) tell which side you would take and why.

To address this item adequately, some understanding of the two distinct sides to the Tasaday controversy was required. Such an understanding involves both (a) thorough comprehension of the relevant materials, and (b) the extraction and coordination of ideas from multiple texts. No single article available to the children presented both sides of the controversy. Rather, each article presented evidence about the tool use, language, or lifestyle of the Tasaday from a single perspective. If students were able to understand two sides of an argument about a piece of evidence (e.g., about tool use), they would have to extract that information from two sources and incorporate it into an integrated commentary on the topic.

Given this perspective, the relevant question with regard to Example 1 was whether the former FCL students were better able to recognize and isolate both sides of the controversy. Toward this end, students' responses were rated on a scale from *no mention* (0) to *good understanding* (3):

0 = The response contained *no mention* of two distinct sides to the controversy.

1 = The existence of two perspectives was mentioned, but *no understanding* of their content was indicated.

2 = The existence of two perspectives was mentioned, and a *fair understanding* of their content was indicated.

3 = The existence of two perspectives was mentioned, and a *good understanding* of their content was indicated.

The former FCL students who responded to this question scored a mean of 2 points. In contrast, their counterparts in the control group scored a mean of 1.1 points.[3] This difference is statistically significant, indicating that the FCL students were better able to comprehend the materials they were asked to read, integrate information from multiple sources, and express their understanding in writing.

Another item on the assessment was designed to probe students' ability to note inconsistencies between pieces of evidence and attempt to resolve them:

Example 2: The claim has been made that the Tasaday are a Stone Age culture that had no contact with the outside world before they were "discovered" in 1971. If someone were to come across pictures from the 1960s of Tasaday people using pocket knives, how would it affect that claim?

Of interest is whether students were able to grasp the tension between the evidence to which they were previously exposed and the hypothetical evidence now being presented. It was clear from the questions the children asked as they worked that their comprehension skills were also tested by this item. Following the temporal sequence of events proposed in this item was no small task for the group as a whole. In the end, however, the former FCL students clearly outperformed their counterparts: 90% of them answered the question correctly, compared with 44% in the comparison group; a statistically significant difference.

The students' written responses also suggested that many of those who were unable to answer this question had difficulty understanding the question itself. The

---

[3] The actual *N*s for the groups were 9 and 10, respectively. The class size was 32. Some of the problems with the incorporation of a set testing schedule in inner-city classrooms are absences on the "designated test day" and the transfer of students from one school to another during even a 1-week period early in the year.

content of many children's incorrect responses reveals that these students often missed the significance of a metal object in a "Stone Age" culture. Rather than addressing the controversy itself, those unable to conclude that either the photographs were forged or these were not Stone Age people tended to focus on the function of the knife. They responded with opinions about hunting or violence. This result is consistent with a trend we observed in responses to another question asking what scientists learned from studying the Tasaday children. Using a rating system to assess how relevant students' responses were to the point of the question, we found that the content of the FCL students' responses were more relevant to the question than that of the remaining students, a marginally significant difference. The suggestion is that the FCL students better understand the questions, and are more able to frame their answers in terms of issues relevant to the question.

Writing. In the case of writing, the data consist of within-subjects changes over the course of a year in the program, including both group-prepared reports and individual students' contributions. The only comparison data we can offer are derived from general norms gleaned from other research. In one iteration of the program, the books the students prepared across three main units reflected increasingly sophisticated use of argument structure, compare and contrast modes, and hierarchical structuring of the content. The students initially produced books that contained a perfectly linear (non)structure of N paragraphs and N animal examples—each paragraph described an animal. By the end of the year they were producing books with a recognizable and complex hierarchical organization. In Fig. 3.2 we show the most complex structure produced by sixth graders at the end of a full year. This passage consists of three types of organization: a hierarchy (waste: the problem), a compare and contrast section (waste: the solution), and an exemplar-based section (hazardous waste). This mixed model is difficult for even college students to handle. Comparing the microgenetic change over a year with existing cross-age norms for writing, we estimate that the best students progressed in a year from poor grade school level to writing levels more typical of young adults (Brown & Campione, 1990).

Understanding Within Domains

The assessment strategy here is similar to that used in the case of reading. We include both general analyses of content acquisition comparing FCL students with a number of control groups. Those differences are then followed up with more detailed analyses investigating their understanding of the content they are acquiring and the ways in which they can apply that understanding to novel tasks. The first question is whether FCL students do indeed learn more about the content. This question was addressed in the same study from which the reading data in Fig. 3.1 were obtained. As shown in Fig. 3.3, the Research group showed significantly larger pretest to posttest gains than did the PCont and ROC groups, with one

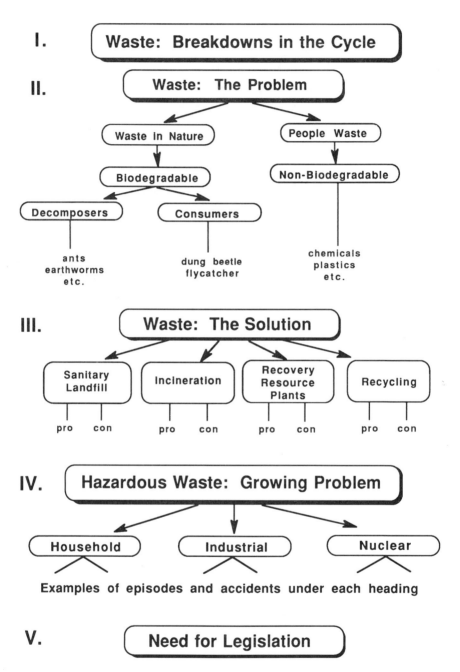

I. **Waste: Breakdowns in the Cycle**

II. **Waste: The Problem**

Waste in Nature

People Waste

Biodegradable

Non-Biodegradable

Decomposers

Consumers

ants
earthworms
etc.

dung beetle
flycatcher

chemicals
plastics
etc.

III. **Waste: The Solution**

Sanitary
Landfill

Incineration

Recovery
Resource
Plants

Recycling

pro con

pro con

pro con

pro con

IV. **Hazardous Waste: Growing Problem**

Household

Industrial

Nuclear

Examples of episodes and accidents under each heading

V. **Need for Legislation**

FIG. 3.2. The organizational structure of one group's final passage.

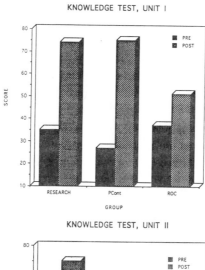

KNOWLEDGE TEST, UNIT I

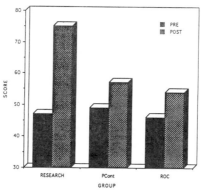

KNOWLEDGE TEST, UNIT II

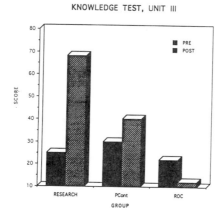

KNOWLEDGE TEST, UNIT III

FIG. 3.3. Proportion of correct responses on tests of content knowledge across three units for Research and Control Groups.

exception: The Research and PCont groups were equivalent following Unit 1. Recall that those groups were treated identically during that phase of the study. Thus, the advantage of the FCL setting was obtained both within groups (PCont students showed significantly more learning when in the FCL environment than when taught according to their teacher's preferred methods) and across groups (Research students outperformed the other groups whenever possible).

Clinical Interviews.   These data were taken from short answer plus justification questions administered to all Research students and a number of control groups. In subsequent studies, we worked only with FCL students and addressed in more detail the depth of their understanding. One strand of data comes from a clinical interview procedure developed by Ash and Brown (1993), in which a series of key questions is raised concerning, for example, the food chain or adaptation. These interviews take place irregularly during the year: at the beginning of the year, after the introduction of some new information, and so forth. In each case, the interviewer elicits basic expository information. If the student cannot answer adequately, the interviewer provides hints and examples as necessary to test the student's readiness to learn that concept. If the student seems knowledgeable, the experimenter might question that understanding by introducing counterexamples to the student's beliefs, and again if appropriate, she might ask the student to engage in thought experiments that demand novel uses of the information.

As one example, shortly after being introduced to the distinction between herbivores and carnivores, the student is asked to sort a set of animals into those categories. When she has done that and provided a good description of the categories, she may be asked, "What would happen on the African plain if there were no gazelles or other meat for cheetahs to eat? Could they eat grain?" At this point, students are far from clear regarding this idea, only about one-third giving correct answers. Students generally answered that the cheetahs could change their diets (become herbivores) if necessary—humans can after all become vegetarians if they choose to do so—and that it would be easier if they were babies at the time (a critical period hypothesis), adults being more set in their ways. Few invoke notions of form and function, such as properties of the digestive tract, to support an assertion that cheetahs could not change.

When asked the same questions at the end of the unit, students are much better able to answer the questions correctly: 60% provide correct answers. Of more interest, they were able to justify those answers. As a concrete example, consider the following excerpts from a sixth grader. During the initial interview, he mentioned speed, body size, mouth size, and tearing teeth as functional physical characteristics of carnivores. He seemed to have the carnivore/herbivore distinction down pat. But when asked about the cheetah thought experiment John mused:

> . . . well I mean if people can, like, are vegetarians, I mean I think a cheetah could change.

This is a good example of a common reasoning strategy: personification as analogy. When asked how this might happen, he said:

> Well . . . just to switch off . . . but um, it would be easier for them to change on to plants than it would be for me; if I had been eating meat . . . because there would still be meat around for me to eat, but for them there wouldn't be . . . so if they wanted to survive, they're going to have to eat grass.

When asked if it would be easier for a baby cheetah to eat grass:

> Well, if it was a baby, it would be easier because it could eat it . . . it would be right there, it would just have to walk a little bit to get it . . . but I think it would be easier. . . . Yeah, and they'd get used to the grass and not care about the animals, because along the line they would forget.

During the posttest clinical interview 6 months later, when asked the same question, he made complex analogies to the cow's intestinal system, arguing that herbivore digestive tracts are more complicated than those of carnivores. By knowing an animal's diet, he argued that he would be able to predict its digestive tract length and how long digestion might take, and vice versa.

This time, when confronted with a variant of the cheetah thought experiment, John responded:

> no . . . no, their digestive system isn't good enough . . . it's too uncomplicated to digest grasses and also their teeth wouldn't be able to chew, so then the grass would overpopulate . . . and the cheetah dies.

When asked if the baby cheetah could survive by eating grass, he asserted that they would probably be the first to die.

A second example involved a question designed to evaluate understanding of the role of the sun's energy in the food chain. Students were asked to predict what would happen to the food chain if the amount of sunlight were suddenly reduced. These data are shown in Fig. 3.4. On the pretest, the students were likely to respond that reduced light from the sun would make it difficult for animals to locate their food, and that nocturnal animals would be less hindered: Only about half the students thought that reducing the sun's energy would disrupt the food chain; and only one in ten acknowledged the role that plants play in generating food with the sun's energy. On the posttests, 80% indicated that the food chain would be disrupted, and about half went on to describe the role played by photosynthesis in supporting the food chain.

To illustrate the character of the improvements, consider the pretest performance of Katy, a sophisticated seventh grader who gave a textbook-perfect description of photosynthesis, one that in traditional tests would certainly be taken as an indication that she fully understood the basic mechanisms (Ash, 1991).

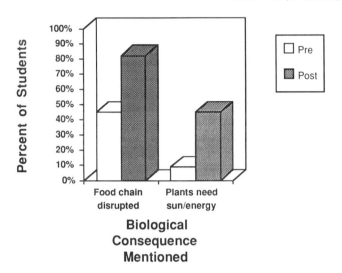

FIG. 3.4.   Pretest and posttest performance of FCL students on "sunlight" thought experiment.

She was then asked the critical question, "What would happen if there were no sunlight?" Katy's response never included the critical information that, as plants make food with the sun's energy, serious reduction in the availability of sunlight would disrupt the entire food chain—no sun, no plants, no food! Instead she concentrated on light to see with:

> That would kill off the plants, beetles, and . . . um . . . nocturnal things would be OK. The dayturnal things . . . snakes, rabbits, hares . . . would be all right, they could be nocturnal. But the dayturnal things would need sunlight to see . . . couldn't find their food in the dark and would eventually starve to death. Hawks would also die out, but owls are nocturnal . . . would be able to see at night and . . . um . . . raccoons would probably be near the top of the food chain.

Katy clearly had not understood the basic place of photosynthesis as the main-spring of life. She can repeat back the mechanisms and form food chains when directly asked, but she cannot yet reason flexibly with her newfound knowledge. On the posttest, however, she gave an accurate account of disruptions that would occur in the food chain and described in some detail the role of photosynthesis.

"Transfer" Projects.   We also evaluate understanding by posing design prob-lems that students work on over extended time. A common theme, from Grades 2 through 7, has involved students in designing animals for different purposes. For example, in several Grade 6 classes, students were asked to "design an animal to fit the following habitat" (desert, tundra, or rain forest). We compared FCL sixth graders with a control group of students who worked on the same design

problem following a summer course on adaptation. The FCL sixth graders outperformed control students in the number of biologically appropriate mechanisms they included in their animals (such as mechanisms of defense, mechanisms of reproductive strategies, etc.). In addition, the research students introduced more novel variations of taught principles along with more truly original ideas. This can be seen in Fig. 3.5. For example, the class had discussed the notion of mimicry as a defense mechanism. In a response scored taught/novel, one student said that the eggs of his animal were placed in a line and the markings made the eggs look like a full-grown cobra, a novel use of the mimicry principle. Another student incorporated the notion of behavioral mimicry that had not been taught, still another introduced the concept of a predator's injecting a poison to which it was itself immune, allowing the predator to devour the stunned prey safely.

A similar task has been used with second graders. After a series of introductory activities, the teacher read them a book called *The Tree of Life* by Barbara Bash stressing the central notion of interdependence—the animals needed the tree to survive for different reasons, but by the same token the tree needed the animals. The students adopted an animal depicted in the book, then drew the animal and wrote a line or two on why it fit the habitat and benefited the tree, after which they placed it on a large mural.

Next the students divided themselves into research teams following the jigsaw method, each researching one aspect of a jigsaw organized around properties of animals necessary for their survival (protection from the elements; animal habitats; protection from predators; animal babies; feeding; and communication). Each child

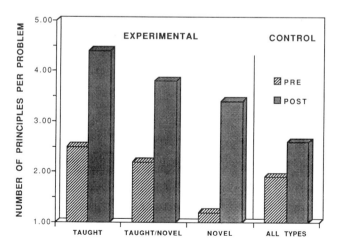

FIG. 3.5. Number of biological principles mentioned on pretest and posttest for the Experimental and Control Groups. For the Experimental Group, the data are further broken down in terms of degree of novelty.

worked individually on his or her own animal example of a theme (e.g., one student selected the dancing bees for communication). The groups prepared to teach all animal examples from their group to children studying another topic. Finally, the groups were asked to design animals of the future that met the six design characteristics that comprised the jigsaw. The main question posed was whether the second graders would be able to benefit from their individual and group work to describe an animal that would embody the critical design features.

We have completed two replications of this task. The first followed a 4-month intervention, where the students had an abbreviated course of study, after which second graders were able to attack the animal of the future task despite their limited introduction to animal/habitat interdependence. We scored their contributions in terms of how many of the design criteria they addressed. The design criteria were solutions to eight issues discussed in class at some time during the intervention: predator/prey relations, defense mechanisms, reproductive strategies (to quote Team B, "reproduction is the science word for having babies"), communication strategies, food getting (carnivore, omnivore, scavenger, etc.), protection from the elements, fit with habitat, and endangerment status. The teams averaged six points out of the possible eight. Verbatim examples of their inventions include:

The Ocrawhale

Our animal of the future lives in a under ground cave with salt water that is 100 feet deep. It is called a ocrawhale.Ocrawhale eats the killer fish and the killer fish eat the little fish. The turtle eats kelp and seaweed.That is called a food chain.

The ocrawhale is like three animals in one. The ocrawhale has crabs pinchers, a tail like an octopus, and a body with balen like a whale.The ocrawhale has a blowhole because he is like a whale and that's how he breathes.

The animal lays its eggs and they sink down in the mud. When they hatch, they swim off on their own.

The animal needs a lot of fat to protect itself from the cold water and from enmies.

The shark is the ocrawhales enemies. If the shark eats the ocrawhale, the ocrawhale uses the octopus tail to fight the shark.

The female ocrawhale isn't the same color as the male ocrawhale because then they can know it its a boy or a girl.

and

The Junkyard Wolf

Are animal of the future lives in the junk yard . It is a amnnore [omnivore] . The babies come out of the side of the mother .It's a scavenger. It camouflages by changing colors and by standing very still. This animal is nocturnal. It has large elephant feetso that it can stomp on the junk to find food.

It communicates by hitting its tail against the [abandoned] cars. The shell protects it from the elements. The animals defense mechanisms are playing dead and ducking its head into its shell. When it needs to fight, it uses its tail. It has a spiked tail.

It eats plants and meat. It eats peoples' scraps and animals that come in. It has a lobster snapper on the back with cheese on it. When the rat sees the cheese it gets caught up in the snapper and the food digests in its stomach. It can also eat things with its mouth.

The ocrawhale example was judged the most coherent and lifelike, while the junkyard monster was the most fantastic. Compared with the compositions of sixth graders on this task, however, the solutions were not weaved into a coherent story. Having chosen a particular habitat—the tundra, a desert, and so on—exerted little constraint on mechanisms for protection from the elements or the nature of the predator/prey relations. On the basis of these initial data, we would conclude that second graders (a) transfer their emergent knowledge of animals in their environment to a novel design task, (b) satisfy design criteria in terms of reasonable biological principles, but (c) are not yet mature enough to weave the design into a coherent, interconnecting whole.

The replication study, where second graders spent an entire year on the project, delving more deeply into the concept of animal/habitat mutuality, produced data that supported points (a) and (b), but not (c). Indeed, second graders can transfer their knowledge and meet the design criteria of finding solutions to the eight problems posed. They scored off the 8-point scale by providing several solutions to some problems. Some animals defended themselves with camouflage, poison sprays, and a combination of protective surfaces and sharp claws and teeth. One invented animal lived in caves and had fur and blubber to protect itself from the elements. One animal had large numbers of eggs, which were themselves camouflaged and kept cool via watering throughout the gestation period.

This cohort of second graders produced compositions more than three times the length of the first set; and, more importantly, their animals were more like those of sixth graders in terms of the overall coherence of the design. Once a habitat was chosen, the other design criteria were suitable for that habitat. The animals were judged much more credible biological adaptations. Consider the cases of the Ripple Green and the Beeper:

The Ripple Green

The description of ripple green is much like the description of an alligator and crocodile. The animal's name is ripple green because it is green and it has ripples all over its body. It is a reptile. It's a medium sized animal. Ripple green has webbed feet to help it swim in the swamp. It has a long tail to help it defend itself. The animal has two scents. It also has sharp teeth to help it carry its food and tear its food apart. One scent is to attract a mate and the other scent is to scare its enemies away.

The animal's habitat is in the swamps of Florida. The ripple green lives in mixed water. In the habitat there are plants, reptiles, birds, fish, amphibians and insects which sometimes can be alligators, frogs, crocodiles, big birds, tall grass, fish, sand and water.

The mother builds the nest high up in the grass so the snakes won't eat the eggs. The mother lays fourteen eggs every summer. It takes three to seven days for the babies to hatch depending on the weather. The mother lays green eggs. The eggs are green so they can camouflage into the grass. Camouflaging protects the eggs. The mother stays with the eggs, close to the edge of the water. She stays close to the swamp in order to get food and water for herself. The mother brings the eggs water to keep them cool. If the eggs get too hot, they will hatch too early and the babies will die. Once the eggs are hatched, the babies stay with their mother for three weeks. After three weeks, the babies are on their own.

Ripple Green communicates with a sweet smelling scent to attract a mate. The scent comes out the back of the tail. They mate once a year in the spring. It sprays a strong smelling scent to communicate to warn other ripple greens that danger is near.

The ripple green is a plant and meat eater or you can say an omnivore. It camouflages the same color as the swamp and has ripples just like the swamp. It quietly swims behind its prey, such as a fish, and then eats the fish. It also eats the grass that is around the swamp.

Since the animal is a reptile, it is a cold blooded animal. It protects itself from the heat by going into the water when it's hot. If the animal gets cold it goes into the tall grass to get cool. It goes on land to get warm.

The animal defends itself by camouflaging. This way it confused is predators, like the alligator and the crocodile. It also uses its long tail to hit its enemy. It can also spray a scent to scare its enemies away.

We think the ripple green will probably be endangered because of the polluting in the swamp. When the swamp is polluted and the ripple green goes under the water, it won't be able to breathe. When people throw trash and other things into the swamp the ripple green thinks it is food and eats it. This will cause the ripple green to get lung cancer. We hope the ripple green will survive.

The Beeper

In describing the beeper, it is important to know that it is part bird and part mammal. The beeper lives in a pond. It's part mammal because it has fur. It has webbed feet to help it swim. It has claws on its webbed feet so it can get out of its shell. It has antennae to communicate. It is very smart. It uses its defense mechanisms very wisely.

The beeper's habitat is a fresh water pond in Northern California. Logs of animals live in the beeper's habitat. Some groups of animals that live in the pond are reptiles like the snake. Amphibians like frogs, toads, and newts also live there. Insects live dragonflies, bees, and caddisflies, also make their home in the pond. Mammals like otters raccoons, deer, foxes and muscrats live near the pond. Birds like dippers, kingfishers, gallinules, swallows, yellow wagtails live there too. Fish like trout and sticklebacks live in the pond too. Plants like grass, flowers, and trees can also be found around the pond.

The beeper is an oviporous animal. It lays eggs. It lays its eggs in a nest. The mother beeper leaves its eggs behind like a turtle. The eggs are protected because they have stone hard shells. It claws its way out of the shell. Once the baby is hatched it doesn't need its mother any more because it can do things that the other and father can do as soon as it is hatched.

Defense mechanisms are important to the beeper because they help it survive. Camouflaging is very useful t the beeper. It helps it defend itself as well as helping it to get food. It camouflages by changing its fur color so its enemy won't see it. When the caddisfly comes near, it changes its fur color in order to catch it. It also defends itself by spitting poison which blinds the enemy.

It needs to get food so it won't starve to death. It is an omnivore. It eats small birds. It also eats caddisflies and flies. It gets its food by camouflaging first and then spitting poison. The poison blinds its prey. Then the beeper kills it with its claws. The poison is harmless to a human.

In order for an animal to protect itself from any element it needs to do either hibernate, migrate, insulate, generate, congregate, or propagate [one student in this group had quite a feel for words]. The beeper has fur and blubber to protect itself from the elements. When it's a baby it only has blubber. It has blubber to keep in warm in the water. In the winter the fur and the blubber keep it warm.

The beeper communicates by making beeps in the air to get a mate. The beeper stays with that mate for life. If the male gets sick the female gets another mate. The communication also warns other beepers that the enemy is near. Its enemy never hears or sees the communication. It knows the difference between the beeps for getting a mate and the beeps for warning.

We doubt that the beeper will become endangered or extinct but there is always the chance that it will. It might become endangered because people might think that the antennae bring good luck and would kill the beeper so they could cut off the antennae and leave the beeper's dead body behind. But the people should know that the antennae aren't good luck because the antennae are only for the beeper to communicate.

Given a sufficient exposure to relevant biological adaptations, second graders delight in displaying their understanding in design tasks of this nature, the very essence of meaningful transfer. The credibility of their creations is attested to by the following anecdote. A visitor talking with the children designing the Ripple Green told the teacher how impressed she was that they knew about animals she had never heard of—she was of the opinion that the ripple green was a real animal.

Reasoning Strategies

The FCL program is highly dialogic: Students spend a considerable amount of time working in their own research groups and teaching others what they are learning. In one particular study (Brown, 1991), student use of analogy and explanation was tracked over the course of a year in which students worked on three major research units. All jigsaw sessions, where the students exchanged information from their individual research groups, were audiotaped and later transcribed. Note that in this case, only a within-subjects comparison was available, as there was no appropriate control group against which to compare any changes. However, in earlier analyses of reading comprehension gain, we did find that FCL students improved more rapidly over time in their ability to notice and exploit analogies than did a number of control groups. The jigsaw analyses were undertaken to track changes in more detail and as they occurred in free-flowing discussions.

Consider first data on the use of analogy. Across the three major instructional units, there was a progression from merely noticing the occurrence of analogies to productive use of analogy to solve problems. Similarly, students progressed from using surface similarities (simple) to a reliance on deep analogies (advanced). For example, children might initially draw an analogy between animals (ladybug and lacewing) that look alike, are both insects, and are examples of a common theme, natural pest control. Later they come to notice the deeper similarity between, say, a crested rat and a viscount butterfly (very dissimilar animals that are both examples of a common theme, visual mimicry). Similarly, children initially make surface analogies, such as between human eyes and the headlights of a car (surface), whereas later they make the analogy between a car's engine and the human heart (deep). With increasing knowledge children progress from accepting superficial analogy to using deep analogy to explain mechanisms. They question initially acceptable surface analogies (such as "plant stems are like straws"), then come to prefer analogies based on deeper understanding of underlying biological mechanisms ("plants are food factories"). This progression, reflecting the increasingly coherent and mechanistic nature of their biological theories, is shown in the top half of Fig. 3.6. Over time, students make more effective use of analogy in their discussions. They use increasingly advanced analogies, both to help them learn new material and to communicate their new understanding to others.

There is a similar development in students' recourse to, and use of, causal explanations, where they go beyond specific facts and set out to understand relations among facts through attempting to explain the relevant mechanisms. As shown in the bottom half of Fig. 3.5, in the first unit of the year, students attempted to generate explanations when faced with an impasse or a breakdown in comprehension; that is, seeking an explanation was a response to a comprehension failure. Later, students resorted to explanations in attempts to resolve inconsistencies. In these cases, they began dealing with sets of facts and principles, rather than more isolated ones; but still the search for explanation was in response to a comprehension failure. Finally, explanation was used spontaneously in the absence of comprehension failure or obvious inconsistencies as learners continually revised and deepened their understanding of complex causal mechanisms. This microgenetic progression is shown in the bottom half of Fig. 3.6.

Reflection and Other-Explanation

One of the major principles on which the program is built is that students should be active participants in the program, aware of their learning processes and progress. They should come to understand why they are engaging in the activities

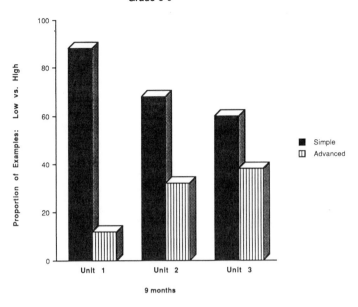

Production of Analogy in Discourse
Grade 5-6

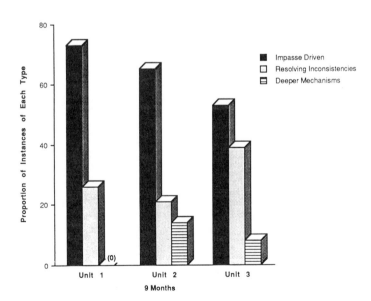

Explanations

FIG. 3.6.   Changes over time in FCL students' production of analogy (top panel) and use of explanation (bottom panel).

that form the basis of the program. What is the purpose of reciprocal teaching? Why might jigsaw activities support their learning? What is the role of writing summaries of what they are working on? Why might they be asked to engage in cross-age, as well as peer, tutoring? We believe that if students do understand the significance of the activities in which they engage, they should be able to serve as collaborators in improving the orchestration of their own learning. Accordingly, a significant portion of FCL assessment efforts involve having students report on both the content they are learning and the processes through which that learning takes place. These reflections are typically quite informal, taking place sporadically in the company of other students, their teacher, or visitors to the classroom. (We have only recently begun to formalize this component of our evaluations, developing specific interview protocols.) Evidence that students do understand the role of the various activities comes from two sources: group modification of standard practices and invention of new ones; and individual students' self-reports on those activities.

Adaptation of Reciprocal Teaching.   When the FCL program began, reciprocal teaching (RT) was introduced by the teacher as a method for helping students understand texts they were reading. She asked students to use RT with the initial texts that were to serve as the basis for their subsequent research. After going through this procedure several times and becoming familiar with RT activities, students spontaneously began using the procedure as a way of monitoring their own learning. When faced with a text that was difficult for individuals to understand, a student would call for an RT session (converting the phrase to a verb, i.e., "We need to RT this passage"), at which time the group would get together and work collaboratively, following RT procedures, to improve their understanding of the passages. Indeed, this decision on the part of students to use RT opportunistically in an attempt to monitor and extend their comprehension has been observed in each fifth- or sixth-grade class in which we have worked. One seventh-grade class also came up with *Seminar*, a version of RT in which the four guiding strategies were complemented by the inclusion of specific forms of argumentation and evidence-seeking.

Invention of Crosstalk.   In the first iteration of FCL, the jigsaw activity—in which research groups reformed into learning groups to teach each other what they had learned—was the culminating activity of an overall unit. It was followed only by a revision of the research groups' final reports, which took into account suggestions and questions raised during the jigsaw discussions.

It was the students themselves who noted that those discussions were very helpful to them in highlighting issues they had not considered, and in noting places where they were unable to answer questions their peers raised. Given that feeling, they argued that the jigsaws should take place more frequently and become a part of the research process itself. They wanted "minijigsaws" in which learning groups would meet periodically to exchange views on progress, to highlight new questions they should consider, and to check on their ability to explain what they were learning to other students.

A further step was taken when the students determined that the minijigsaws were not the most efficient way to proceed. Reorganizing into different learning groups took time, and the discussions in the different groups varied, making it difficult for all students to benefit from the combined set of discussions—each student would have to debrief his colleagues on the issues raised in his or her jigsaw group. The solution, again proposed by the students, was to exchange group progress in a whole-class setting, which they termed *crosstalk*, referring of course to talk across the different research groups. In this variant, the research groups would take turns reporting on their topics, their guiding questions, and their progress; the remaining students would react to their work, ask questions of clarification, and suggest information they had learned that seemed relevant to the presenting group. Thus, in addition to serving a comprehension-monitoring function, crosstalk also functioned as a method for discussing commonalties across groups and focusing attention on higher order relations among the research strands. Crosstalk is now a regular feature of FCL classes.

Individual Descriptions of RT.   The first two examples involved group reflections and inventions, but we also are interested in the reactions of individual students. The data on individual students come from both formal interviews and from ethnographic observations taken at various points throughout the year. As one example, consider the following interchange (reconstructed from field notes) between a visiting educational researcher (R) who had just observed an RT session and a sixth-grade student (S).

R: Do you use reciprocal teaching when reading alone?

S: Oh, yes, I use it all the time.

R: (skeptically) How do you do that?

S: When I read hard things, I use the strategies. I try to remember what has happened so far and ask myself what the major questions are. I try to think about what is not clear—clarifying is where my team helps me the most. A lot of time, I wish my teammates were with me because they always help me understand what we're reading. Sometimes I try to think about the questions they might ask me because they often look at things in different ways than me.

This seems as clear a description of internalization as one could hope for!

Comments on Teaching and Explanation.   The crosstalk discussion itself indicates students' awareness of the ways in which teaching and explaining to others contributes to learning. Beyond group data, there are also many instances of individual students making similar points. We conclude with a summary of comments obtained from interviews conducted by members of the FCL research staff; statements noted by researchers monitoring ongoing classroom activities; and a videotape that a group of fifth- and sixth-grade students made about tutoring. There is a clear consensus on the role and importance of teaching others. First, one learns from teaching, for example, a fifth grader reporting on cross-age tutoring, "I think tutoring is a great experience because they will not only learn from you, but you can learn from them. Not until I began to tutor did I find out that second and third graders can be as smart as sixth graders. They know a lot, and they are very smart kids who ask you questions that make you think hard." The second point that emerges is that effective teaching involves posing questions, not providing answers, for example, from the student-prepared video, "Good teaching is asking good questions, not giving answers."

CONCLUSIONS

Analyses of classroom performance are notoriously difficult. In this chapter, we have described the ways in which we search for evidence of transfer, conceived as understanding and flexible use of resources. Our view is that there are multiple manifestations of transfer, ranging from the understanding of domain-specific concepts through the deployment of relatively domain-general reading and argumentation strategies. Our emphasis is on both the use of concepts and strategies and on the ability of students to explain both those concepts, and the conditions of use of the strategies, to themselves and others.

Within this framework, we have reviewed data indicating that FCL students show impressive degrees of transfer. We have also described a number of experimental approaches we have used, ranging from comparisons between FCL students and those in a variety of control groups through detailed microgenetic analyses of individual students and small groups of students. Although none of the approaches is without fault, we argue that the picture obtained across the set of converging operations affords an accurate view of the nature and extent of transfer in these environments.

ACKNOWLEDGMENTS

The research in this manuscript was supported by grants from the James S. McDonnell Foundation, the Andrew W. Mellon Foundation, Grant HD-06864 from the National Institutes of Health, and an award to ALB from the Evelyn Lois Corey Research Fund. To provide an overview of the research, this report draws heavily on a series of earlier papers (Brown, 1992; Brown & Campione, 1990, in press; Brown et al., 1993).

REFERENCES

Aronson, E. (1978). *The jigsaw classroom.* Beverly Hills, CA: Sage.

Ash, D. (1991). *A new guided assessment of biological understanding.* Unpublished manuscript, University of California, Berkeley.

Ash, D., & Brown, A. L. (1993, April). *After the jigsaw is over: Children's learning in socially and informationally rich environments.* Paper presented at the meetings of the American Educational Research Association, Atlanta.

Brown, A. L. (1974). The role of strategic behavior in retardate memory. In N. R. Ellis (Ed.), *International review of research in mental retardation* (Vol. 7, pp. 55–111). New York: Academic Press.

Brown, A. L. (1978). Knowing when, where, and how to remember: A problem of metacognition. In R. Glaser (Ed.), *Advances in instructional psychology* (Vol. 1, pp. 77–165). Hillsdale, NJ: Lawrence Erlbaum Associates.

Brown, A. L. (1989). Analogical learning and transfer. What develops? In S. Vosniadou & A. Ortony (Eds.), *Similarity and analogical reasoning* (pp. 369–412). Cambridge: Cambridge University Press.

Brown, A. L. (1991, October). *Explanation, analogy, and theory in children's spontaneous learning.* Paper presented at the Kenneth Craik Memorial Lecture Series, St. John's College, Cambridge.

Brown, A. L. (1992). Design experiments: Theoretical and methodological challenges in creating complex interventions in classroom settings. *The Journal of the Learning Sciences, 2*(2), 141–178.

Brown, A. L., Ash, D., Rutherford, M., Nakagawa, K., Gordon, A., & Campione, J. C. (1993). Distributed expertise in the classroom. In G. Salomon (Ed.), *Distributed cognitions: Psychological and educational considerations* (pp. 188–228). New York: Cambridge University Press.

Brown, A. L., Bransford, J. D., Ferrara, R. A., & Campione, J. C. (1983). Learning, remembering, and understanding. In P. H. Mussen (Series Ed.) & J. H. Flavell & E. M. Markman (Vol. Eds.), *Handbook of child psychology: Vol. 3. Cognitive development* (4th ed., pp. 77–166). New York: Wiley.

Brown, A. L., & Campione, J. C. (1981). Inducing flexible thinking: A problem of access. In M. Friedman, J. P. Das, & N. O'Connor (Eds.), *Intelligence and learning* (pp. 515–530). New York: Plenum.

Brown, A. L., & Campione, J. C. (1984). Three faces of transfer: Implications for early competence, individual differences, and instruction. In M. Lamb, A. Brown, & B. Rogoff (Eds.), *Advances in developmental psychology* (Vol. 3, pp. 143–192). Hillsdale, NJ: Lawrence Erlbaum Associates.

Brown, A. L., & Campione, J. C. (1990). Communities of learning and thinking, or A context by any other name. *Human Development, 21,* 108–125.

Brown, A. L., & Campione, J. C. (1994). Guided discovery in a community of learners. In K. McGilly (Ed.), *Classroom lessons: Integrating cognitive theory and classroom practice* (pp. 229–270). Cambridge, MA: MIT Press/Bradford Books.

Brown, A. L., & Kane, M. J. (1988). Preschool children can learn to transfer: Learning to learn and learning from example. *Cognitive Psychology, 20,* 493–523.

Brown, A., Kane, M. J., & Echols, C. (1986). Young children's mental models determine analogical transfer across problems with a common goal structure. *Cognitive Development, 1*(2), 103–122.

Brown, A. L., Kane, M. J., & Long, C. (1989). Analogical transfer in young children: Analogies as tools for communication and exposition. *Applied Cognitive Psychology, 3,* 275–293.

Brown, A. L., & Palincsar, A. S. (1989). Guided, cooperative learning and individual knowledge acquisition. In L. B. Resnick (Ed.), *Knowing, learning, and instruction: Essays in honor of Robert Glaser* (pp. 393–451). Hillsdale, NJ: Lawrence Erlbaum Associates.

Campione, J. C. (1973). The generality of transfer: Effects of age and similarity of training and transfer tasks. *Journal of Experimental Child Psychology, 15,* 407–418.

Campione, J. C., & Beaton, V. L. (1973). Transfer of training: Some boundary conditions and initial theory. *Journal of Experimental Child Psychology, 13*, 94–114.

Campione, J. C., & Brown, A. L. (1973). The role of contextual cues in mediating transfer. *Journal of Experimental Child Psychology, 16*, 217–224.

Campione, J. C., & Brown, A. L. (1974). The effects of contextual changes and degree of component mastery on transfer of training. In H. W. Reese (Ed.), *Advances in child development and behavior* (Vol. 9, pp. 69–114). New York: Academic Press.

Campione, J. C., & Brown, A. L. (1977). Memory and metamemory development in educable retarded children. In R. V. Kail, Jr. & J. W. Hagen (Eds.), *Perspectives on the development of memory and cognition* (pp. 367–406). Hillsdale, NJ: Lawrence Erlbaum Associates.

Campione, J. C., & Brown, A. L. (1978). Toward a theory of intelligence: Contributions from research with retarded children. *Intelligence, 2*, 279–304.

Campione, J. C., Brown, A. L., & Ferrara, R. A. (1982). Mental retardation and intelligence. In R. J. Sternberg (Ed.), *Handbook of human intelligence* (pp. 392–490). Cambridge: Cambridge University Press.

Campione, J. C., Brown, A. L., & Jay, M. (1992). Computers in a community of learners. In E. DeCorte, M. Linn, H. Mandl, & L. Verschaffel (Eds.), *Computer-based learning environments and problem solving* (NATO ASI Series F: Computer and Systems Science, *84*, pp. 163–192). Berlin: Springer-Verlag.

Erickson, F., & Schultz, J. (1977). When is a context? Some issues and methods on the analysis of social competence. *Quarterly Newsletter of the Institute for Comparative Human Development, 1*, 5–10.

Fish, S. (1980). *Is there a text in this class? The authority of interpretive communities.* Cambridge: Harvard University Press.

Flavell, J. H. (1970). Developmental studies of mediated memory. In H. W. Reese & L. P. Lipsitt (Eds.), *Advances in child development and behavior* (Vol. 5, pp. 181–211). New York: Academic Press.

Gick, M. L., & Holyoak, K. J. (1980). Analogical problem solving. *Cognitive Psychology, 12*, 306–355.

Goodwin, C. (1987, June). *Participation frameworks in children's argument.* Paper presented at International Interdisciplinary Conference on Child Research, University of Trondheim, Norway.

Judd, C. H. (1908). The relation of special training to general intelligence. *Educational Review, 36*, 28–42.

Palincsar, A. S., & Brown, A. L. (1984). Reciprocal teaching of comprehension-fostering and monitoring activities. *Cognition and Instruction, 1*(2), 117–175.

Pylyshyn, Z. W. (1978). When is attribution of beliefs justified? *Behavioral and Brain Sciences, 1*, 93–99.

Scardamalia, M., & Bereiter, C. (1991). Higher levels of agency for children in knowledge building: A challenge for the design of new knowledge media. *The Journal of the Learning Sciences, 1*, 37–68.

Thorndike, E. L. (1913). *Educational psychology* (Vol. 2). New York: Teachers College, Columbia University.

Thorndike, E. L., & Woodworth, R. S. (1901). The influence of improvement in one mental function upon the efficiency of other functions. *Psychological Review, 8*, 247–261, 384–395, 553–564.

Wertsch, J. V. (1991). *Voices in the mind.* Cambridge: Cambridge University Press.

Vygotsky, L. S. (1978). *Mind in society: The development of higher psychological processes* (M. Cole, V. John-Steiner, S. Scribner, & E. Souberman, Eds. and Trans.). Cambridge, MA: Harvard University Press.

CHAPTER 4

Promoting Transfer Through Model Tracing

Mark K. Singley
Educational Testing Service

THE GHOST OF GENERAL TRANSFER

Lave (1988) argued that our formal educational system is predicated on a mistaken belief in the transfer of abstract knowledge from one situation (the classroom) to another (e.g., the home, the job, the marketplace). Indeed, nearly a century of research in psychology has generated a depressing lack of evidence for the notion of general transfer. Thorndike (1924), the first psychologist to study transfer systematically, showed that training in formal subjects like Latin and geometry had no effect on performance in reasoning tasks relative to training in more mundane subjects like bookkeeping and shopwork. More modern attempts at showing transfer have also been discouraging. For example, there are the classic studies of Hayes and Simon (1977) showing little transfer between isomorphs of the tower of Hanoi puzzle. Continuing in this vein, Jeffries (1978) found little transfer between missionaries and cannibals and waterjug problems, although according to her simulation model, both involved use of a means–ends analysis strategy. Gick and Holyoak (1983) observed little transfer between isomorphs of Duncker's radiation problem. Aside from these laboratory studies of puzzle problems, studies of transfer in more realistic school settings have also been largely unsuccessful. For example, Post and Brennan (1976) trained students for several weeks on a general heuristic procedure for solving algebra word problems. Their instructions included such things as "determine what is given" and "check your result." On a problem-solving posttest, the performance of the trained subjects was no better than that of a control group. Other attempts at teaching general problem-solving strategies have been largely negative (Polson & Jeffries, 1985). Finally, despite early claims that computer programming would emerge as the mental discipline that would revolutionize children's thinking (Papert, 1980), empirical studies have shown little benefit of learning to program on general problem-solving abilities (for a useful review, see Mayer, Dyck, & Vilberg, 1986).

Against this backdrop of failed experiments and the apparent failure of our educational system, we see the recent emergence of the situated learning movement. Some within the movement (e.g., Lave, 1988) deny the existence of abstract cognitive tools that can be applied in diverse situations and are thus seemingly denying the possibility of transfer entirely. Others have remained within the cognitive tradition but have adopted a more realistic view of what kinds of transfer are possible. There is a new realism in transfer research that is informed by recent advances in the understanding of task structure and the mechanisms of transfer.

THE NEW REALISM IN TRANSFER RESEARCH

In the last decade, some exciting progress has been made in codifying and teaching moderately general skills, which represents a turnaround of sorts of the historical trend. Here is a brief review of a handful of examples from a wide range of domains (for a more thorough review, see Singley & Anderson, 1989). First, in the domain of mathematics, Schoenfeld (1985), after numerous failed attempts by other researchers, has been moderately successful in teaching abstract heuristic strategies to college students. His basic strategy has been to take the heuristics of Polya (1957) as a starting point and to elaborate them with more specific rules and guidelines. Reflecting on his success, Schoenfeld (1985) concluded that "heuristics are complex and subtle strategies, and it is dangerous to underestimate the amount of knowledge and training required to implement them" (p. 210). In physics, Larkin and her colleagues (Larkin, Reif, Carbonell, & Gugliotta, 1986) codified general principles and mechanisms of interpretation that apply across subdomains like fluid statics and electricity. Larkin (1989) described the computer simulation that applies the general principles as follows: "FERMI is *not* an entirely general problem-solving system, but it does contain general knowledge that is separate from the more specific knowledge of a domain and that the system can apply to solve problems in several domains in the physical sciences" (p. 289). In computer programming, Klahr and Carver (1988) taught an abstract debugging strategy to elementary school children and observed transfer to the debugging of plans outside of a programming context. Finally, Palincsar and Brown (1984) successfully taught general comprehension strategies that apply broadly across contexts. What characterizes these successful studies, and how do they differ from previous attempts? These studies share three important and interrelated features. They are as follows:

1. *Importance of explicit task analysis.* These studies all stress the importance of a thorough and accurate task analysis as a necessary precondition to teaching for transfer. In the cases of Larkin et al. (1986) and Klahr and Carver (1988), these task analyses were expressed as simulation models that could perform the task, which is the ultimate check on the sufficiency of a proposed method. Although simulation models are neither a necessary nor sufficient condition for success, the kind of explicit task analysis that they require does seem to drive out the unsubstantiated wishful thinking that characterizes some of the previous work on transfer.

2. *Appreciation of computational demands.* One consequence of a serious attempt at task analysis is an enhanced appreciation of how difficult it is to apply abstract knowledge across contexts. This leads to moderated expectations about what kinds of transfer are possible, and also to an enhanced appreciation of the importance of control knowledge. For example, one analysis of Schoenfeld's (1985) success is that, through painstaking task analysis, he was able to specify some of the conditions under which Polya's heuristics should be used. In defining a strategy, the researcher must be explicit about when the strategy is useful and when it is not. An inability to specify these conditions is a sure sign that the strategy is deficient.

3. *Enhanced role for the teacher.* In much of the experimental work on transfer, the mode of operation has been to present problems to students that, under the experimenter's analysis, shared elements or were amenable to a similar mode of attack. After doing little or nothing to codify the similarities between problems, the experimenters would then lament the depressing lack of spontaneous transfer observed. These studies place the researcher in a much more proactive position, following the lead of the Gestalt psychologists (e.g., Katona, 1940), who countered Thorndike by attributing low levels of observed transfer to the lack of quality instruction.

The message from these three studies is that, not only must the teacher scope out the domain and codify the abstract strategy, the teacher must also successfully communicate that strategy to students. Each of these steps is difficult and prone to error. It seems, however, that students need help formulating and managing abstractions if transfer is the desired outcome.

PROMOTING TRANSFER THROUGH MODEL TRACING

This chapter reports on attempts to teach abstract problem-solving strategies in the domains of mathematics and programming. Like the aforementioned studies, this work stresses the importance of an explicit task analysis, and teaching the products of that analysis directly to students. In fact, these two concerns are forged together in the approach. In this work, model-tracing intelligent tutoring systems (Anderson, Boyle, Farrell, & Reiser, 1989) are used to teach the students. In a model-tracing tutor, problem-solving strategies are specified in the form of running cognitive simulations of ideal student performance. These strategies are typically defined through detailed cognitive task analyses informed by verbal protocols of more and less proficient students solving problems in the domain, as well as protocols drawn from experts. The resulting ideal student model is used as a benchmark against which actual student performance can be judged. As students solve problems with a model-tracing tutor, the simulation of the ideal student is run simultaneously in the background, and student input is checked against simulated input from the ideal model. In the case of a discrepancy, the student is interrupted with tutoring designed to remedy the deficit. The strength of the model-tracing paradigm is that, when one of these discrepancies is detected, the tutor can pinpoint the problem very precisely. The tutor determines which knowledge should have been brought to bear by examining the ideal model, and then tailors instruction to increase the probability of that knowledge being brought to bear at appropriate times in the future. As should be apparent, the success of the model-tracing paradigm is heavily dependent on getting the "correct" representation of cognitive skill. Building a robust student model is labor intensive: If one wants to avoid having an autocratic and limiting system, it is important to be able to at least recognize (if not support) all viable solution paths and strategies in the domain of instruction. This means accommodating differences in both the general approach taken to solve a problem as well as the ordering and/or grain size of steps within a particular approach. Ultimately, however, there is a lot of indeterminacy in what constitutes a "correct" representation. But this indeterminacy is a potential strength if the goal is to engineer transfer. Even if a tutor can accommodate different strategies for solving a problem, it should prefer and encourage those strategies that are cast at a high enough level of abstraction so that they apply across a wide variety of problems.

How do students learn in a model-tracing tutor? Model tracing is closely related to the notions of apprenticeship learning (Brown, Collins, & Duguid, 1988) and scaffolding (Vygotsky, 1978). However, these processes are typically mediated by human tutors, are poorly understood, and are characterized by lots of implicit intelligence (Day, Cordon, & Kerwin, 1989). Model tracing, on the other hand, demands precise operationalization because it is mediated by a computer. It is precise in both its conceptualization of what is being taught and its method of teaching. Of course, precision is not necessarily an overriding virtue: Given the lack of understanding of what constitutes good tutoring and technological limitations, the instructional strategies currently employed by model-tracing tutors are almost certainly precisely limited and precisely nonoptimal. But being precise is a virtue in the sense that it defines a starting point from which one can make comparisons and incrementally improve learning outcomes.

Model-tracing tutors as a class subscribe to the theory of learning by doing (Anzai & Simon, 1979). They promote learning through the means discussed here.

Instruction in Problem-Solving Context

The theory of learning by doing holds that instruction should take place primarily during problem solving, not before or after. In a model-tracing tutor, this instruction primarily takes the form of help to perform the next step of a problem or remediation following an errorful step. Depending on the situation, this instruction could be quite strategic or conceptual, for example, the next "step" could be construed as setting a high-level goal structure for solving the problem. In these contexts, students see knowledge applied immediately and forcefully to solve real problems, and can quickly apply it for themselves. In contrast, standard textbook instruction is sometimes characterized as conveying inert knowledge that must be "bridged" to actual problem-solving situations, which is an uncertain and errorful process (Pea, 1989). By presenting information just as it is needed to solve a problem, the gap between abstract knowledge and its application is minimized. However, the danger is that knowledge can become overly situated, with students failing to appreciate its range of application. Model-tracing tutors should promote generality by exemplifying abstractions in a variety of concrete problem-solving situations.

Successive Approximation to the Target Skill

As in apprenticeship learning, the instructional approach in model tracing is to place students in real problem-solving situations and encourage them to do as much as they can as soon as they can. The tutor is there to provide scaffolding when it is needed and to adjust problem content and difficulty so that students can make steady progress toward mastery. Typically, the skill is not broken down into prerequisites that are practiced in isolation and then recombined (Gagne & Briggs, 1979). Mastery is achieved through more of a task-oriented, spiral curriculum, which has motivational as well as cognitive benefits (Carroll, 1990). Students begin by solving simple but nevertheless full-blown problems, not meaningless exercises.

Individualization

The defining feature of a model-tracing tutor is the individualization of feedback and practice based on an articulate model of proficient performance. This goes beyond the individualization offered in traditional computer-based instruction, in that feedback is delivered on actual task performance, and not on just the exhibition of knowledge that underlies task performance. Pinpointing and remediating specific weaknesses in task performance maximizes productive learning time and minimizes frustration.

Individualization takes a variety of forms. As mentioned earlier, the system can provide help (requested by the student) or remediation (delivered following an errorful action) geared toward getting students to resolve a problem-solving impasse and provide the next step. To do this, the system must understand what work the student has already done (or is salvageable) and be able to describe and, most importantly from the standpoint of transfer, motivate which step to perform next. This involves anchoring the step in the context of some larger plan or goal structure. Additionally, the system can recognize and respond to specific errors a student is making. To do this, the system must maintain a catalogue of prestored errors that students are likely to commit or be equipped with some generative theory of errors (VanLehn, 1990).[1] Finally, model-tracing tutors could teach different subpopulations of students with different techniques, but the paucity of well-documented aptitude-treatment interactions on which to base customized interventions makes this largely unrealized potential at this time.

Reification and Exemplification of Abstract Cognitive Structures

The model-tracing approach inherits the aforementioned three features from more conventional, human-mediated forms of individualized instruction, such as apprenticeship learning. But the computer medium in which model-tracing tutoring takes place affords a unique kind of support that is not readily available in human tutoring: the reification of problem-solving goals and actions. In most conventional instruction, as students solve problems, the abstract goals and plans (or strategies) that organize and motivate low-level problem-solving actions are often implicit. As students solve problems with a model-tracing tutor, however, these abstract goals and plans can be reified as graphical objects in the user interface and become the focus of tutorial discourse. Students may be asked not only to perform a sequence of actions that will solve the problem, but also to produce the higher level abstractions, the goals and plans, that organize those actions. Of course, it is just these abstract goals and plans that represent the deep structure of the domain and form the basis for transfer across problems, so it is critically important to make them explicit during practice. The goal structures provide the rationale for taking a particular problem-solving action, and thereby support reasoning about the range of application of that action in other problems. Once reified at the user interface, the goal and plan structures provide an abstract

---

[1]There is some debate about whether it is pedagogically effective to characterize students' errors ("this is what you are doing wrong") or whether it is sufficient to simply provide remediation ("this is what you should be doing"; Sleeman, Kelly, Martinek, Ward, & Moore, 1989). Presently, there seems to be little evidence to support the additional burden of bug diagnosis, although the definitive experiment has probably not yet been performed.

annotation on the problem-solving trace, and the trace itself becomes an exemplification of the abstraction. This reification and exemplification of abstractions is useful not only when the problem-solving actions are being generated in the first place, but also after the problem has been solved and students are reflecting on their work (Collins & Brown, 1988).

AN EXAMPLE: ALGEBRA WORD PROBLEM SOLVING

As an example of the model-tracing approach, I now describe the development of a tutoring system for algebra word problems (Singley, Anderson, Gevins, & Hoffman, 1989). First, I describe our cognitive task analysis and subsequent codification of abstract strategies for algebra word problem solving. Then I briefly describe the system we used to teach those strategies, and finally an experiment we conducted to assess the effectiveness of those strategies.

Task Analysis of Algebra Word Problem Solving

As previously mentioned, the first step in promoting transfer through model tracing is to perform a thorough task analysis to determine the component steps of problem solving, and more importantly, some overall strategy for generating and sequencing those components. To solve an algebra word problem, students must first derive a representation of the elements of the problem, and then do a considerable amount of problem-solving search to put the elements together. One of the many reasons why word problem solving is so difficult is that in most cases these two phases of problem solving (representation and search for solution) are nearly independent. Mistakes in the representation phase can lead to impasses in the solution phase, but rarely do these impasses reveal anything about the nature of the underlying misconception.

I develop the task analysis in the context of an example problem, the classic picture frame problem:

> A picture frame measures 20 cm by 14 cm. 160 sq cm of picture shows. What is the width of the frame?

Generally, to solve an algebra word problem, one must bring to bear a set of constraints that serve to express the answer of the problem in terms of known quantities (we view equations as quantitative constraints among variables). I examine the five steps a hypothetical ideal student might take in solving such a problem. In our description, the steps are presented in a certain well-defined order, where one stage of processing finishes before the next begins. In fact, the students we have observed interleave the components discussed here a fair amount.

Step 1: Define the Problem Situation. As a first step, it is helpful to represent the qualitative relationships between the various elements of the problem. This set of qualitative relationships (e.g., the picture is centered inside the frame, the frame has equal width on all four sides, etc.) has been called the *problem situation* (Reusser, 1985). In line with the work of Larkin and Simon (1987), we view a pictorial diagram as being a powerful and compact representation of this set of relationships. Once constructed, the diagram not only provides useful cues for generating constraints but also acts as a kind of search control mechanism for combining constraints.

Step 2: Map Known Quantities Onto the Problem Situation. Once the elements of the problem have been identified and the qualitative relationships between them established, it is then necessary to map the known quantities provided in the problem statement onto the elements. If a diagram is being used, this amounts to labeling elements of the diagram with the givens, and finally, labeling the goal of the problem with a variable. Needless to say, the correct construction of the diagram does not logically imply the correct labeling of the diagram.

Step 3: Generate Constraints. One important feature of the more difficult algebra word problems is that much of the information required for their solution is not stated explicitly in the problem text. Important quantitative relationships are missing from the problem statement and must either be derived from the problem situation or retrieved from the problem schema. For example, in the picture frame problem, the text simply provides a series of variable assignments. Not stated explicitly are the three primitive constraints that are critical for solution:

- The area of the picture equals the length of the picture times the width of the picture.
- The length of the picture equals the longer dimension of the frame minus two times the width of the frame.
- The width of the picture equals the shorter dimension of the frame minus two times the width of the frame.

When properly combined, these three primitive constraints are sufficient for the solution of this problem. However, many more constrains can be derived from the problem situation, such as the area of the picture equals the total area minus the area of the frame, and the total area equals the longer dimension of the frame times the shorter dimension of the frame. Before solving the problem, it is impossible to know which of these constraints will be useful.

Step 4: Combine Constraints. A very important component of word problem solving that has been largely overlooked is search. Singley (1986) found that, in the domain of calculus-related rates word problems, the representation phase was not the most difficult to master. Rather, the search through the system of equations took the most time and was the locus of most errors.

According to our task analysis, algebra word problems involve the solution of systems of equations, too. For example, in our picture frame problem, the three constraints presented here must be combined in such a way that the goal of the problem is expressed in terms of known quantities. The search problem is that there are more than just these three constraints that are potentially relevant and there are untold ways of combining the constraints. Indeed, it is rather impressive that beginning algebra students can solve these problems at all, given that this search process has been largely hidden from them in standard instructional texts. Given that students have no systematic method for dealing with search, it is no wonder that performance in word problem solving is often brittle and shows little transfer to new problem types. Given the lack of strategic instruction, students must learn particular solution patterns for particular problems.

Step 5: Solve the Final Equation. Once an equation is written that incorporates all the necessary constraints, the problem is finished except for algebraic solution. The details of this process have been explored in other work in our laboratory (Lewis, Milson, & Anderson, 1987). We have concluded that algebraic solution is largely decoupled from the other components of word problem solving skill and can be profitably ignored in a word problem curriculum (Heid & Kunkle, 1988; Singley, 1988).

In summary, our task analysis claims that word problem solving is difficult because it is a knowledge-intensive task that involves a number of difficult components, not the least of which is the search through the space of constraints (Steps 3 and 4). Indeed, data from an initial study we conducted showed that students make 10 times as many errors on word problems that involve systems of equations, and that the difficulty of a problem is directly related to the number of primitive equations that make up the solution. This is consistent with the results of a relatively recent National Assessment of Educational Progress, a national survey of mathematical problem-solving abilities (Carpenter, Corbitt, Kepner, Lindquist, & Reys, 1980). The survey showed that performance on one-step word problems was quite good, but that performance on multistep problems was quite bad.

These results all suggest that students need help managing their search processes, and this is what we chose to focus on. Through our task analysis, we defined three distinct strategies for the generation and combination of constraints: skeletal strategy, means–ends strategy, and diagram strategy.

Skeletal Strategy

The skeletal strategy is a working-forward strategy that most closely approximates the kinds of example solutions presented in textbooks (e.g., Forester, 1984). In the skeletal strategy, one first writes the primitive equation that is in some sense key to solving the problem. This primitive equation in most cases does not contain the goal variable, and its presentation is entirely unmotivated except for the fact that it "works." For example, to solve the example problem, one would first recognize that the area of the picture is equal to the length of the picture times the width of the picture:

$$length * width = 160. \tag{1}$$

Notice that this equation makes no reference to the goal variable, the width of the frame (x), and at first blush seems irrelevant. However, this is the skeletal equation, the equation that provides the structure that allows students to simply work forward to solve the problem. At this point, one would then realize that the length of the picture equals $20 - 2x$, and the width of the picture equals $14 - 2x$, and suddenly one has an equation that is solvable for x:

$$(20 - 2x)(14 - 2x) = 160. \tag{2}$$

The skeletal strategy gets its name from the fact that the first equation written is the easily identified skeleton of the final equation (i.e., the equation can easily be seen as a *length * width = area* equation). It is easily identified because the skeletal equation (which again typically does not contain the goal variable) provides for a parse tree that has minimal depth and maximal breadth. Thus, the skeletal strategy generates final equations whose structures are easily understood. This may be why it is popular in terms of exposition: It provides the most easily understood postmortem of how a problem was solved. However, the strategy is not generative in that particular skeletal equations and subsequent solution steps are largely unmotivated. The search problem is totally ignored; learning is reduced to the more-or-less rote acquisition of specific problem-solution patterns or schemas.

Means–Ends Strategy

Means–ends analysis is a working-backward strategy that has been well documented as a novice strategy for solving systems of equations (Larkin, McDermott, Simon, & Simon, 1980). However, to my knowledge, it has never before been taught directly to algebra students. In means–ends analysis, one first writes a primitive equation that contains the goal variable. Given this equation, subgoals are set to find values for the remaining unknowns. Additional constraints are generated that contain the unknowns and are substituted into the equation containing the goal. The problem is solved when the goal variable is stated in terms of knowns. Here is a solution trace of the picture frame problem using the means–ends strategy:

$$14 - 2x = w \text{ (where } w \text{ is the width of the picture)} \tag{3}$$

$$w = 160/\ell \text{ (where } \ell \text{ is the length of the picture)} \tag{4}$$

$$14 - 2x = 160/\ell \text{ (substitute 4 into 3 to eliminate } w) \tag{5}$$

$$\ell = 20 - 2x \tag{6}$$

$$14 - 2x = 160/(20 - 2x) \text{ (substitute 6 into 5 to eliminate } \ell) \tag{7}$$

The advantage of means–ends analysis over the skeletal strategy is that the first as well as all subsequent steps are well motivated. However, the resulting final equation is difficult to understand because the strategy generates a tree structure that has maximal depth and minimal breadth. Thus, it is hard to understand the solution once it is generated. Indeed, Sweller, Mawer, and Ward (1983) claimed that means–ends analysis interferes with learning because it makes heavy demands on working memory and obscures the underlying problem schemas. Nevertheless, when the goal of instruction is not the acquisition of a catalogue of schemas but rather an abstract strategy that applies broadly across problem types, means–ends analysis seems superior to the standard textbook strategy.

Diagram Strategy

Another strategy we have defined makes direct use of the diagram. It involves the repeated labeling of objects in the diagram using only the goal variable and known quantities until an equation can be written that makes use of the labels and contains the goal variable. For example, Fig. 4.1 shows the labeling of a diagram for the picture frame problem using this strategy. At this point, an equation can be written that states the area of the picture (160) in terms of the length of the picture (20 – 2x) and the width of the picture (14 – 2x). The virtue of this strategy is that it introduces no extra variables and thus places a smaller burden on working memory. In addition, the diagram provides at least heuristic guidance about which object to label next, so the search problem is somewhat mitigated.

In problems involving tables, the search problem is reduced further. Each row and column in the table represents a separate primitive equation that is potentially

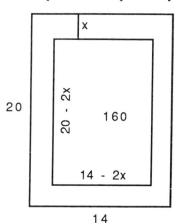

FIG. 4.1. The diagram strategy applied to the picture frame problem.

relevant, and the two-dimensional structure of the table reveals the systematicity of the primitive equations, most importantly which equations share variables and therefore can be combined.

The drawback of the diagram strategy is that the termination point is unclear. One must continually monitor the diagram to see when the final equation can be written. Also, the diagrams themselves vary between problem types, and the strategy is not enabled until a correct diagram is constructed. This limits the generality of the strategy somewhat.

Design of the Tutor

The Algebra Word Problem Tutor is designed to support each of the five components of word problem-solving skill previously outlined. Figure 4.2 shows the interface of the tutor following solution of the picture frame problem using the means–ends strategy. Although the means–ends strategy is shown, the system was programmed to tutor on any of the three strategies described. Interestingly, the tutor can generate answers to problems using either the means–ends strategy or the diagram strategy. It must be preprogrammed with solutions using the skeletal strategy.

I now describe the tools provided by the tutor for the five problem-solving components. For the first step, defining the problem situation, the tutor simply presents students with appropriate diagrams in a separate diagram window. Thus, students are not actively involved in the construction of diagrams.[2] Once the diagram is displayed, students are encouraged to label its lines and shapes with either numbers, variables, or expressions. This is done simply by first telling the system the kind of object to be labeled (line or shape), selecting the particular object with the mouse, and entering the new label on a keypad. The system is very flexible in terms of the labels it accepts. For example, the following are just a few of the valid labels for the leftmost vertical line in Fig. 4.2: (a) 20, (b) y, (c) $2x + p$ (where p is the length of the picture), (d) $(160 + f)/14$ (where f is the area of the frame), (e) $[p * (14 - 2x) + f]/(w + 2x)$ (where w is the width of the picture).

If a student asks for help and all known quantities are not posted on the diagram, the tutor will help the student post the missing quantities through a succession of hints. The tutor does no work directly for the student.

The tutor allows students to write primitive (or composed) constraints at any time during the solution of the problem. There are two ways to write constraints: either by writing a full-fledged equation (in support of the means–ends or skeletal strategies) or by labeling the diagram with an expression (in support of the diagram strategy). In Fig. 4.2, we see that the student has not labeled the diagram with expressions, but has instead written three primitive equations. If a student

---

[2]We have experimented somewhat with providing diagram construction tools to students, but I do not report on this work here (see Singley & Anderson, in prep).

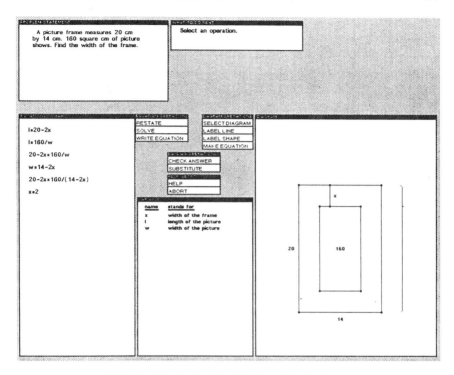

FIG. 4.2.   The Algebra Word Problem Tutor interface.

asks for help and not all the necessary constraints have been generated, the tutor recommends different things depending on the strategy being used:

• Skeletal strategy. If no constraints at all have been generated, the tutor recommends writing the so-called skeletal equation. This is followed by recommendations to perform the predetermined substitutions required by the skeletal strategy.

• Means–ends strategy. The tutor first recommends writing the primitive equation that contains the goal variable and the fewest number of unknowns. Once such an equation exists, the tutor recommends that students write additional primitive equations that can be used to replace the remaining unknown variables with either known values or expressions containing known values and the goal variable.

• Diagram strategy. The tutor recommends labeling the diagram with an expression involving only known values and the goal variable (no new variables are recommended). At any point in the solution process, a very limited number of objects can be labeled in this way. Thus, constraints are generated in an order that is determined by the givens of the problem, which gives the diagram strategy a decidedly working-forward flavor.

To support the combination of constraints, the tutor supplies a substitution operator that can be used to eliminate an unwanted variable in the target equation by replacing it with either its numeric value or an equivalent symbolic expression. For example, given the equations $160 = \ell * w$ and $\ell = 20 - 2x$, the substitution operator returns $160 = (20 - 2x) * w$.

In addition, the tutor supplies students with a symbolic calculator that solves any equation containing a single variable. The focus in the tutor, then, is on deriving a solvable equation, not on solving it.

Evaluation of Strategies

Having identified three distinct strategies for constraint generation and combination, we were interested in comparing them in terms of both ease of learning and range of transfer. To recap our task analysis, we determined that the skeletal strategy, although good for explaining the solution trace for a particular problem, was not generative and should show poor transfer. The means–ends and diagram strategies were both generative in that each step could be well motivated. The diagram strategy, however, required a well-formed diagram to enable it, and as we have not yet defined a generative strategy for diagram construction, its range of transfer should be somewhat limited. On the other hand, the lack of variable proliferation and subgoaling in the diagram strategy should make it easy to learn and perform.

We performed an experiment comparing the strategies. The students were 24 Grade 7 children who were concurrently taking their first course in algebra. All had had some exposure to work problems and had been taught how to solve linear and quadratic equations. Students were assigned to one of the three strategies, and additionally, to one of four training problem schemas: coin mixture, liquid mixture, rectangular frame, or two-sided frame. Participants solved problems drawn from one of the four schemas using the tutor until a training criterion was achieved: two consecutive problems with a total of two or fewer errors and no help requests. Following training, participants solved problems from each of the other three types, in addition to more problems of the same type. The other three types of problems represented near and far transfer problems. For example, if a student were trained on coin-mixture problems, then the liquid-mixture problems would represent near transfer problems, and the two types of frame problems would represent far transfer problems. *Near transfer* is defined by the sharing of some (but not all) of the underlying primitive equations that define a problem schema. *Far transfer* is defined by disjoint sets of underlying primitive equations.

The mean number of trials to criterion for the diagram, means–ends, and skeletal strategies were 7.8, 8.9, and 11.1, respectively. A post hoc t test revealed that the diagram strategy took significantly fewer trials to reach criterion than the skeletal strategy ($t = 2.32$, $df = 16$, $p < .05$). Figure 4.3 shows comparisons of the strategies on the transfer problems in terms of help requests per problem.

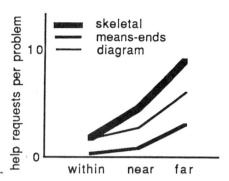

FIG. 4.3. Performance of the three strategies on transfer problems in terms of help requests per problem. The "within" category refers to problems of the same type seen in training.

(Other dependent measures, such as time per problem and errors per problem, yielded no significant effects.) As shown, the means–ends strategy emerges as the superior strategy on both near and far transfer problems. Analyses of covariance and subsequent t tests revealed that students taught the means–ends strategy asked for help significantly fewer times than students taught the skeletal strategy in both the near transfer ($t = 3.2$, $df = 16$, $p < .05$) and far transfer ($t = 2.7$, $df = 16$, $p < .05$) problems.

Thus, it appears that the diagram and means–ends strategies are superior to a formalization of the standard textbook strategy in terms of both learning and transfer. The diagram strategy leads to the fastest criterion performance, and the means–ends strategy leads to the fewest requests for help in both near and far transfer situations. It is interesting that the same strategy was not superior in terms of both learning and transfer. The Gestalter Katona (1940) first hinted at this trade-off between learning and transfer when he observed that a rote strategy for solving matchstick problems was easier to learn but showed less transfer than a more meaningful strategy. Singley and Anderson (1989) showed that, in production system simulations, general methods require more rules than specific methods because they generate deeper goal structures, which again implies a learning-transfer trade-off. These results place an important restriction on the work of Sweller and his colleagues (Sweller, Mawer, & Ward, 1983). Sweller's position is that means–ends analysis is a poor strategy for novices, in that it places undue demands on working memory and interferes with schema acquisition. Given the present results, however, perhaps we should question whether schema acquisition is a proper goal of instruction. Sweller's position is reminiscent of the situated learning position, in that issues of learning dominate at the expense of issues of transfer.

REIFICATION OF GOAL STRUCTURES

As argued earlier, a great deal of instructional leverage comes from an accurate and complete task analysis of the domain and the successful communication of that analysis to the student. This is especially true for the more strategic aspects of a skill. Abstract goal structures and plans are what drive problem solving, and are at the root of problem-solving transfer, yet their explication is typically absent from traditional pedagogy. Because the reification and communication of goal and plan structures hold such promise for promoting transfer, and are particularly possible in model-tracing tutors, this topic deserves further attention.

Reactive and Proactive Reification

As stated previously, if transfer is the goal, then attempts should be made to codify problem-solving strategies at high levels of abstraction in the ideal model. However, just because the strategic knowledge in an ideal model is cast at a certain level of abstraction does not mean that students will learn those abstractions through their interactions with the tutor. There is no way to pour the contents of the ideal model directly into the students' heads, as was the case in the classical image of the Nurnberg funnel (Carroll, 1990). The challenge to model-tracing tutors is to structure the interface and the interaction between system and student such that these abstractions are communicated effectively and become an integral part of problem solving. This is largely an interface design problem, and many approaches are possible.

Minimally, it seems a tutor should reference goal and plan structures in any help, feedback, and remediation messages it delivers. This is what was done in the algebra word problem tutor. For example, if a student had difficulty writing a primitive equation to further the means–ends strategy, the system would identify the "best" equation that the student had written (the one that contained the answer variable and the fewest other unknowns) and would remind the student that the goal was to eliminate all variables other than the answer variable in that equation. Couching feedback in terms of goals and plans is well exemplified in Proust, a semantic program checker for Pascal programming (Johnson, 1986). In Proust, students submit small programs for semantic analysis (much as one would submit a program to a compiler for syntactic analysis) and are given feedback on their solutions in terms of goals and plans improperly realized or not realized at all. The system induces the overall strategy the student used to solve the problem from the surface-level code produced, and then judges the solution in terms of that strategy. For example, it may be determined that the student was trying to shield the program against bad input, but that the implementation failed to treat a certain case. Feedback would make reference to the overall goal, point out places in the program where the goal was inadequately addressed, and suggest fixes. The operative principles here are that, first of all, problem-solving actions (in this case, lines of Pascal code) can only be understood and judged in terms of how they contribute to the realization of goals and plans, and that, second, feedback on those actions is most meaningful and effective if it makes reference to goals and plans.

Goal and plan discourse in the context of error feedback and help messages can be characterized as reactive reification. Students either need help correcting a faulty move, or generating the next step of a solution, and the tutor brings to bear its underlying goal and plan abstractions to structure the situation and render its advice in a more conceptually rich context. Except for these breakdown situations, however, the goal and plan abstractions are kept "under the covers." But another possibility is proactive reification, in which the system imbeds the goal and plan abstractions directly into the interface and makes their manipulation an integral part of problem solving.

One example of proactive reification is in the interface of the Related Rates Tutor (Singley, 1990). The Related Rates Tutor helps first-year calculus students solve related rates word problems. Through initial verbal protocol analyses of problem solving in the domain, it was discovered that students were attempting to execute what was the standard chain-rule strategy for solving these problems, but were having trouble formulating and maintaining the requisite subgoals. To remedy this problem, an enhancement to the interface of the tutor was designed that allowed students to post and display the subgoals required by the chain-rule strategy.

Figure 4.4 shows the goal blackboard at two different points in the solution process. Related rates problems typically involve the application of the chain rule to relate variables that are otherwise unrelated in any of the equations given. For example, one could chain together a derivative describing changes in p with respect to s (dp/ds) with another relating changes in s with respect to t (ds/dt) to yield a derivative relating changes in p with respect to t (dp/dt). Thus, in this case, if the goal is to find dp/dt, possible subgoals are to find dp/ds and ds/dt and then combine them with the chain rule. Before solving the problem, the tutor first asks that students state their plan in terms of the simple goal structures shown in the figure. The tutor provides feedback on the adequacy of the goal structure to solve the problem, and all subsequent actions taken by the student are judged in relation to the goal structure. For example, a particular action may be flagged by the system as not contributing to any of the subgoals. The interface also helps the student with goal management, a serious problem plaguing novice performance (Anderson, Farrell, & Sauers, 1984). As students progress through problems, individual subgoals are boxed and shaded to indicate which are active and which have been satisfied, respectively.

An experiment testing the effects of this type of planning discourse showed that student problem-solving performance improved in terms of both speed and quality of moves while the goal blackboard was present during training. Furthermore, many of the positive effects persisted after the goal blackboard was taken away in a posttest, suggesting that the blackboard was not only a performance aid but also a learning catalyst. Finally, and perhaps most importantly, use of the goal blackboard improved transfer to other kinds of calculus problems not involving the chain rule but amenable to solution with an analogous goal structure.

The usefulness of proactive reification may be limited by the fact that it may be difficult to find a transparent representation for goals and plans that are easily

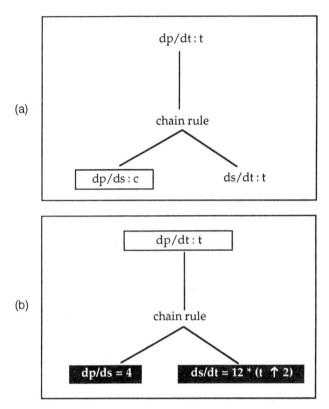

FIG. 4.4. The goal blackboard in the Related Rates Tutor. (a) Here the goal structure has been posted and it is time to satisfy the first subgoal, finding *dp/ds*. (b) The two subgoals have now been satisfied and it is time to apply the chain rule to derive *dp/dt*.

manipulable by the student in some domains. The problem is that the planning space is typically positioned at a level of abstraction far above what Newell and Simon (1972) called the physical problem space, the space where actual operations are carried out. It may be that the goal blackboard worked in the Related Rates Tutor simply because the usual distinction between the planning space and the physical problem space is for the most part degenerate in this domain: The goals themselves are very similar to the kinds of objects that students were manipulating in the physical problem space. This meant that students are not burdened with learning a new and abstract vocabulary for conversing about goal structures in this domain. However, in other domains, such as programming, the planning structures are more abstract and may have little meaning to the novice. The danger of goal reification in these domains is that it may overwhelm students with additional complexity. Whether this additional burden in some sense pays for itself in terms of enhanced transfer outcomes is unclear at present.

Bridge (Bonar, 1988) is an interesting example of a system that attempts proactive reification in the domain of Pascal programming. Bridge first asks students to state their solution plan for a program in terms of a sequence of English phrases, such as "read in . . ." or "keep the count of . . . ," which are selected from a menu. The student is then asked to transform this representation into an abstract goal-plan structure. Plans are graphical schemalike structures that are selected from a catalogue and whose slots are filled in by the student to fit the situation. For example, the New Value Controlled Loop Plan has four slots. Three of these take other plans with slots as fillers (plans to get new input, to perform computations inside the loop, and to perform computations once the loop is exited); the last specifies the loop test. Once completed, the student uses these abstract structures to organize the generation of actual Pascal code. The system provides feedback on the construction of the plans, and then uses them for conceptual leverage in the delivery of feedback on subsequent Pascal coding.

Incidental Reification

Although the benefits in terms of transfer from proactive reification may be great, it may be prohibitively expensive to ask students to learn to construct solutions with an abstract planning language in some domains. As an alternative, we have recently been experimenting with yet another kind of goal reification, something we have dubbed incidental reification. In contrast to the approach where goal structures are constructed directly by the learner, the approach in incidental reification is to have the system take responsibility for generating and displaying the goals. As students take actions in the physical problem space, a goal-plan parser automatically updates the contents of a goal blackboard to reflect the system's current interpretation of what the student is doing. The interpretation may be that the student is on track and pursuing a reasonable goal given the current problem, or perhaps the student is pursuing an inappropriate goal or pursuing a reasonable goal in an inappropriate way. Once displayed, the goal structures can become the focus of tutorial discourse just as if the student had generated them. The defining feature of incidental reification is that the goal structures are updated automatically and incidentally in response to the student's conventional problem solving in the domain.

We have been exploring the use of incidental reification in the development of a tutor of Smalltalk[3] programming called Molehill (Singley, Carroll, & Alpert, 1991). The component of Molehill that implements incidental reification is an information display called the Goalposter. The Goalposter displays the system's ongoing interpretation of the students' actions in terms of inferred goals and

---

[3]Smalltalk is an object-oriented, rapid-prototyping environment with a large number of built-in object classes and methods that are meant to be selected and combined to build applications quickly. Unlike learning a procedural language like Pascal or C, learning Smalltalk is dominated by browsing through the class hierarchy and becoming familiar with the extensive code library.

plans, a kind of goal blackboard that maintains the students' current goal tree. As students browse the class hierarchy or write code, the display updates automatically to reflect the system's current interpretation of the students' actions. Although textual, the presentation of individual goals is telegraphic: several words at most. Goals are displayed in a hierarchical list structure, with goal–subgoal relationships denoted by indentation. The Goalposter is useful after a project is finished in that goal traces are saved for later inspection. It is our hope that these goal traces will support analogical problem solving both inside and outside of the context of the tutor. Presently, only the Goalposter is permitted to post goals to the display. In order to get support from the tool, students are only required to recognize the posted goals and make the correspondence between the posted structures and their own behavior.

Figure 4.5 shows a screen image of Molehill. The Goalposter resides in the lower left pane; most remaining panes belong to the class hierarchy browser, a Smalltalk system tool that supports browsing through the code library. Here, the student is looking for character input functionality to create a new kind of window that displays all of its input in upper case, which is one of the initial projects

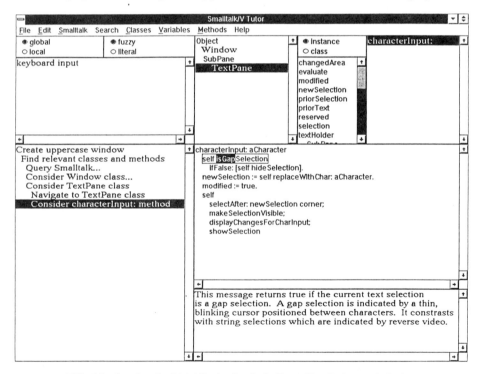

FIG. 4.5. Interface for Molehill, the Smalltalk Tutor. The Goalposter is in the lower left pane.

defined in the tutor. The student has just selected the characterInput: method defined in the TextPane class.

The Goalposter provides feedback on the correctness of goals and actions but it remains in the background of the student's work and does not prescribe action. The Goalposter displays the text of an inferred goal colored either red or green. Green signifies an appropriate goal for the user to attempt, and red indicates a "buggy," or incorrect or irrelevant, goal. The aim of this coloring scheme is to make salient whether the goal should be pursued. To gain a fuller understanding of the current goal state, the user may expand any red or green goal (by double-clicking on its text) to display an explanation of why the goal is worthwhile or not.

We display correct goals because, even when students are correct, feedback can be useful. Such feedback encourages learners to pursue appropriate courses of action and builds feelings of confidence. In the case of the Goalposter, the system provides feedback not only on the correctness of an action but also an interpretation of why it is correct and where it fits into the overall solution. We hope this will help communicate the conceptual structure of the solution as it develops.

The Goalposter employs a variety of goal management techniques. As appropriate goals become active, they are posted to the display in green. They remain in green until they are satisfied, at which time their color changes to black. Whenever a goal is suspended in favor of some other goal, its structure collapses, that is, only the top-level goal is shown in the display. The retention of the top-level goal in green serves as a reminder that the goal had been pursued but is now suspended. Once the goal is resumed, the structure expands and new subgoals are added to the existing structure. Thus, the Goalposter provides a kind of fish-eye view (Furnas, 1986) of the current state of the project, with higher resolution shown for the currently active goal. The current goal is automatically selected in the display, which means that all Goalposter menu operations by default apply to the current goal. To the extent that goals are unordered, the tutor applies a recency principle in the delivery of help: provide the next step for the most recently posted unsatisfied goal.

A major concern we have had is the comprehensibility of the Goalposter display. This concern centers on the complexity of the structure as a whole as well as the transparency of names of individual goals. We have already discussed our use of color coding and fish-eye views to try to manage the complexity of the display. A great danger is that the display will be viewed by learners as a complex addition to an already complex programming environment. In an attempt to avoid this pitfall, we have tried at every turn to simplify hierarchical relationships and use straightforward names for individual goals. However, we must conclude that, with incidental reification as well as reactive and proactive reification, interface design issues deserve lots of attention. We must strive to make the reification of goals illuminate rather than cloud the fundamental structure of problem solving.

CONCLUSION

In this chapter, I have tried to argue for the usefulness of model tracing as an approach for promoting both learning and transfer. Effective model tracing involves two difficult yet potentially rewarding tasks: the conceptualization and codification of problem-solving strategies in the domain and successful communication of those strategies to students. Ultimately, promoting transfer through model tracing is largely an engineering problem, and there will always be room for improvement.

There is always the possibility of discovering new, useful abstractions. One approach is to draw from pedagogical pioneers, as Schoenfeld did from the work of the eminent mathematician George Polya (Schoenfeld, 1985). But simply the exercise of building a model-tracing tutor often leads to the discovery of useful abstractions in the domain. We have discussed several simple examples of this in this chapter. Other examples include the evolution of more abstract and generative models of geometry problem solving in the context of the Geometry Tutor (Koedinger & Anderson, 1990) and the development of a cognitive model of programming recursion in the context of the Lisp Tutor (Pirolli, 1986).

Once discovered and codified, abstract strategies must be communicated effectively to students. We have discussed the potential benefits and drawbacks of three different communication techniques: reactive, proactive, and incidental reification. Again, the big challenge in each of these is to make the reifications reveal rather than obscure the essential nature and power of the abstraction. We have just begun exploration of the design space for reification, and much work remains to be done to realize the full potential of the approach.

REFERENCES

Anderson, J. R., Boyle, C. F., Farrell, R., & Reiser, B. J. (1989). Cognitive principles in the design of computer tutors. In P. Morris (Ed.), *Modelling cognition* (pp. 93–134). New York: Wiley.

Anderson, J. R., Farrell, R., & Sauers, R. (1984). Learning to program in LISP. *Cognitive Science, 8*, 87–129.

Anzai, Y., & Simon, H. A. (1979). The theory of learning by doing. *Psychological Review, 86*, 124–140.

Bonar, J. (1988). Intelligent tutoring with intermediate representations. *Proceedings of ITS '88 Intelligent Tutoring Systems Conference.* New York: ACM.

Brown, J. S., Collins, A., & Duguid, P. (1988). *Cognitive apprenticeship, situated cognition, and social interaction* (Institute for Research on Learning Report No. IRL88-0008). Palo Alto, CA: Institute for Research on Learning.

Carpenter, T. P., Corbitt, M. K., Kepner, K. S., Lindquist, M. M., & Reys, R. (1980). Results of the second NAEP mathematics assessment. *Mathematics Teacher, 73*, 329–338.

Carroll, J. M. (1990). *The Nurnberg funnel: Designing minimalist instruction for practical computer skill.* Cambridge, MA: MIT Press.

Collins, A., & Brown, J. S. (1988). The computer as a tool for learning through reflection. In H. Mandl & A. Lesgold (Eds.), *Learning issues for intelligent tutoring systems* (pp. 1–18). New York: Springer-Verlag.

Day, J. D., Cordon, L., & Kerwin, M. L. (1989). Informal instruction and development of cognitive skills: A review and critique of research. In C. McCormick, G. Miller, & M. Pressley (Eds.), *Cognitive strategy research: From basic research to educational applications* (pp. 83–103). New York: Springer-Verlag.

Forester, P. (1984). *Algebra I.* Menlo Park, CA: Addison-Wesley.

Furnas, G. (1986). Generalized fish-eye views. *Proceedings of CHI '86 Human Factors in Computing Systems.* New York: ACM.

Gagne, R. M., & Briggs, L. J. (1979). *Principles of instructional design* (3rd ed.). New York: Holt, Rinehart and Winston.

Gick, M., & Holyoak, K. (1983). Schema induction and analogical transfer. *Cognitive Psychology, 15,* 1–38.

Hayes, J. R., & Simon, H. A. (1977). Psychological differences among problem isomorphs. In J. Castellan, D. Pisoni, & G. Potts (Eds.), *Cognitive theory* (Vol. 2). Hillsdale, NJ: Lawrence Erlbaum Associates.

Heid, K. & Kunkle, D. (1988). Computer-generated tables: Tools for concept development in elementary algebra. In *Ideas for algebra: National Council of Teachers of Mathematics yearbook.* Reston, VA: NCTM.

Jeffries, R. (1978). *The acquisition of expertise on missionaries-cannibals and waterjug problems.* Unpublished doctoral dissertation, University of Colorado, Boulder.

Johnson, W. L. (1986). *Intention-based diagnosis of errors in novice programs.* Unpublished doctoral dissertation, Yale University, New Haven, CT.

Katona, G. (1940). *Organizing and memorizing.* New York: Columbia University Press.

Klahr, D., & Carver, S. (1988). Cognitive objectives in a LOGO debugging curriculum: Instruction, learning, and transfer. *Cognitive Psychology, 20,* 362–404.

Koedinger, K., & Anderson, J. R. (1990). Abstract planning and perceptual chunks: Elements of expertise in geometry. *Cognitive Science, 14,* 511–550.

Larkin, J. (1989). What kind of knowledge transfers? In L. Resnick (Ed.), *Knowing, learning, and instruction: Essays in honor of Robert Glaser* (pp. 283–306). Hillsdale, NJ: Lawrence Erlbaum Associates.

Larkin, J., McDermott, J., Simon, D. P., & Simon, H. A. (1980). Models of competence in solving physics problems. *Cognitive Science, 4,* 317–345.

Larkin, J., Reif, F., Carbonnell, J., & Gugliotta, A. (1986). *FERMI: A flexible expert reasoner with multi-domain inferencing* (Carnegie Mellon Department of Psychology Technical Report). Pittsburgh, PA: Carnegie Mellon University.

Larkin, J., & Simon, H. A. (1987). Why a diagram is (sometimes) worth ten thousand words. *Cognitive Science, 11,* 65–99.

Lave, J. (1988). *Cognitive in practice.* Cambridge, England: Cambridge University Press.

Lewis, M., Milson, R., & Anderson, J. R. (1987). The teacher's apprentice: Designing an intelligent authoring system for high school mathematics. In G. Kearsley (Ed.), *Artificial intelligence and instruction: Applications and methods* (pp. 269–302). Menlo Park, CA: Addison-Wesley.

Mayer, R., Dyck, J., & Vilberg, W. (1986). Learning to program and learning to think: What's the connection? *Communications of the ACM, 29,* 605–610.

Newell, A., & Simon, H. A. (1972). *Human problem solving.* Englewood Cliffs, NJ: Prentice-Hall.

Palincsar, A., & Brown, A. L. (1984). Reciprocal teaching of comprehension-fostering and comprehension-monitoring activities. *Cognition and Instruction, 1,* 117–176.

Papert, S. (1980). *Mindstorms: Children, computers, and powerful ideas.* New York: Basic Books.

Pea, R. (1989). *Socializing the knowledge transfer problem* (Institute for Research on Learning Report No. IRL89-0009). Palo Alto, CA: Institute for Research on Learning.

Pirolli, P. (1986). A cognitive model and computer tutor for programming recursion. *Human-Computer Interaction, 2*, 319–355.

Polson, P., & Jeffries, R. (1985). Instruction in general problem solving skills: Analysis of four approaches. In I. Segal, S. Chipman, & R. Glaser (Eds.), *Thinking and learning skills, Vol. I: Relating instruction to research*. Hillsdale, NJ: Lawrence Erlbaum Associates.

Polya, G. (1957). *How to solve it*. Garden City, NY: Doubleday/Anchor.

Post, T., & Brennan, M. L. (1976). An experimental study of the effectiveness of a formal vs. an informal presentation of a general heuristic process on problem solving in tenth grade geometry. *Journal for Research in Mathematics Education, 7*, 59–64.

Reusser, K. (1985). *From situation to equation: On formulation, understanding and solving situation problems* (Tech. Rep. No. 143, Institute of Cognitive Science). Boulder: University of Colorado.

Schoenfeld, A. (1985). *Mathematical problem solving*. New York: Academic Press.

Singley, M. K. (1986). *Developing models of skill acquisition in the context of intelligent tutoring systems*. Unpublished doctoral dissertation, Carnegie-Mellon University, Pittsburgh, PA.

Singley, M. K. (1988). The relationship between operator selection and application in mathematics problem solving. *Proceedings of ITS '88 Conference*. New York: Association for Computing Machinery.

Singley, M, K. (1990). The reification of goal structures in a calculus tutor: Effects on problem solving performance. *Interactive Learning Environments, 1*, 102–123.

Singley, M. K., & Anderson, J. R. (1989). *The transfer of cognitive skill*. Cambridge, MA: Harvard University Press.

Singley, M. K., & Anderson, J. R. (in prep.). *Learning and transfer of abstract strategies in algebra word problem solving*.

Singley, M. K., Anderson, J. R., Gevins, J., & Hoffman, D. (1989). The algebra word problem tutor. *Proceedings of the 4th International Conference on AI and Education*. Amsterdam: IOS.

Singley, M. K., Carroll, J. M., & Alpert, S. (1991). Psychological design rationale for an intelligent tutoring system for Smalltalk. In J. Koenemann-Belliveau, T. Moher, & S. Robertson (Eds.), *Empirical studies of programmers: Fourth workshop* (pp. 196–209). Norwood, NJ: Ablex.

Sleeman, D., Kelly, A., Martinek, R., Ward, R., & Moore, J. (1989). Studies of diagnosis and remediation with high school algebra students. *Cognitive Science, 13*, 551–568.

Sweller, J., Mawer, R., & Ward, M. (1983). Development of expertise in mathematical problem solving. *Journal of Experimental Psychology: General, 112*, 639–661.

Thorndike, E. L. (1924). Mental discipline in high school studies. *Journal of Educational Psychology, 15*, 1–22.

VanLehn, K. (1990). *Mind bugs: The origins of procedural misconceptions*. Cambridge, MA: MIT Press.

Vygotsky, L. S. (1978). *Mind in society: The development of higher psychological processes*. Cambridge, MA: Harvard University Press.

CHAPTER 5

Derived Structural Schemas and the Transfer of Knowledge

Donald F. Dansereau
Texas Christian University

OVERVIEW

These days almost every apartment or house has a thermostat. It controls the heater and the air conditioner. You set it for the temperature you want and it tries to keep the temperature near that. Inside it has a thermometer that measures the room temperature. It compares that with its goal, the temperature you set. If the room temperature does not match the goal, the thermostat turns on the right equipment to correct things. This pattern is shown as a flow diagram in Fig. 5.1.

If you lift the top of the tank on your flush toilet, flush it, and observe how the plumbing keeps the water at the right level, you will see that the pattern is similar to that of a thermostat. Only the names of the parts and the details of how they work are different.

This same pattern or schema applies to a lot of other things. In biology, it describes the way the body regulates water intake and blood sugar, and the muscle movements needed to push an elevator button. In engineering, it describes the way the elevator stops at the right place so you don't trip when you get in it. And in psychology, it describes how people who decide to take the stairs for exercise learn to control their climbing rate so they get their exercise and still can stand up when they get to the top.

Knowing this homeostasis schema in the form of the general diagram gives you some power (see Fig. 5.1). If you are trying to learn about a new process that you know is homeostatic in nature, the structural schema will provide a ready-made organization for capturing and cataloging the new ideas no matter

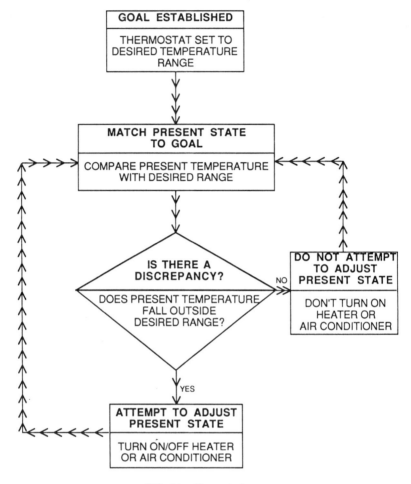

FIG. 5.1. Homeostasis map.

how they are presented. If you are trying to teach someone else about a homeostatic process, you can use the schema to organize the presentation and draw
parallels between this process and ones that are more familiar to the student. If
you are trying to think more deeply about a homeostatic process, you can use
elements of the structural schema as departure points ("How are the goals
established?" "How often does the matching process take place?") and as points
of comparison with similar processes. In general, a coherent schema of this type
provides a manageable structure for organizing knowledge and for relating it to
analogous domains.

There is good evidence that we use schemas all the time in our everyday
activities. These schemas contain the common elements that recur over a number
of similar episodes. For example, we have a schema for houses that contain the

aspects that are common to all houses we have experienced. We also have event schemas (sometimes called scripts) for going to restaurants, driving a car, and so on. Except when we need to be systematic (e.g., when choosing a house to buy, or teaching someone else to drive), we typically use these schemas without awareness, and in appropriate, but unsystematic ways. As is seen here, most of the previous thinking and research has dealt with these "naturally" acquired schemas. The homeostatic schema is a little different in that it was consciously derived and its use will likely be conscious and systematic. The use and study of "derived" structural schemas of this sort has been much less prevalent. These schemas apply to processing objects and procedures that either are infrequently experienced or are ones whose common elements are not obvious. In either case, natural, unconscious statistical averaging will not be effective; conscious derivation of schema categories is necessary. The focus of this chapter is to take a closer look at these schemas, their derivations, and their use in learning, thinking, and communicating.

Before proceeding further, I describe research with another derived structural schema (Brooks & Dansereau, 1983) in order to provide an example of the usefulness of this class of schemas. The specific schema for this research was created by asking upper level college students and instructors what categories and subcategories of information a well-informed individual needed to know about any scientific theory. Their responses were synthesized and condensed into a hierarchical structure with the following upper level categories:

<u>D</u>escription:	What phenomena does it attempt to explain? What are the theoretical principles? and How do they operate?
<u>I</u>nventor and history:	Who is responsible for the theory and what are its antecedents?
<u>C</u>onsequences:	What effects has it had on science and other aspects of the world?
<u>E</u>vidence:	What is the evidence for or against the theory?
<u>O</u>ther theories:	Are there other analogous, complementary, or competing theories?
<u>X</u>-tra information:	Is there any additional information about the theory that does not fit into one of the above slots?

These main categories were labeled using the acronym DICEOX (the first letter of each), to help people remember the schema.

In the Brooks and Dansereau (1983) study, college students were taught the main DICEOX categories, their subcategories, and their relationships. They were then taught how to use this schema in studying and recalling a text excerpt on a scientific theory. They were taught to take notes by filling in the DICEOX categories as they read the text. They were also instructed to use the DICEOX categories to cue their recall during testing. On a test of free recall, the DICEOX group significantly outperformed control groups who used their own study and testtaking methods (which typically included notetaking, underlining, and standard recall strategies).

I have taught DICEOX and a variety of other derived structural schemas (e.g., system, technique, and event schemas) to college students in my freshman-level techniques of college learning course. They are instructed to use them in studying for their regular courses. Feedback from students over five iterations of this course indicate that the derived schemas are usable and beneficial. They report that the schemas help them decide what they need to know, help them determine gaps and inconsistencies in their knowledge, and assist them in recalling and organizing information for tests and papers. Some students indicate that they feel less intimidated by teachers and textbooks because they have some advance knowledge about the structure of the content.

To balance the ledger, however, it is necessary to point out some of the dangers and shortcomings associated with these schemas. The following list was distilled from comments by students and other instructors who have used derived structural schemas:

- The schema may subdivide a topic inappropriately (i.e., the schema categories may cut the knowledge pie into pieces that are too large, too small, and/or the wrong shape).

- The wrong schema may be selected for a particular topic (e.g., a theory schema may be used when an event schema is most appropriate).

- Many topics are hybrids (i.e., combinations of schemas and schema segments). Application of a particular schema to the domain may be impossible or misleading.

- Placing information in schema categories may produce artificial conceptual boundaries and mask detailed interconnections between ideas located in different categories.

- Schema application may lead to relatively superficial treatment of a topic and may interfere with the formation of other, more appropriate mental models (e.g., a homeostatic schema may interfere with the development of a realistic mental image of the workings of a thermostat).

I believe these problems can be circumvented by the appropriate construction, selection, and application of these derived schemas. Schemas should be sufficiently detailed and precise to validly capture a knowledge domain, but simple and coherent enough to be manageable by a novice. The remainder of this chapter provides background on schema theory and research, and information on the development and use of derived structural schemas.

TERMINOLOGY

This chapter is about a particular type of schema. To provide a basis for a discussion of this concept and its history, we need to agree on some terminology. The following "working glossary" should be reviewed before proceeding (the alphabetizing has been contorted to reflect the priority of the terms in the subsequent discussions):

Schema, Natural

Description: A set of relatively abstract categories or placeholders and their interrelations. These schemas typically are formed by repeated experiences with the object, action, or event. Category labels are typically not used.

Examples: face schema, building schema, car schema

Comments: Most people do not use the term *natural schema*, but rather, just *schema*. I use the modifier and also use schemas rather than schemata as the plural.

Key References: Head (1920); Bartlett (1932); R. C. Anderson (1984).

Schema, Derived (structural)

Description: Similar to natural schemas, except that the underlying structural components of a set of instances are usually *consciously* derived and labeled by experts.

Examples: the DICEOX theory schema, homeostatic schema, and certain text and story grammars (see grammar entry)

Comments: This type of schema is the focus of this chapter.

Key References: Brooks and Dansereau (1983); Ohlhausen and Roller (1986); Bean, Singer, Cowen, and Rowan (1986).

Script, Natural

Description: A dynamic schema (see entry on natural schemas) that typically portrays a series of related actions. This script emerges typically from statistical averaging of a large number of episodes.

Examples: "Washing clothes," "Going to a restaurant"

Comments: Some writers do not distinguish between schema and script. I do.

Key References: Bransford and Johnson (1972); Schank and Abelson (1977); Bower, Black, and Turner (1979); Dansereau and Armstrong (1986); Abbott, Black, and Smith (1985); and Maki (1990).

Script, Derived (structural)

Description: Same as natural script, except that the underlying structural components of a set of instances (episodes) are usually *consciously* derived and labeled by experts.

Examples: the SQ3R and SCOUT study scripts (see Fig. 5.7)

Comments: This type of script is the focus of this chapter.

Key References: Robinson (1946) and Dansereau (1985).

Prototype

Description: The most salient representative of a class of objects. The set of features from which other members of the class can be derived by adding correction factors.

Examples: prototypical dog, face, car

Comments: Sometimes used synonymously with schema. Most used in perception and pattern recognition. Sometimes called a template.

Key References: Posner (1973); Evans (1968).

Grammar, Story, Text, and Case

Description: A derived schema for verbal materials. Contains elements common to a collection of stories and/or text.

Examples: Rumelhart's (1975) story grammars

Comments: These usually are derived by expert analysis, and, as a consequence, are strongly related to derived schemas.

Key References: Rumelhart (1975); Fillmore (1968; case grammar).

Frames

Description: According to Minsky (1975), "A frame is a data-structure for representing a stereotyped situation, like being in a certain kind of living room or going to a child's birthday party."

Examples: recognition frames

Comments: Rooted in an artificial intelligence (computer) perspective. For my purposes, frames are schemas.

Key Reference: Minsky (1975).

This listing should give you a good feel for the terminology used by schema theorists and researchers.

As another example of a derived schema, the discussions of these terms were organized into subheadings by a simple structural schema consisting of Descriptions, Examples, Comments, Key References (DECK). Using the DECK schema helped me provide consistent and relatively complete coverage of each of the terms.

SCHEMA AND SCRIPT THEORIES

The concept of *schema* as a generic representation of a collection of objects, events, procedures, concepts, and so forth, can be traced back to Head (1920), Piaget (1926), and Bartlett (1932). Then, after almost 30 years of dormancy, interest in this concept and theories related to it resurged in the early 1960s, peaked from the mid-1970s to mid-1980s, and waned in the last half of the 1980s.

Generally, the notion has been that schema and script systems (collections of superordinate, subordinate, complementary, and competing schemas, and their associated correction factors that allow for the generation of specific instances) provide, at a minimum, functionally valid models of human knowledge representation, and economical arrangements for artificial intelligence programs. As with most theories, the early writings heralded the promise of schema theory (e.g., Spiro, 1980), the middle writings attempted to demonstrate its validity and boundary conditions (e.g., Anderson, Pichert, & Shirey, 1983), and the later writings have tended to disparage it and offer alternatives (e.g., Alba & Hasher, 1983; Kardash, Royer, & Greene, 1988).

Both psychologists and cognitive/computer scientists have developed schema theories. As is usually the case in such matters, the psychologists' models are typically broad, informal, verbal descriptions designed to guide research (e.g., R. C. Anderson, 1984), whereas the models that have emerged from cognitive science are more precise, formal, and focused on specific domains (e.g., Minsky, 1975; Schank & Abelson, 1977). There is a certain synergy between these two modeling approaches: The psychologists broaden and loosen the ideas emerging from cognitive science, whereas the cognitive scientists restrict and tighten the concepts developed by psychologists.[1] However, it should be noted that even with these efforts, it is widely agreed (e.g., Alba & Hasher, 1983; Brewer & Treyens, 1981; Maki, 1990; Taylor & Crocker, 1981) that schema and script theories are generally nebulous and only loosely related to one another.

In general, schema theories contain both structure and process considerations. The *structural* aspects are focused on how the information is represented and organized in memory (human or computer), whereas the *processing* aspects are focused on how these structures are developed, updated, and used. The cognitive science models have tended to be heavy on structure, whereas the psychological models have been heavy on process.

A flavor of the structural oriented models can be gleaned from Abelson's work (1981) on scripts. He defined a script as a "hypothesized cognitive structure that, when activated, organizes comprehension of event-based schematas. . . . In a strong sense, it involves expectations about the order as well as the occurrence of events" (p. 717). He proposed eight factors that characterize script representations:

1. Equifinal actions: different script actions that accomplish the same result.
2. Variables: slots that allow for different objects or people to play the same roles in different script episodes. However, within an episode the variables are fixed (bound).
3. Paths: action routes that serve as alternatives to normal procedures.

---

[1]The history of schema theory provides a good example of the positive results that can emerge from separate, but complementary examinations of the same domain by psychologists and cognitive/computer scientists.

4. Scene selection: a specific set of slots that can be filled to establish location, settings, and so on.
5. Tracks: subscripts that are applicable to particular situations.
6. Interferences: typical obstacles and errors and what to do about them.
7. Distractions: events that interrupt or preempt the execution of a script.
8. Free behaviors: additional nonscript behaviors that may occur during script execution.

Abelson also talked about prevalent knowledge script systems in which the "tracks" are subcategories and "metascripts," abstractly stated scripts with a minimum of specification, serve as superordinate categories. For example, a person might have a "going to a restaurant" metascript with subordinate scripts for "going to fancy restaurants" and "going to fast food" restaurants. Further, there may be tracks subordinate to the "fast food" script for "drive-in" versus "walk-up" script variations.

Other examples of structure-heavy schema models are Minsky's (1975) frame theory for visual perception, and Rumelhart's (1975) story grammars for the structure of narrative text. These structural models and others emerging from cognitive/computer science have helped indirectly to inform thinking about the processing aspects of schema theory.

As might be expected, the development of process models has been less systematic and precise. Evans (1968) suggested that humans form natural schemas by statistical-like averaging of attributes across a series of exposures. Similarly, Thorndyke (1984) hypothesized that schemas are "formed by induction from numerous previous experiences with various exemplars of the general concept. Presumably, schemata develop through a process of successive refinement—as one accumulates additional experiences with a concept, expectations for the expected properties of the concept become more clearly defined" (p. 173). Rumelhart and Norman (1981) speculated that schemas change and develop via three processes:

- Accretion: assimilation of additional information within categories.
- Tuning: changes in the schema categories themselves: resulting in improved categorization accuracy.
- Restructuring: development of new structures or radical reorganization of old ones.

Of these three processes, restructuring has received the most attention. It has been hypothesized to account for dramatic changes in knowledge that appear to occur with age or with expertise. Vosniadou and Brewer (1987) discussed two major types of restructuring: global restructuring of schemas brought about by changes in the general logical capabilities of the individual, and domain-specific restructuring based on increased knowledge of a specific domain. In recent years, Piaget's (1929) stage theory, which is based on global restructuring, has been seriously attacked by investigators who suggest that domain-specific restructuring better represents developmental changes (Carey, 1985). This domain-specific view also has been shared by researchers in science education (e.g., Novak, 1977) and by those studying the differences between novices and experts (e.g., Chi, Glaser, & Rees, 1982). From this view, naive theories (or schemas) of a specific domain like physics are restructured into more sophisticated theories as domain knowledge is increased by experience and/or instruction.

Carey (1985) described two types of domain-specific restructuring: weak restructuring, which involves the addition of categories and relationships between categories, and radical restructuring, which involves dramatic changes in the nature of the categories and their overall organization, similar to the changes observed in the history of science (e.g., paradigm shifts, Kuhn, 1962). As Vosniadou and Brewer (1987) pointed out, these two forms of domain-specific restructuring do not need to be mutually exclusive. Weak restructuring can explain mundane learning that involves elaboration of existing schemas, and radical restructuring can explain the more dramatic changes in children's and adults' thinking.

In addition to models of natural schema acquisition and change, there also have been speculations as to how stored schemas influence processing during the comprehension and recall of text, pictures, and events; and during the performance of various skilled activities. Alba and Hasher (1983), in analyzing the schema-theory literature, identified five ways schemas influence general processing. On the encoding side are: *selection* of only schema-relevant information for storage or further processing, *abstraction* of the message from its presentation form so that only meaning is carried forth, *integration* of the new with the old to form a "holistic representation," and *interpretation* of the message to add inferences, omitted details, and relevant prior knowledge. On the retrieval side is the *reconstruction* of a stored memory or skill by using remembered details and general knowledge to fabricate a recall and/or performance. Presumably these five factors combine to determine what we learn, what we remember, and how we perform.

In this subsection, I have overviewed the status of schema and script theories. These theories have focused on three separable aspects: the structure and representation of schemas in memory, the development and modification of schemas, and the impact of schemas on general processing. Although these theories are generally imprecise and only loosely related to one another, they have provided useful frameworks for designing and analyzing research on learning, memory, and performance. In the next subsection, I review briefly some of the experimentation examining the psychological reality of natural schemas and scripts.

RESEARCH ON NATURALLY ACQUIRED SCHEMAS AND SCRIPTS

A Cursory Review

The research on schemas and scripts can be subdivided loosely into the examination of effects on comprehension/encoding and retrieval/performance.

Comprehension and Encoding. In general, appropriate activation of relevant prior knowledge, presumably in schematic form, has been shown to be critical for the acquisition of new knowledge (e.g., Bransford & Johnson, 1972; Bransford & Nitsch, 1978; Dooling & Lachman, 1971; Pichert & Anderson, 1977; Thorndyke, 1977). This activation of existing schemas can be either top–down (e.g., the use of a disambiguating title; Bransford & Johnson, 1972), or bottom–up (e.g., use of story characters with certain physical attributes; Morris, Stein, & Bransford, 1979). Without the activation of an appropriate schema, comprehension and encoding of new material is strongly impeded (Alba & Hasher, 1983).

Once activated, the schema or script is hypothesized to exert great influence on the selection of new information for encoding. Information that instantiates important schema categories (i.e., fills schema slots) presumably has a high priority in the encoding process (R. C. Anderson & Pichert, 1978; Owens, Bower, & Black, 1979).

In addition, some investigators have noted that special selection priority is accorded instantiating information that is atypical of the activated schema or script. This notion, which has been termed the *typicality effect*, was originally described by Schank and Abelson (1977), and verified experimentally by Smith and Graesser (1981) and Hudson (1988). One explanation for schema selection effects is that important (and especially atypical) information fills empty slots in existing memory structures and thus inherits the rich interconnections that already have been established (Pichert & Anderson, 1977; Rumelhart & Ortony, 1977). A second explanation is that selection is influenced through allocation of attention (R. C. Anderson & Pearson, 1984). Those important elements that have been identified as important to the schema are allocated additional attention. Because of the extra attention, important elements are comprehended and encoded more thoroughly. At this point, there is no compelling evidence to suggest that either or both of these explanations are valid (Kardash, Royer, & Greene, 1988).

Regardless of how it occurs, the selection process presumably can lead to incomplete memory representations of new events. In recalling these events, people apparently reconstruct by adding "probable detail" from their general schematic knowledge (Bartlett, 1932). Distortions will occur whenever the probable detail produced was not actually part of the original event. There is evidence that people remember typical actions or elements that never actually occurred in a specific episode (e.g., Graesser, Woll, Kowalski, & Smith, 1980).

This recall of typical, but not occurring, elements is a special case of schema-guided inference. Johnson, Bransford, and Solomon (1973) reported that respondents who hear a passage describing a person pounding a nail will infer the presence of a hammer as the probable instrument and incorporate the instrument into their representation of the passage. Minsky's (1975) frame theory predicts a related type of inference. If a stimulus generally conforms to an existing frame but does not contain all the information categories specified by the frame, missing information will be filled in by "default values." These are values typically associated with the missing categories in other stimuli.

In the examples of inference just given, it is not clear whether they occur during encoding, during retrieval, or both. Some investigators (e.g., Alba & Hasher, 1983; Kardash et al., 1988; McDaniel & Kerwin, 1987) have severely questioned the validity of schema theory, especially as it relates to comprehension and encoding. Comparing recognition and recall performance, they suggested that both schema-relevant and schema-irrelevant information is encoded, but that primarily schema-relevant information is recalled. The initial storage of schema-irrelevant information would argue against the selection process that is germane to most schema theories (e.g., R. C. Anderson, 1984). Although these analyses weaken the apparent validity of schema effects on encoding, they do not detract from schematic effects during retrieval and performance.

Retrieval and Performance. A number of investigators (e.g., R. C. Anderson & Pichert, 1978; Kardash et al., 1988; McDaniel & Kerwin, 1987; Yekovich & Thorndyke, 1981) expressed the view that schemas are particularly useful as a scaffolding for accessing and/or generating information at retrieval. This is illustrated clearly in the now classic set of studies by R. C. Anderson and associates (R. C. Anderson et al., 1983; Pichert & Anderson, 1977). In these studies, participants read a passage describing a home. In some conditions, after recalling as much as they could about the passage, they were told to think about the material from a new viewpoint (i.e., as either a home buyer or a burglar). They were then asked to write down any additional information they could remember. Typically, participants in this "new schema" condition recalled more additional information than those just exhorted to "recall more." Presumably the home buyer or burglar schema provided an effective structure or plan for searching existing memories and thus enhanced recall. However, it should be noted that some of the additional recall may have come from their generating appropriate default values for some of the schema slots.

This same effect appears to occur with nonverbal materials. For example, Brewer and Dupree (1983) compared recall of actions that were embedded in a goal-directed script (e.g., "reached up with a ruler to adjust the hands of a high clock") with the same action not embedded in a goal-directed script (e.g., reached up with a ruler). They found that immediate recall for an action was more than twice as good if it occurred in a plan schema. However, they also found that on an immediate visual recognition test the two types of actions were recognized equally well. This implies that the actions were stored regardless of context, but that the existence of a script helped to retrieve them.

In general, there is much greater agreement among investigators that schemas and scripts impact recall than there is that they affect selective encoding (see Kardash et al., 1988). The extreme view, following the lead of Penfield and Roberts (1959), would suggest that everything encountered is encoded and that apparent differences in memory are due to the availability or unavailability of appropriate retrieval schemas and scripts.

The effects of schemas and scripts on task performance have received much less attention than their presumed effects on memory. Abelson (1981) informally described the role of scripts in the enactment of various types of social behaviors (e.g., helping, cooperating, and forming attitudes). He offered compelling arguments that the script concept has explanatory power in these situations. Thorndyke (1984) described experiments examining the working of schemas in real-world problem solving (e.g., air traffic control problems; Thorndyke, McArthur, & Cammarata, 1981) and in situation assessment (e.g., weather evaluation; Hayes-Roth, 1980). However, to date, the efforts to assess the roles of scripts and schemas in task performance are at best provocative. The work is too sketchy at this point to draw any conclusions.

Shortcomings

Schema and script theories have substantial face validity as both models of human memory and as economical architectures for artificial intelligence programs. However, their status as psychological constructs is questionable. First, the theories are not defined precisely enough to be testable at a detailed level. Second, the research on some of the basic schema and script tenets suggest strong limitations. Although apparently operative at retrieval, there is little evidence to support their impact on encoding or storage. Third, newer theories of memory (e.g., production systems; J. R. Anderson, 1983; and proposition-specific processing; McDaniel & Kerwin, 1987) have been proposed as being more valid alternatives to scripts and schemas.

From a practical perspective, the use of natural schemas/scripts to enhance education has been limited by the fact that naturally formed schemas/scripts most likely vary in detail from individual to individual. Furthermore, most educationally relevant schemas/scripts are not experienced frequently or contiguously enough to be induced through pure experience only. In addition, many of the common elements of schemas and scripts are hidden beneath diverse surface representations (e.g., homeostasis and production patterns).

One approach to ameliorate these practical difficulties has involved the guided induction of schemas. This approach, which usually falls under the rubric of analogy training, is described briefly in the next section.

RESEARCH ON SCHEMAS ACQUIRED
BY GUIDED INDUCTION: ANALOGY TRAINING

A Cursory Review

Most of the naturally derived schemas and scripts that have been investigated presumably have arisen from the averaging of a collection of examples that have both surface and structural similarities (e.g., several instances of washing clothes or going to a fancy restaurant). That is, they have similar perceptual qualities and their parts have similar underlying relationships. On the other hand, analogies, especially those that are used educationally, often are similar structurally but are not similar in terms of surface features (e.g., they don't look alike; the solar system and an atom, the heart and a pump, a thermostat and the hypothalamus). As a result, the type of schema that captures the common elements among a set of analogs can be called, appropriately, a "structural" schema. Acquiring this type of schema is extremely difficult because of the lack of perceptual similarity among instances of the schema.

Recently, there has been extensive investigation of the use of analogies in learning and problem solving. Experiments on their spontaneous use by novices (Gick & Holyoak, 1980, 1983; Holyoak, 1984; Holyoak & Koh, 1987) found that these individuals were unlikely to use an analogous solution from structurally similar problems without explicit hints. When college students are provided with hints, they are more likely to remember the analogy when it is similar in both surface and structural dimensions to the problem to be solved, but once the analogy is recognized, it is structural similarity that is most important for its effective use.

A number of studies have shown that the use of analogies can be facilitated by manipulations that encourage the formation of structural schemas. The most direct manipulation of this sort involves explicit instructions in abstract rules, coupled with examples (analog problems), in domains such as statistics and algebra. Such abstract training can produce substantial spontaneous transfer (e.g., Bassok & Holyoak, 1989; Fong, Krantz, & Nisbett, 1986). There is also evidence that provision of multiple analogs without explicit instruction in generalized rules can facilitate transfer (Gick & Holyoak, 1983). In these situations, giving students explicit instructions to compare analogs structurally further enhances transfer to superficially dissimilar situations (Brown, Kane, & Echols, 1986; Catrambone & Holyoak, 1989).

In addition to the findings that the formation of a structural schema enhances analogical transfer, it also has been suggested that engaging in analogical transfer further enhances the induction of a structural schema (e.g., R. C. Anderson & Thompson, 1989; Holyoak, 1984, 1985; Novick & Holyoak, 1991; Ross & Kennedy, 1990). This, in turn, may facilitate more flexible transfer to other situations.

Schemas derived in this way are thought to underlie experts' ability to categorize problems based on their structural features (e.g., Chi, Feltovich, & Glaser,

1981; Schoenfeld & Herrmann, 1982), and to remember large amounts of meaningful information in their domain of expertise after only a brief presentation (e.g., Chase & Simon, 1973; Egan & Schwartz, 1979).

The underlying structural characteristics of analogies and their parent schemas have been given prominence in Gentner's structure mapping theory of analogies (Gentner, 1982; Gentner & Gentner, 1983) and have been shown to directly promote comprehension of and memory for scientific text (Halpern, Hanson, & Riefer, 1990).

Gaps and Shortcomings

Except for the few studies on problem solving where abstract rules and examples were presented (e.g., Bassok & Holyoak, 1989), approaches to analogy training have involved primarily indirect attempts at guiding students to induce and use structural schemas (e.g., multiple analogs and comparison instructions). These indirect or guided approaches, because they depend on the skills and experiences of the students, may lead to the induction and use of incomplete, incorrect, or poorly structured schemas. Also, the effort and difficulty involved in deriving and representing these schemas may prohibit their use outside of experimental settings.

An alternative approach is to instruct students directly on the use of expert-derived structural schemas. This approach would insure the use of appropriate and well-formed schemas in the learning of new information. These expert schemas also could be used to provide students with general information about the nature of structural schemas as a prelude to having them devise their own. The remainder of this chapter focuses on expert structural schemas.

RESEARCH ON EXPERT-DERIVED SCHEMAS

A Cursory Review

There has been very little research on the impact of expert structural schemas such as the homeostasis and theory (DICEOX) schemas introduced earlier in this chapter. However, as is seen here, the results of this research are sufficiently suggestive to warrant cautious application of this approach in educational settings.

Brooks and Dansereau (1983) investigated the DICEOX schema described earlier. After deriving the DICEOX schema, they trained half of their participants to use the DICEOX schema over a 2-week period. The remaining participants received support strategy training (e.g., study time management). Both groups then studied a theory passage (plate tectonics), which they later recalled. Brooks and Dansereau found that the DICEOX group recalled more of the main ideas than did the control group. There were no differences recalled in details.

Similar results have been reported for schema- or script-organized passages (Brooks & Dansereau, 1983, experiment 2; Ohlhausen, 1985). Brooks and Dansereau reorganized the plate tectonics passage from their first study to reflect the DICEOX schema. Half of the participants received the DICEOX-organized passage and the remaining participants received the original passage. Participants reading the DICEOX-organized passage recalled more main ideas than those reading the original passage. Again, there were no differences in the detail ideas recalled between the groups.

In a similar study, Ohlhausen (1985) tested a "nation" schema for geography passages with fifth, seventh, and ninth graders, and adults. The nation schema was composed of two superordinate categories with seven subordinate categories. They were physical geography (including location, landforms, and climate) and cultural geography (including history, culture, economy, and government). The participants read a passage on a fictitious Polynesian country that either was organized or was not organized according to the nation schema. Ohlhausen found, first, that schema recognition and use increases with age. She also found that participants who read the schema-organized passage outperformed those who read the nonschema-organized passage.

Skaggs, Rewey, and Paulus (1990) compared the relative efficacy of two different structural schemas (production vs. homeostasis) for use in general biology classes. Results indicated a preference difference and slight performance advantage for the production schema/script over the homeostasis schema/script. In a second experiment, one general biology class received production schemas (see Fig. 5.2 for an example) during instruction and as a review tool, and the other class received "traditional" instruction. Results indicated that the students in the schema class performed significantly better on various measures of learning than students in the traditional class.

Derived structural schemas also have been shown to be effective in presenting personally relevant information on drugs and alcohol (Dees, 1991; Dees, Dansereau, Peel, Boatler, & Knight, 1991; Dees et al., 1992; Patterson & Dansereau, 1991). A derived self-schema and a behavior pattern schema (see Figs. 5.3 & 5.4) were used in the aforementioned studies to present reasons and consequences associated with alcohol use, and information relevant to the development and maintenance of an alcohol pattern, respectively. Compared to traditional methods of instruction, these methods led to better recall of the information and greater positive shifts in awareness and intentions.

Derived schemas of this type also have been shown to be useful in helping college students analyze their own personal knowledge and experiences (Dees, Dansereau, Peel, & Knight, 1993; Dees et al., 1992; Peel & Dansereau, 1991; Peel, Dansereau, & Dees, 1991). Student-completed schemas are seen by prospective counselors as more informative (e.g., revealing more gaps and stimulating more questions) than student-produced essays. Also, the completion of schemas is viewed by the students as more effective than essay writing, especially by low verbal ability participants.

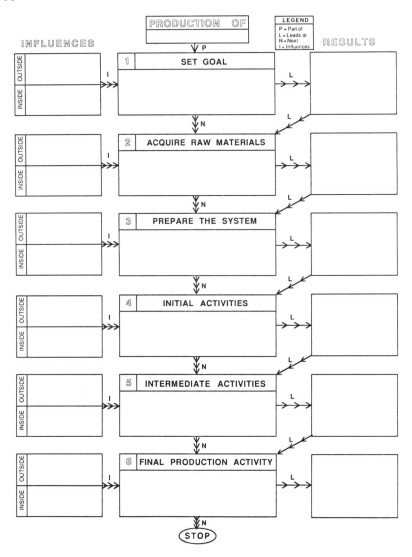

FIG. 5.2.   Production schema.

Gaps and Shortcomings

Although the derived structural schema research is in its infancy, the findings to date are encouraging. However, a substantial amount of additional research is needed to establish the parameters and boundary conditions associated with effective schema usage. In addition, the derivation and representation of structural schemas is, at present, much more of an art than a technology. Principles need

DIVISIONS OF THE SELF	STRENGTHS	WEAKNESSES	GOALS
Social Interactions and relationships with other people (e.g., level of comfort in social situations; ability to make and keep friends). 			
Cognitive Ways of thinking, learning, and solving problems (e.g., ability to understand books and lectures; ability to come up with creative solutions to problems). 			
Overt Behavioral Verbal and physical skills and actions (e.g., ability to speak and write effectively; ability to play sports, dance, etc.). 			
Physical Health, strength, endurance, energy level (e.g., tendency to get sick; need for sleep). 			
Emotional Moods and feelings (e.g., tendency to get angry, anxious, or depressed; ability to be happy). 			
Motivational Wants and needs, and the determination to meet them (e.g., ability to set and reach personal goals). 			
Spiritual/ Philosophical Morals, ethics, religion, and life view (e.g., sense of "fair play," views of "right and wrong"). 			

FIG. 5.3. Self-schema (reduced version).

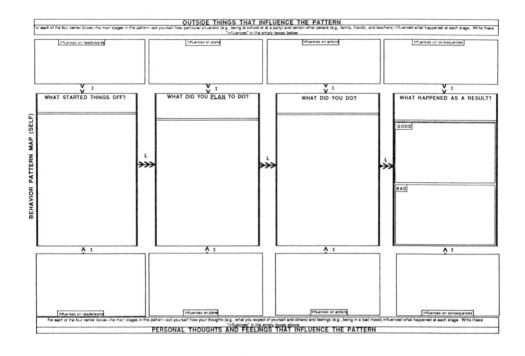

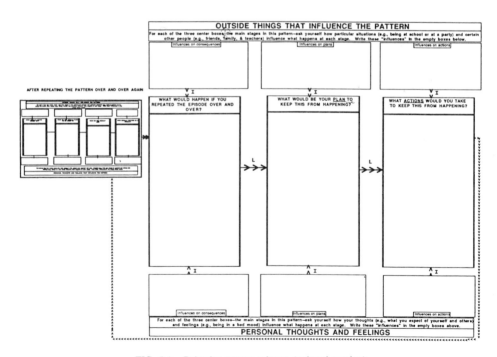

FIG. 5.4.　Behavior pattern schema (reduced version).

to be developed to guide their induction and presentation. The next section of this chapter provides some preliminary ideas on how this might be done.

DERIVATION, REPRESENTATION, AND USE OF EXPERT-DERIVED SCHEMAS

Structural schemas can be viewed as "generic analogs." They provide bridges that can be used to relate structurally similar knowledge domains. If properly constructed, they distill the essence of an analogy. Structural schemas differ from simple hierarchical categorization schemes in their representation of lateral (horizontal) connections between categories or items at the same hierarchical level. As we will see in a subsequent subsection, this potential richness of interconnections makes the effective representation and communication of structural schemas particularly challenging.

Structural schemas can be a descriptive set of interrelated categories that capture the important aspects of a knowledge domain (e.g., the DICEOX theory schema). They can also represent dynamic procedures (e.g., study strategies) and processes (e.g., production and homeostasis) in script form. Although specialized structural schemas are used heavily in most technically rich domains (e.g., medical practice and the military), there is very little information available on how to derive, represent, and use generalizable structural schemas.

Derivation of Structural Schemas

Before describing a derivation process, it is important to identify some characteristics of a "good" structural schema.

1. The schema forms a hierarchical partition of the relevant aspects of the structure of a set of information domains. That is, the structural schema categories are mutually exclusive and exhaustive, so that instantiating (filling in) a schema with information from a particular domain will be feasible and relatively unambiguous.

2. The partitioning chosen is appropriate to the tasks to be performed by the schema users.

3. At each level of the hierarchy, the number of steps or categories are cognitively manageable (i.e., they do not exceed short-term memory capacity).

4. Category or step labels are appropriate and communicative (i.e., they facilitate correct categorization and/or action).

5. Where possible, mnemonic aids, such as acronyms, are used to make the schema memorable and accessible.

In order to create structural schemas with these characteristics, the following derivation procedure can be used as a guide:

1. Choose two or three analogs from the class of information structures you are wanting to communicate.
2. Extract common categories (or steps) from the set of analogs. If possible, meet the "partition" criteria described earlier.
3. Repeat Step 2 to create alternative categorization schemes.
4. Select best scheme.
5. Establish connections between categories and derive subcategories. Maintain cognitive manageability.
6. Develop appropriate set of labels using the criteria of descriptiveness and mnemonic value.

In some cases, the derivation of structural schemas may be facilitated by schema experts and a content expert working cooperatively. The following steps were taken in developing biological schemas for the Skaggs et al. (1990) study described earlier:

1. Schema experts (the experimenters) and content experts (biology professors) collaborated to identify relatively difficult, but well-bounded domains of biological information (i.e., photosynthesis, maintenance of blood pressure, hormonal control);
2. Schema and content experts collaborated to determine the types of systems or classes of activities involved within these domains (i.e., production of glucose, balancing of hormonal levels).
3. The experts generated other exemplars of these "systems" to draw parallels and to solidify generic schema/script titles (i.e., production, homeostasis).
4. A set of schemas and scripts were generated by the schema experts and subsequently modified by the content experts.
5. Biology graduate students reviewed and annotated the resulting schemas and scripts.
6. A Macintosh SE computer was used to produce final copies of the schemas and scripts.

In discussing these derivation procedures, I have not dealt with formats for representing these schemas (e.g., category lists vs. outlines, vs. matrices vs. maps). The next subsection takes up this critical issue.

Representation of Structural Schemas

Although lists and outlines and other linear formats may be used occasionally to represent aspects of structural schemas (e.g., the DICEOX list presented earlier), the rich interconnections (especially the lateral connections) between schema categories and steps often make these formats inappropriate. Two-dimensional representations (matrices, charts, or maps) offer more flexibility in this regard. Although concept-attribute matrices (e.g., the self-schema matrix in Fig. 5.3) and standard flow charts and hierarchical charts provide some relief from the restrictions inherent in linear formats, we have found node-link knowledge maps (see Figs. 5.2 & 5.4) to offer the most advantages in schema representation.

Our research with knowledge maps (see Fig. 5.5 for a map of maps and Fig. 5.6 for the canonical set of links used in mapping) has indicated that this format has substantial advantages over linear formats such as text in presenting complex information (Lambiotte, Dansereau, Cross, & Reynolds, 1989; McCagg & Dansereau, 1991; Rewey, Dansereau, & Peel, 1991; Rewey, Dansereau, Skaggs, Hall, & Pitre, 1989; Reynolds & Dansereau, 1990; Reynolds, Patterson, Skaggs, & Dansereau, 1991; Skaggs, Dansereau, & Hall, 1989; Wiegmann, Dansereau, McCagg, Rewey, & Pitre, 1992).

Selected results of these experiments are as follows:

- Individuals are able to acquire more effective metaknowledge about a domain of information from a brief exposure to a map than from a brief exposure to text.
- Maps are generally more effective than their text counterparts for the recall of main ideas. No differences are found between maps and text on the recall of details. The visually salient parts of the maps appear to be recalled better.
- Students with relatively low verbal ability appear to benefit most from map presentations.

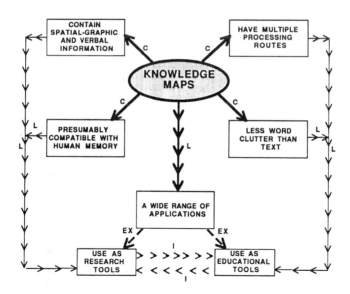

FIG. 5.5. A map of maps.

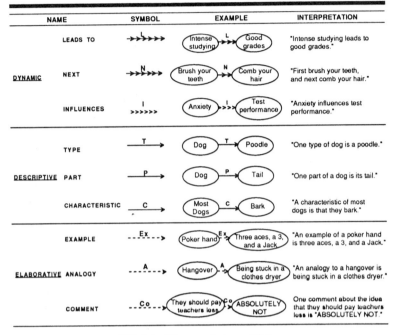

FIG. 5.6. The canonical set of links.

- Information is recalled better when presented in maps that conform to good gestalt principles (as opposed to maps that are unstructured).
- Maps are more effective than pure text when used as performance and reference aids.
- Individuals with low prior knowledge benefit from the use of maps as visual aids in lectures.
- Participants in cooperative (e.g., peer tutoring) activities benefit more from map communication aids than from text-based aids.

In addition to these empirical findings, knowledge maps have a number of pragmatic advantages.

1. They can be introduced and used as easily as other materials, such as texts, handouts, overhead transparencies, self-tests, or student notes, and don't require heavy reliance on expensive technology.

2. They are content flexible. Knowledge maps can be made to communicate a wide variety of content domains. We have developed maps to cover topics in biology, probability and statistics, psychology, engineering, computer science, and education. Instructors and students can tailor their maps to fit their own

needs; thus, although maps have direct pedagogical value, they also give instructors and students a sense of ownership of whatever material is mapped.

3. They are multipurpose. Maps can serve a variety of purposes in the teaching/learning process; for example, maps can be: placed on an overhead and used as lecture aids; made into handouts for notes, reference materials, and as aids to cooperative learning; made into posters for orientation and for showing progress through a semester course; designed for homework assignments and tests by leaving out important nodes or links that require student completion; and produced by students to review content or to facilitate self- or instructor diagnosis of learning difficulties.

4. They are easy to understand and produce. Although map "literacy" improves with experience, individuals can learn to understand and create coherent maps after about an hour of training and practice.

5. They can be merged easily with existing instructional practices. Because there are no rigid conditions associated with inserting mapping activities into a course, map activities can supplement or substitute for current approaches throughout a curriculum, to provide a change of pace or shift in perspective when most appropriate.

6. They are low cost. Given computer graphics capabilities, they are no more expensive than text. Even without computers, handmade maps are not difficult to produce.

These general advantages of knowledge maps, coupled with our preliminary success in using them as formats for representing structural schemas (see section "Research on Expert-Derived Schemas"), have made us firm believers in the mapping approach. For those interested, additional information is available on making and using knowledge maps (see Dansereau & Cross, 1990; Evans & Dansereau, 1991).

Use of Structural Schemas

Structural schemas can be used by instructors and tutors during the presentation of new information to enhance its organization and to illustrate its relationships to other knowledge domains. For example, in the Skaggs et al. (1990) study, the biology professor introduced the production schema (see Fig. 5.2 for an example), showed how it could be instantiated (filled in) with simple information about the production of pencils, and then used it to review information on photosynthesis (i.e., additional blank schema maps were instantiated with the steps in plant production of glucose and oxygen).

Students can be provided with blank schema maps to use as notetaking and study tools. This was the approach used in the first experiment on the DICEOX theory schema (Brooks & Dansereau, 1983). The student can use the schema maps as a basis for asking the instructor questions and for self-testing. The schema categories can be used also as retrieval cues during actual testing and performance situations. Providing students with structural schemas prior to content instruction can serve as an empowerment. The students have a sense of what is to be covered, and they intelligently probe the instructor for information needed to complete the schema.

Structural schemas for analyzing personal problems can be used in personal counseling and in objective problem solving. These types of schemas (see Fig. 5.4) facilitate the organization and categorization of episodic knowledge so that more general semantic information can be brought to bear in identifying warning signals, insufficient planning, inappropriate actions, pattern escape routes, and alternative solutions. Our research (e.g., Dees et al., 1993) has indicated that this use of structural schemas may have important implications for drug, alcohol, and other forms of personal education.

Another important use of a particular type of structural schema, the derived structural script, is as an action guide. In this case, a series of generic steps and substeps are provided to guide an individual through learning or problem-solving activities. An example derived from our mapping research and teaching is presented in Fig. 5.7. There is substantial evidence that the use of these expert-derived scripts leads to better performance than the use of scripts naturally acquired by students.

Although there appears to be sufficient evidence to warrant greater use of derived structural schemas, there are some major cautions. As mentioned in the overview of this chapter, schemas can be inappropriately structured and inappropriately applied. In these cases, the schema may actually be a hindrance to learning and performance. Even appropriate schemas should be used heuristically and tailored to the individual and the task at hand. Robotic use of these devices is ill-advised. As described earlier, structural schemas are primarily information scaffolds. As with all good scaffolds, they probably need to be torn down once the target structure is firmly in place so that the beauty of the underlying edifice can be seen.

ACKNOWLEDGMENTS

This chapter and some of the research it describes is based on work supported partially by the National Institute on Drug Abuse under Grant #5-R01 DA04987-02A1. The government has certain rights in this material. Any opinions, findings, and conclusions or recommendations expressed in this material are those of the author and do not necessarily reflect the views of NIDA.

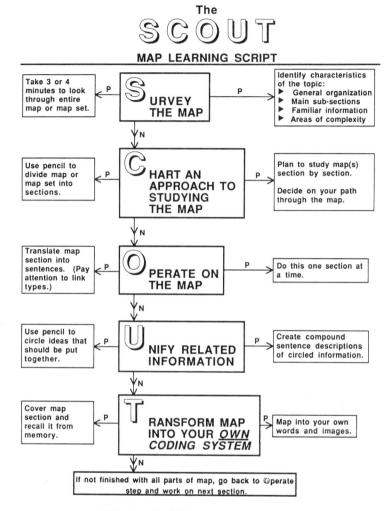

FIG. 5.7. The SCOUT map learning script.

REFERENCES

Abbott, V., Black, J. B., & Smith, E. W. (1985). The representation of scripts in memory. *Journal of Memory and Language, 24*(2), 179–199.

Abelson, R. P. (1981). Psychological status of the script concept. *American Psychologist, 36,* 715–729.

Alba, J. W., & Hasher, L. (1983). Is memory schematic? *Psychological Bulletin, 93,* 203–231.

Anderson, J. R. (1983). Acquisition of proof skills in geometry. In R. S. Michalski, J. G. Carbonell, & T. M. Mitchell (Eds.), *Machine learning: An artificial intelligence approach* (Vol. 1, pp. 191–220). Palo Alto: Tioga.

Anderson, R. C. (1984). Role of the reader's schema in comprehension, learning, and memory. In R. C. Anderson, J. Osborn, & R. J. Tierney (Eds.), *Learning to read in American schools: Basal readers and content texts*. Hillsdale, NJ: Lawrence Erlbaum Associates.

Anderson, R. C., & Pearson, P. D. (1984). A schema-theoretic view of basic processes in reading comprehension. In P. D. Pearson, R. Barr, M. L. Kamil, & P. Mosenthal (Eds.), *Handbook of reading research* (pp. 255–291). New York: Longman.

Anderson, R. C., & Pichert, J. W. (1978). Recall of previously unrecallable information following a shift in perspective. *Journal of Verbal Learning and Verbal Behavior, 17*, 1–12.

Anderson, R. C., Pichert, J. W., & Shirey, L. L. (1983). Effects of the reader's schema at different points in time. *Journal of Educational Psychology, 75*, 271–279.

Anderson, J. R., & Thompson, R. (1989). Use of analogy in a production system architecture. In S. Vosniadou & A. Ortony (Eds.), *Similarity and analogical reasoning* (pp. 267–297). Cambridge: Cambridge University Press.

Bartlett, F. C. (1932). *Remembering: An experimental and social study*. Cambridge, England: Cambridge University Press.

Bassok, M., & Holyoak, K. J. (1989). Interdomain transfer between isomorphic topics in algebra and physics. *Journal of Experimental Psychology: Learning, Memory, and Cognition, 15*, 153–166.

Bower, F. H., Black, J. B., & Turner, T. J. (1979). Scripts in memory for text. *Cognitive Psychology, 11*, 177–220.

Bransford, J. D., & Johnson, M. K. (1972). Contextual prerequisites for understanding: Some investigations of comprehension and recall. *Journal of Verbal Learning and Verbal Behavior, 11*, 717–726.

Bransford, J. D., & Nitsch, K. E. (1978). Coming to understand things we could not previously understand. In J. F. Kavanagh & W. Strange (Eds.), *Speech and language in the laboratory, school and clinic*. Cambridge, MA: MIT Press.

Brewer, W. F., & Dupree, D. A. (1983). Use of plan schemata in the recall and recognition of goal-directed actions. *Journal of Experimental Psychology: Learning, Memory, and Cognition, 9*, 117–129.

Brewer, W. F., & Treyens, J. C. (1981). Role of schemata in memory for places. *Cognitive Psychology, 13*, 207–230.

Brooks, L. W., & Dansereau, D. F. (1983). Effects of structural schema training and text organization on expository prose processing. *Journal of Educational Psychology, 75*, 811–820.

Brown, A. L., Kane, M. J., & Echols, C. H. (1986). Young children's mental models determine analogical transfer across problems with a common goal structure. *Cognitive Development, 1*, 103–122.

Carey, S. (1985). Are children fundamentally different kinds of thinkers and learners than adults? In S. F. Chipman, J. W. Segal, & R. Glaser (Eds.), *Thinking and learning skills* (Vol. 2, pp. 485–517). Hillsdale, NJ: Lawrence Erlbaum Associates.

Catrambone, R., & Holyoak, K. J. (1989). Overcoming contextual limitations on problem-solving transfer. *Journal of Experimental Psychology: Learning, Memory, & Cognition, 15*(6), 1147–1156.

Chase, W. G., & Simon, H. A. (1973). The mind's eye in chess. In W. G. Chase (Ed.), *Visual information processing* (pp. 215–281). New York: Academic Press.

Chi, M. T. H., Feltovich, P. J., & Glaser, R. (1981). Categorization and representation of physics problems by experts and novices. *Cognitive Science, 5*, 121–152.

Chi, M. T. H., Glaser, R., & Rees, E. (1982). Expertise in problem solving. In R. Sternberg (Ed.), *Advances in the psychology of human intelligence* (pp. 7–76). Hillsdale, NJ: Lawrence Erlbaum Associates.

Dansereau, D. F. (1985). Learning strategy research. In J. W. Segal & S. F. Chipman (Eds.), *Thinking and learning skills, Vol. 1: Relating instruction to research* (pp. 259–290). Hillsdale, NJ: Lawrence Erlbaum Associates.

Dansereau, D. F., & Armstrong, D. R. (1986). Evaluation of a verbal report inventory through script memory and learning strategies research. *Journal of Experimental Education, 54*(3), 129–133.

Dansereau, D. F., & Cross, D. R. (1990). *Knowledge mapping: A handbook for improving thinking, learning, and communicating.* Fort Worth: Department of Psychology, Texas Christian University.

Dees, S. M. (1991, August). *Using knowledge maps to develop understanding of personal behavior and behavior related to drug use: An overview.* Paper presented at the annual meeting of the American Psychological Association, San Francisco, CA.

Dees, S. M., Dansereau, D. F., Peel, J. L., Boatler, J. G., & Knight, K. (1991). Using conceptual matrices, knowledge maps, and scripted cooperation to improve personal management strategies. *Journal of Drug Education, 21,* 211–228.

Dees, S. M., Dansereau, D. F., Peel, J. L., & Knight, K. (1993). Using scripted cooperation to communicate information about the consequences of alcohol and cocaine use. *International Journal of the Addictions, 28*(2), 153–166.

Dees, S. M., Dansereau, D. F., Peel, J. L., Knight, K., Boatler, J. G., & Loftis, M. (1992). Using knowledge maps and scripted cooperation to inform college students about patterns of behavior related to recurring abuse of alcohol. *Addictive Behaviors, 17,* 307–318.

Dooling, D. J., & Lachman, R. (1971). Effects of comprehension on retention of prose. *Journal of Experimental Psychology, 88,* 216–222.

Egan, D. E., & Schwartz, B. J. (1979). Chunking in the recall of symbolic drawings. *Memory & Cognition, 7,* 149–158.

Evans, S. H. (1968). Chemical programming in the brain: Speculations. *Journal of Biological Psychology, 10,* 10–14.

Evans, S. H., & Dansereau, D. F. (1991). Knowledge maps as tools for thinking and communication. In R. F. Mulcahy, R. H. Short, & J. Andrews (Eds.), *Enhancing learning and thinking* (pp. 97–120). New York: Praeger Publishers.

Fillmore, C. J. (1968). The case for case. In E. Bach & R. Harms (Eds.), *Universals in linguistic theory.* New York: Holt, Rinehart & Winston.

Fong, G. T., Krantz, D. H., & Nisbett, R. E. (1986). The effects of statistical training on thinking about everyday problems. *Cognitive Psychology, 18*(3), 253–292.

Gentner, D. (1982). Are scientific analogies metaphors? In D. S. Miall (Ed.), *Metaphor: Problems and perspectives* (pp. 106–132). Great Britain: The Harvester Press Limited.

Gentner, D., & Gentner, D. R. (1983). Flowing waters or teeming crowds: Mental models of electricity. In D. Gentner & A. L. Stevens (Eds.), *Mental models* (pp. 99–129). Hillsdale, NJ: Lawrence Erlbaum Associates.

Gick, M. L., & Holyoak, K. J. (1980). Analogical problem solving. *Cognitive Psychology, 12,* 306–355.

Gick, M. L., & Holyoak, K. J. (1983). Schema induction and analogical transfer. *Cognitive Psychology, 15,* 1–38.

Graesser, A. C., Woll, S. B., Kowalski, D. J., & Smith, D. A. (1980). Memory for typical and atypical actions in scripted activities. *Journal of Experimental Psychology: Human Learning & Memory, 6,* 503–515.

Halpern, D. F., Hanson, C., & Riefer, D. (1990). Analogies as an aid to understanding and memory. *Journal of Educational Psychology, 82*(2), 298–305.

Hayes-Roth, F. (1980). Artificial intelligence for systems management. In J. Prewitt (Ed.), *Machine intelligence 1980.* Washington, DC: American Association for the Advancement of Science.

Head, H. (1920). *Studies in neurology.* Oxford: Oxford University Press.

Holyoak, K. J. (1984). Analogical thinking and human intelligence. In R. J. Sternberg (Ed.), *Advances in the psychology of human intelligence* (Vol. 2, pp. 199–230). Hillsdale, NJ: Lawrence Erlbaum Associates.

Holyoak, K. J. (1985). The pragmatics of analogical transfer. In G. H. Bower (Ed.), *The psychology of learning and motivation* (Vol. 19, pp. 59–87). New York: Academic Press.

Holyoak, K. J., & Koh, K. (1987). Surface and structural similarity in analogical transfer. *Memory & Cognition, 15,* 332–340.

Hudson, J. A. (1988). Children's memory for atypical actions in script-based stories: Evidence for a disruption effect. *Journal of Experimental Child Psychology, 46,* 159–173.

Johnson, M. K., Bransford, J. D., & Solomon, S. K. (1973). Memory for tacit implications of sentences. *Journal of Experimental Psychology, 98,* 203–205.

Kardash, C. A. M., Royer, J. M., & Greene, B. A. (1988). Effects of schemata on both encoding and retrieval of information from prose. *Journal of Educational Psychology, 80*(3), 324–329.

Kuhn, T. S. (1962). *The structure of scientific revolutions.* Chicago: University of Chicago Press.

Lambiotte, J. G., Dansereau, D. F., Cross, D. R., & Reynolds, S. B. (1989). Multidimensional semantic maps. *Educational Psychology Review, 1*(4), 331–367.

Maki, R. H. (1990). Memory for script actions: Effects of relevance and detail expectancy. *Memory & Cognition, 18*(1), 5–14.

McCagg, E. C., & Dansereau, D. F. (1991). A convergent paradigm for examining knowledge mapping as a learning strategy. *Journal of Educational Research, 84*(6), 317–324.

McDaniel, M. A., & Kerwin, M. L. (1987). Long-term prose retention: Is an organizational schema sufficient? *Discourse Processes, 10*(3), 237–252.

Minsky, M. (1975). A framework for representing knowledge. In P. H. Winston (Ed.), *The psychology of computer vision.* New York: McGraw-Hill.

Morris, B., Stein, C., & Bransford, J. (1979). Prerequisites for the utilization of knowledge in the recall of prose passages. *Journal of Experimental Psychology, Human Learning, & Memory, 5*(3), 253–261.

Novak, J. D. (1977). An alternative to Piagetian psychology for science and mathematics education. *Science Education, 61,* 453–477.

Novick, L. R., & Holyoak, K. J. (1991). Mathematical problem solving by analogy. *Journal of Experimental Psychology: Learning, Memory, and Cognition, 17*(3), 398–415.

Ohlhausen, M. M. (1985). The effects of reader and text structure variables on the ability to identify the important information in social studies text: The existence and acquisition of text structure and content schemata (Doctoral dissertation, University of Iowa, 1985). *Dissertation Abstracts International, 46,* 2983-A.

Ohlhausen, M. M., & Roller, C. M. (1986). Teaching students to use a nation schema to learn about countries. *Journal of Reading, 30*(3), 212–217.

Owens, J., Bower, G. H., & Black, J. B. (1979). The "soap opera" effect in story recall. *Memory & Cognition, 7,* 185–191.

Patterson, M. E., & Dansereau, D. F. (1991, August). *Knowledge maps and cooperative learning: Potential tools for drug education.* Paper presented at the annual meeting of the American Psychological Association, San Francisco, CA.

Peel, J. L., & Dansereau, D. F. (1991, August). *Prevention of personal problems via schematic maps and peer feedback.* Paper presented at the annual meeting of the American Psychological Association, San Francisco, CA.

Peel, J. L., & Dansereau, D. F., & Dees, S. M. (1991). *Identifying the best scenario for using schematic organizers as integration tools for alcohol related information.* Unpublished manuscript.

Penfield, W., & Roberts, L. (1959). *Speech and brain mechanisms.* Princeton, NJ: Princeton University Press.

Piaget, J. (1926). *The language and thought of the child.* New York: Harcourt, Brace.

Piaget, J. (1929). *The child's conception of the world.* Totowa, NJ: Littlefield, Adams.

Pichert, J. W., & Anderson, R. C. (1977). Taking different perspectives on a story. *Journal of Educational Psychology, 69,* 309–315.

Posner, M. I. (1973). *Cognition: An introduction.* Glenview, IL: Scott, Foresman.

Rewey, K. L., Dansereau, D. F., & Peel, J. L. (1991). Knowledge maps and information processing strategies. *Contemporary Educational Psychology, 16,* 203–214.

Rewey, K. L., Dansereau, D. F., Skaggs, L. P., Hall, R. H., & Pitre, U. (1989). Effects of scripted cooperation and knowledge maps on the processing of technical material. *Journal of Educational Psychology, 81,* 604–609.

Reynolds, S. B., & Dansereau, D. F. (1990). The knowledge hypermap: An alternative to Hypertext. *Computers & Education, 14*(5), 409–416.

Reynolds, S. B., Patterson, M. E., Skaggs, L. P., & Dansereau, D. F. (1991). Knowledge hypermaps and cooperative learning. *Computers & Education, 16*(2), 167–173.

Ross, B. H., & Kennedy, P. T. (1990). Generalizing from the use of earlier examples in problem solving. *Journal of Experimental Psychology: Learning, Memory, and Cognition, 16*(1), 42–55.

Rumelhart, D. E. (1975). Notes on a schema for stories. In D. Bobrow & A. Collins (Eds.), *Representation and understanding: Studies in cognitive science*. New York: Academic Press.

Rumelhart, D. E., & Norman, D. A. (1981). Accretion, tuning, and restructuring: Three modes of learning. In J. W. Cotton & R. Klatzky (Eds.), *Semantic factors in cognition* (pp. 37–60). Hillsdale, NJ: Lawrence Erlbaum Associates.

Rumelhart, D. E., & Ortony, A. (1977). The representation of knowledge in memory. In R. C. Anderson, R. J. Spiro, & W. E. Montague (Eds.), *Schooling and the acquisition of knowledge* (pp. 99–135). Hillsdale, NJ: Lawrence Erlbaum Associates.

Schank, R. C., & Abelson, R. P. (1977). *Scripts, plans, goals, and understanding*. Hillsdale, NJ: Lawrence Erlbaum Associates.

Schoenfeld, A. H., & Hermann, D. J. (1982). Problem perception and knowledge structure in expert and novice mathematical problem solvers. *Journal of Experimental Psychology: Learning, Memory, and Cognition, 8*, 484–494.

Skaggs, L. P., Dansereau, D. F., & Hall, R. H. (1989, March). *The effects of knowledge maps and pictures on the acquisition of scientific text*. Paper presented at the annual meeting of the American Educational Research Association, San Francisco, CA.

Skaggs, L. P., Rewey, K. L., & Paulus, P. (1990, June). *Using derived schemas and scripts to improve learning of biological information*. Paper presented at the annual meeting of the American Psychological Society, Dallas, TX.

Smith, D. A., & Graesser, A. C. (1981). Memory for actions in scripted activities as a function of typicality, retention interval, and retrieval task. *Memory & Cognition, 9*, 550–559.

Spiro, R. J. (1980). *Schema theory and reading comprehension: New directions* (Tech. Rep. No. 191). Champaign: University of Illinois, Center for the Study of Reading.

Taylor, S. E., & Crocker, J. (1981). Schematic bases of social information processing. In E. T. Higgins, C. P. Herman, & M. P. Zanna (Eds.), *Social cognition: The Ontario Symposium* (Vol. 1, pp. 89–134). Hillsdale, NJ: Lawrence Erlbaum Associates.

Thorndyke, P. W. (1977). Cognitive structures in comprehension and memory of narrative discourse. *Cognitive Psychology, 9*, 77–110.

Thorndyke, P. W. (1984). Applications of schema theory in cognitive research. In J. R. Anderson & S. M. Kosslyn (Eds.), *Tutorials in learning and memory* (pp. 167–191). San Francisco, CA: W. H. Freeman.

Thorndyke, P. W., McArthur, D., & Cammarata, S. (1981). AUTOPILOT: A distributed planner for air fleet control. *Proceedings of the International Joint Conference in Artificial Intelligence* (pp. 171–177).

Vosniadou, S., & Brewer, W. F. (1987). Theories of knowledge restructuring in development. *Review of Educational Research, 57*(1), 51–67.

Wiegmann, D. A., Dansereau, D. F., McCagg, E. C., Rewey, K. L., & Pitre, U. (1992). Effects of knowledge map characteristics on information processing. *Contemporary Educational Psychology, 17*, 136–155.

Yekovich, F. R., & Thorndyke, P. W. (1981). An evaluation of alternative functional models of narrative schemata. *Journal of Verbal Learning and Verbal Behavior, 20*, 454–469.

CHAPTER 6

Teaching for Understanding: The Importance of the Central Conceptual Structures in the Elementary Mathematics Curriculum

Sharon Griffin
Clark University

Robbie Case
Stanford University

Allesandra Capodilupo
Brock University

Giving students knowledge that is useful outside of the specific context in which learning occurs has been a central goal of education for as long as classrooms have existed. However, in spite of the efforts that have been devoted to this subject for much of the previous century, in the 1990s one has only to listen to any representative of the workplace to realize that this objective has not yet been met in the field of mathematics education. In the public press, there is mounting evidence that the mathematical knowledge U.S. students acquire in school does not prepare them to meet the demands of an increasingly sophisticated workplace or to compete successfully in a global economy. In a less public but equally concerned quarter, university faculty have also expressed dismay that U.S. students who demonstrate mathematical knowledge on standardized tests in high school are unable to use this knowledge to acquire the advanced mathematical understandings expected in college-level courses. Although both of these concerns suggest a problem in knowledge transfer, another body of evidence has accumulated over the past decade that points to a deeper problem: one that involves knowledge acquisition itself and one that may be centrally related to the issue of transfer. These findings are described here.

Results of recent assessments of U.S. children's mathematical understanding have been disturbing. SAT scores are markedly lower than they were 20 years ago. Our children's mathematics achievement compares unfavorably to that of peers in other developed societies (Stevenson, Lee, & Stigler, 1986). Too many children are not acquiring the kinds of mathematical concepts presented in their textbooks or the kinds of mathematical skills needed to succeed in a technologically advanced society (National Assessment of Educational Progress [NAEP], 1983). Of further concern, the problem is especially great among lower socioeconomic status (SES) children. Differences among SES groups are apparent before children begin school (Griffin, Case, & Siegler, 1994; Saxe, Guberman, & Gearhart, 1989), are more striking by the middle of first grade (Case, 1975), and become progressively greater during the course of schooling (NAEP, 1988). A major reason for the low level of mathematical achievement seems to be the increasing separation between children's intuitive, informal understanding of mathematics and the algorithms they need to learn in their formal schooling (Ginsburg & Russel, 1981).

The program that is described in this chapter was designed to attack this problem at its source—by preventing the problems from developing in the first place. In particular, the objective was to develop diagnostic and instructional procedures that—if implemented—would permit the vast majority of first graders to understand the conceptual basis of addition and subtraction and to acquire a higher degree of skill in these processes as a consequence. The long-term result, we hoped, would be to provide a more solid intellectual and motivational foundation for acquiring more advanced mathematical understanding that would be useful in a wide range of circumstances.

THEORETICAL FRAMEWORK

After reviewing the literature on young children's arithmetic, Resnick (1983) concluded that children represented the addition process in terms of something like a mental number line, and that this number line provided the conceptual underpinning for children's use of arithmetic strategies. According to her analysis, children see the use of a strategy such as counting on their fingers as being justified, because it is like traversing a mental number line and arriving at the answer. The lack of such a representation may be part of the reason that some students have difficulty learning to add or subtract, or are poor at executing these strategies; lack of understanding of why the strategies work may interfere with the skillful execution of the strategies. This in turn may lead to such strategies not being used very often, and prevent a core set of problems from being learned "by heart." Three issues that this analysis raises are: (a) What sort of conceptual knowledge does a "mental number line" entail?; (b) how is this knowledge organized and represented?; and (c) can this knowledge be taught? In the past few years, a potential answer to all three of these questions has come from our research on children's cognitive development.

In the past decade or so, a number of neo-Piagetian theories have been proposed whose goal has been to preserve the insights of Piaget's theory, while eliminating its weaknesses (Case, 1985; Fischer, 1980; Halford, 1982). Interestingly, although Piaget himself placed the major stage division in middle childhood at about 7 or 8 years of age, most neo-Piagetian theorists have suggested that a more major reorganization in children's thought actually takes place at about the age when arithmetic is normally introduced, namely 5 or 6 years.

What exactly does this reorganization entail? Although a number of answers to this question have been proposed, our answer is perhaps most directly relevant to early math education, because we have concentrated so much of our research on children's understanding of quantitative problems. Our proposal is that, at about this age, children develop a set of powerful organizing schemata that we refer to as *central conceptual structures*.

Our investigation of these structures started with Siegler's (1976) observation that 6-year-olds use a quantitative rule for solving balance-beam problems (Pick the side that has the greater number of weights as the one that will go down). Four-year-olds cannot usually solve balance-beam problems that demand a rule of this sort. However, they can solve problems that are solvable by a qualitative version of the rule; that is, problems where one side has a very large weight and the other side a very small one (Liu, 1981). Four-year-olds also can solve problems where their only task is to count small arrays of objects. Given this pattern of strengths and weaknesses, we have proposed that what 4-year-olds lack is the ability to coordinate these two schemes into what we termed a "dimensional structure"; that is, a structure in which properties such as weight are represented as quantitative dimensions with two poles and a continuum of values in-between (Case & Griffin, 1990).

In a series of studies completed just before the present project began, this difference between 4- and 6-year-olds was found to be quite general, applying to children's problem-solving on logical-mathematical, social-scientific, and everyday time-telling and money-handling tasks (Case, 1985; Case, Sandieson, & Dennis, 1986; Griffin, Case, & Sandieson, 1992). These findings suggested that a "dimensional representation" might mediate children's performance on a wide range of quantitative tasks. To identify prerequisites for making the transition to this sort of thought, training studies were next conducted. These studies focused on training core elements of a dimensional representation and, to heighten the educational relevance of this work, the children included in these studies were drawn from lower SES communities.

These training studies produced three findings that were of direct relevance to the present project.

1. When low SES children who were four were assessed, they were found to lack several key elements of the dimensional structure. Unlike their high SES peers, they often could not count reliably beyond very small set sizes. In addition,

even when they could count, they often could not accurately compare numerical magnitudes. Thus, they could not answer questions such as, "Which is bigger, 6 or 5?"

2. This lack of knowledge could be remedied by a series of about twenty 10-minute instructional sessions, each of which could be placed in a game context and made highly enjoyable.

3. Once the children acquired this knowledge, they began spontaneously to demonstrate performance characteristics of middle-class 6-year-olds on a wide range of tasks, even such tasks as the balance beam, which had not been introduced in the training sessions. In short, the children showed remarkably broad transfer (Case & Sandieson, 1987).

These findings may help to clarify why many children begin to experience difficulty in learning mathematics as early as Grade 1. Typically, first-grade exercises briefly focus on numerical representation (e.g., count these apples and write the proper numeral above them), and then move quickly to operations and their corresponding symbols (e.g., 2 + 3 = ?). Regardless of a child's social class, if all the child knows is how to count, that child will be missing precisely the sort of representation that the research on addition and subtraction suggests is necessary for solving these problems in a meaningful and reliable fashion. In short, the child will be missing the equivalent of a mental number line.

This is not to say that the components of dimensional structure as we first conceived them are all there is to the sort of mental number line on which addition and subtraction depend. For subtraction, children also need to learn how to count backwards. They must also learn to map addition and subtraction operations onto their numerical representations. An expanded number line that contains these components, as well as those that were trained in the earlier studies, is illustrated in Fig. 6.1.

Given the hypothesized importance of this structure, we decided that it would be worthwhile to develop a math "readiness" curriculum that would enable kindergarten children who did not already possess this structure to acquire it before they started first grade. The Rightstart program was designed to accomplish this objective.

To summarize: The theoretical assumptions on which the present project was based may be summarized, in point form, as follows.

1. In the course of their preschool experience, many (but not all) children develop powerful organizing schemata that are central to their understanding of the school tasks that they encounter in subsequent years. These schemata may be called *central conceptual structures* (Case & Griffin, 1990).

2. The central conceptual structure on which early addition and subtraction are dependent is one for conceptualizing the world in terms of quantitative di-

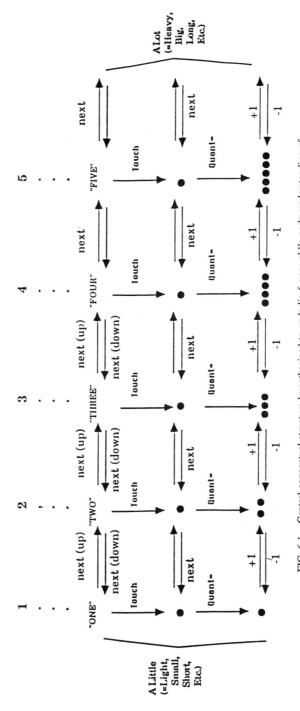

FIG. 6.1. Central conceptual structure hypothesized to underlie 6-year-old's early understanding of mathematics (dotted lines indicate "optional"—i.e., nonuniversal—notional knowledge).

mensions. Once this structure is in place, children see the world as comprised of dimensions having two poles, and a large number of points between these poles, whose relative magnitude can be indexed by the number system (see Fig. 6.1).

3. Children who experience difficulties with early arithmetic during their formal schooling are quite likely not to have developed this quantitative central conceptual structure, whereas their successful peers typically have this structure firmly in place by first grade.

4. If these children are provided with experience that enables them to develop this structure—before they enter first grade—their ability to learn addition and subtraction should improve considerably.

5. It therefore seems worthwhile to develop a curriculum that will provide this experience.

CURRICULUM MATERIALS

Because our goal was to help kindergarten children acquire each of the components of the structure illustrated in Fig. 6.1, and to assemble these components into a coherent whole, the materials that we developed were based on this figure. The content that we covered in the curriculum (referred to hereafter as the Rightstart program) was the set of nodes and relations illustrated in the figure. These were partitioned into instructional units as follows.

1. Number sequence (up) from 1 to 10.
2. Number sequence (down) from 10 to 1.
3. One-to-one mapping of numbers on to objects, when counting in either direction.
4. Mapping of each number on to canonical set of appropriate size.
5. Increment rule (i.e., knowledge that each number up in sequence has been incremented by one [+1]).
6. Decrement rule (i.e., knowledge that each number down in sequence has been decremented by one [−1]).
7. Mapping of relative numerosity on to number sequence (because this set [XXX] has more than this set [XX] one can say that 3 is "more" than 2).
8. Use of information regarding relative numerical magnitude to make dimensional judgments (e.g., A weighs more than B because A contains 3 identical objects and B only contains 2).
9. Numerals 1 to 10.

The principles that were followed in devising materials to teach this content were as follows. *Affective engagement:* First, each exercise should be affectively engaging. *Representational congruence:* Second, the visual props for representing numerical change should be congruent with children's internal representation of number. This means that they should indicate numbers of increasing magnitude as lying along a line that increases in length. *Representational diversity:* Third, a variety of external forms of representation should be utilized (e.g., thermometers, board game, "number lines," rows of objects, etc.). *Developmental sequencing:* Fourth, the materials should be sequenced in their normal order of developmental acquisition. *Multiple levels of understanding:* Finally, wherever possible, multiple levels of learning should be possible. Thus, even in the early exercises where the explicit activity is counting, the props and general context should be such as to permit some implicit learning of the higher order concepts by the more capable children. Similarly, even in the later exercises that are devoted to such topics as the increment or decrement rule, children who are still consolidating their counting should be able to do so, and should be able to get some fun and knowledge out of the exercise.

The materials that were developed to help children acquire each of the above elements of knowledge, and to integrate them into a coherent structure, were assembled together into a set of 20 lessons for teachers to follow. To maximize affective engagement, the majority of the activities included in these lessons were set in a game format. As an example, one of the early lessons was presented as follows:

Explicit Objective: For the numbers 1 to 5 (or 1 to 10), children will know that each number maps onto an object when counting, and that each number maps onto a set. Children will gain beginning experience of "take-away" operation and predictability of results.

Implicit Objective: More capable children will have a chance to compare quantities, to use the generative rule, and to make dimensional assessments.

Materials Needed: Poker chips (5 colors); Plastic jar (bank); Cloth; Mask

Activity 1: Specific objective: Can count a set of objects and compute quantity; Can identify the primary colors.

Procedure: Drop poker chips on the table in a heap and place plastic jar in the center. Ask first child to get 1 red chip and place it in the jar. Ask second child to get 2 blue chips and place them in the jar, counting them out loud as they are dropped in. Ask third child to get 3 white chips and place them in the jar, and so on, until fifth child gets 5 of a different color (e.g., yellow). Everyone has to watch to make sure each child puts the right color and the right number in and doesn't make any mistakes. When all are in, hold up the jar and ask children, "Which color has the most? Are there more red chips or more yellow chips?" Let children answer and then say, "Let's dump them out and count them to find out." Dump them out and have children count the red chips and the yellow chips to see which ones have the most. (Note: Pick an extreme contrast for this task.) Repeat with different quantities of chips (up to 10), allowing the more capable children to count the larger sets.

Activity 2: "Superboy/girl Game." Specific objective: Can count a set of objects and compute quantity. Beginning experience with "take-away" operation.

Procedure: "Now we're going to play the Superboy game. One person (instructor chooses and gives mask) will be Superboy/girl. We're going to pretend these chips are money and this jar is a bank. (Give each child 5 chips, and each child a different color of chips.) Everyone count your money to see how much you have—remember how much money you have and what color your money is. Now each of you count your money into the bank. Does everyone remember their color and number? (Confirm that they do. If not, empty bank and count again.) Now, Superboy/girl is going to come and borrow someone's chip and we have to figure out whose chips s/he borrowed. (All close eyes—Superboy/girl removes *one* chip.) Now, did s/he borrow one of yours, or yours, or yours? How can we figure this out? Let's take all of the chips out of the bank (empty bank) and everyone count their chips to see if they are all there." Have children count, determine which set is missing one, and predict what color chip Supergirl/boy must have borrowed. When a prediction is made, Superboy/girl must return the borrowed chip so prediction can be tested. Repeat, giving each child a turn playing Superboy/girl.

Variations: Repeat with different quantities of money put into the bank (e.g., from 6 to 10 chips each). When children are comfortable with this level of play, repeat with increasing quantities of money (2 to 4 chips) borrowed from the bank. These variations can be introduced at selected points in the training sequence (e.g., when children are comfortable counting sets of six or more), interspersed with other activities specified in later lessons.

Reinforcement Activity: "Five Little Children Line-up Game." Specific Objective: Provide daily experience with "take-away" operation.

Procedure: Tell children, "When I tap you on the shoulder, it's your turn to leave the group to line up at the door to go back to your classroom. But first, let's see how many children are in this group. (Let children count to determine quantity.) O.K., let's sing our song (use tune of Ten Little Indians). Five little children doing their work. (Tap one child on the shoulder and let him/her leave group.) One lines up and then there are __. (Let children compute or predict quantity.) Four little children doing their work. (Tap another child on the shoulder.) Another lines up and then there are __." Continue until all children are lined up.

The instructions that teachers were given for following the lessons always stressed that there were two objectives: namely, helping the children acquire the number line structure, and helping them realize that numbers could be fun. A more detailed description of the curriculum is available upon request from the senior author.

YEAR 1 TRIAL OF THE CURRICULUM

Study 1

For the first year trial of the Rightstart program, we wanted to test the theoretical assumptions on which it was based, and to obtain measures of its educational utility. Specifically, we wanted to obtain answers to the following questions: (a)

Can the knowledge implied in the "central dimensional structure" be taught? (b) Is the Rightstart program more effective than traditional kindergarten mathematics programs, or other forms of special instructional attention, in enabling children to acquire this knowledge? (c) Will the knowledge gained transfer to a wide range of quantitative tasks for which no special training was provided? (d) Will the knowledge gained enhance children's ability to profit from brief instruction in formal first grade arithmetic?

Although the first and third questions just posed had been addressed in the earlier training studies, and affirmative answers had been provided, these results were unusual when compared to the training and transfer effects typically reported in the literature. The present study also differed from the previous ones in significant ways, in that the structure we were attempting to teach and the curriculum we had designed to teach it, were considerably more complex. For both of these reasons, we felt it was worthwhile to submit these questions to a more rigorous test and to institute the controls and the further tests implied in the second and fourth questions just posed. To address these questions, two control treatments were designed and several assessment measures were constructed or adopted for use in the present study. These are described in the following sections.

The Sample

The Rightstart program was implemented in three kindergarten classes serving families who had immigrated from rural Portugal to Toronto. In November of the kindergarten year, children in these classes appeared to be missing many of the components of the dimensional structure portrayed in Fig. 6.1. On a number knowledge test constructed to measure predimensional, dimensional, and bidimensional numerical understanding (see Table 6.1), the majority of these children performed at or below the predimensional level (i.e., the level typically achieved by middle-class 4-year-olds).

Two control treatments were also implemented in the same three classes. One of the control treatments was a traditional early math curriculum. This program was based on the best existing materials we could find; however, it differed from the Rightstart program in that it provided less emphasis on the conceptual underpinnings of number. The other control treatment was a reading readiness module, designed on the basis of Bradley and Bryant's (1985) hypothesis that a major component of reading readiness is the ability to differentiate the sound of language from its meaning. To ensure comparability across treatments in the amount of special attention children received and their level of engagement in the activities presented, the three instructional modules were identical in length and comparable in the game format employed for the majority of the activities.

The sample of 60 kindergarten students was divided into three matched groups on the basis of their pretest number knowledge scores. A rank-ordering procedure

TABLE 6.1
Number Knowledge Test

Preliminary:

1. Let's see if you can count from 1 to 10. Go ahead.

Level 0: (Predimensional: 4-yr.-old level)

2. I'm going to show you some poker chips (show mixed array of 3 red and 4 blue chips). Count the blue chips and tell me how many there are.
3. I'm going to give you 1 candy and then I'm going to give you 2 more (do so). How many do you have altogether?
4. I'm going to show you two piles of poker chips (show stacks of 5 and 2, same color). Which pile has more?
5. Here are some circles and triangles (show mixed array of 7 circles and 8 triangles). Count the triangles and tell me how many there are.

Level 1: (Dimensional: 6-yr.-old level)

6. If you had 4 chocolates and someone gave you 3 more, how many chocolates would you have altogether?
7. What number comes right after 7?
8. Now, what number comes two after 7?
9a. Which is bigger: 5 or 4?
9b. Which is bigger: 7 or 9?
10a. Now I'm going to ask you something different: Which is smaller: 8 or 6?
10b. Which is smaller: 5 or 7?
11. (Present visual array) Which number is closer to 5: 6 or 2?

Level 2: (Bidimensional: 8-yr.-old level)

12. How much is 54 + 12?
13. Which is bigger: 69 or 71?
14. Which is smaller: 27 or 32?
15. (Present visual array) Which number is closer to 21: 25 or 18?

---

was used to assign children to groups, with the child receiving the lowest ranked score assigned to the Rightstart group (i.e., the treatment group); the child receiving the second lowest ranked score assigned to the traditional math group (i.e., Control Group 1); and the child receiving the third lowest ranked score assigned to the reading readiness group (i.e., Control Group 2); and so on. This method was adopted in order to give the "neediest" children the benefit of the Rightstart program, and in order to provide a conservative rather than liberal estimate of the effectiveness of this training.

The mean chronological ages of the three groups were very similar. The treatment group was 5.23 years at the beginning of training. Control Group 1 was 5.26 years. Control Group 2 was 5.30 years.

The Training

Training was provided by the senior research officer of the project and two graduate research assistants. Each trainer was assigned to one of the three classrooms and was responsible for the training of all the children in it, in small groups. Because children from each of the three treatment groups were represented in each classroom, each trainer provided training in all three instructional modules. This design permitted us to assess the effectiveness of the Rightstart program, not only in relation to the other training modules, but also across classrooms and across trainers.

Each child received 40 group training sessions, with each session lasting approximately 20 minutes. The size of the training groups was five children, and for the most part training was done in a corner of the regular classroom. Visual distractions were minimized by the use of room dividers. Auditory distractions were unfortunately plentiful and could not be controlled.

The Rightstart group received training in all the components of the number line in Fig. 6.1. Control group 1 received the traditional math module, which incorporated some of the components of the Rightstart module (e.g., counting, understanding cardinality), although eliminating other components not typically taught in kindergarten and, within our framework, considered central to a mental number line conceptual structure (e.g., the generative rule; relative quantity). Control group 2 received the language module and no number training whatsoever.

The fact that there was considerable overlap in the training provided to the Rightstart group and the traditional math group (i.e., control group 1) minimized our chances of finding posttraining differences between these two groups. At the same time, it offered two advantages. First, it enabled us to determine if the Rightstart module was in any way superior to good math curricula currently in existence. Second, it enabled us to pinpoint more precisely the ways it was superior, if this should turn out to be the case.

Posttesting

Transfer Tests to Assess the Centrality of the Dimensional Structure. Our battery of tests yielded pre- and posttraining scores in number knowledge, and in several other domains of knowledge postulated to be related to number knowledge (e.g., time-telling skills, money-handling skills, balance-beam understanding, conservation of number). No specific training was provided for any of the tasks drawn from related domains (i.e., mention of time concepts, money concepts, weight displacement, etc., was carefully avoided in all instructional modules) and these tasks served as transfer tests to assess the centrality of the dimensional structure, and the generality of training effects. These tasks are described in the following:

Balance Beam. On this task, children are presented with a conventional balance beam with washers on each side, and asked which side they think will go down (Siegler, 1978). Their answers are considered to be *predimensional* if they can only make predictions when one side has a large weight on it and the other side has a small weight on it, based on global comparisons of quantity. By contrast, their answers are considered *unidimensional* if they can assess weights of nearly equal magnitude by counting them, and predict that the side with the greater number of weights will go down.

Birthday Party. In an analogous task to the balance beam, children are shown pictures of two children (Marini, in press). They are then told the following story about the two children in the pictures: "These children are going to their birthday party. Before they arrive they each want to get some marbles. At the birthday party the children get some marbles. Here are the marbles this child wanted, and here's what he got. Here are the marbles this child wanted, and here's what she got. Who do you think is happier?" Answers were considered to be predimensional if the respondent could only make predictions based on global comparisons of gifts received, but this comparison made no mention of the number of marbles (e.g., "He has a lot of marbles and she doesn't so he is happier."). Answers were considered dimensional if they contained some evidence of counting (e.g., "He is happier because he has 4 marbles and she has 3.").

Money Knowledge. This task tests basic understanding of the values associated with U.S. coins and folding money (Case & Sandieson, 1985). The questions are read from a testing sheet, and real money is either presented or referred to, as specified by the question. The children respond with short answers. As with all the other tasks, the items on the test are designed so that children's answers can be classified as predimensional or unidimensional. Predimensional items can be passed with a global judgment of quantity. (For example, the child is shown two piles of pennies, one of which has eight pennies and the other of which has two pennies. The child is then asked to determine which pile is worth more.) Items requiring unidimensional understanding present tasks that cannot be completed successfully by a global perceptual scan and that require, instead, a careful assessment of relative magnitude.

Time Knowledge. This task tests children's time discrimination and time-telling knowledge (Case, Sandieson, & Dennis, 1986). A paper clock with movable hands is presented for some of the items, whereas other items simply make reference to time. As with the money knowledge task, the items are read from a testing sheet and the children respond with short answers. Again, predimensional items require global judgments of absolute quantity. Unidimensional items require a careful assessment of relative magnitude. For example, children are told a visitor is coming to their house to play. The visitor says she will come over at 5 o'clock, but arrives at 6 o'clock, and the question is whether she arrives early or late.

Posttest Instructional Units. It was postulated that the Rightstart module would give children a central conceptual structure that would enhance their ability to profit from instruction in formal first-grade arithmetic. To test this prediction, first-grade instructional units in addition and subtraction were designed and were taught to all children in the sample at the end of the kindergarten year. Each of these was designed to teach children to manipulate formal symbols, a level of problem solving that had not been included in any of the three training modules.

Because Capodilupo (1992) had postulated that musical sightreading was also facilitated by a dimensional structure (i.e., it permitted children to determine which keys to play by counting the spaces and bars on the staff and by mapping these intervals on to the keyboard), a unit to teach this skill, and to test this prediction, was also included in the present study.

These instructional units were designed with three constraints in mind. First, due to constraints on the time that children could be absent from their regular classroom activities, each unit had to be extremely brief (i.e., 30–45 minutes). Second, to simulate a real-life situation, each unit had to conform to traditional teaching practices. Third, to be effective within the first constraint, each unit had to be sensitively geared to the conceptual level of the child.

As is no doubt apparent, these constraints produced conflicting demands. The traditional curriculum typically teaches addition and subtraction (and musical sightreading as well) over a period of several months, and is often insensitive to the general conceptual level of the child. To resolve this conflict, a developmentally appropriate framework was adopted for each unit. Within this framework, every attempt was made to incorporate as many "traditional" components as possible.

The instructional units were taught to children in small groups of three to four, in a quiet room in the school, 1 month after training was completed. As a partial control for teacher bias (i.e., teacher's expectancy that the Rightstart group would show superior learning), each group was composed of children from each of the three training groups. Within this constraint, the groups were matched for ability level as much as possible. Teaching was performed by the three trainers, who had administered the training modules over the course of the school year. A brief description of each unit is provided here:

The Addition Unit. In essence, children were given a story line to make the formal problem format (e.g., $2 + 2 = \_$) sensible to them and to serve as a "conceptual bridge" between the concrete problems presented early in the sequence and the abstract problems presented later. Instruction provided a graded sequence of steps designed to help children map symbolic notation onto the concrete representation of the problem.

At the end of this instructional unit, children were presented with four criterion problems written in traditional notation (e.g., $4 + 3 = \_$). They were given an opportunity to solve each problem with no prompts and, if unsuccessful, were given a prompt in the form of a word story. Children were credited with understanding the material if they provided the correct answer to three of these four problems, with or without prompts.

The Subtraction Unit. This unit followed the same general format as the addition unit, with the story line and the problems adjusted to teach subtraction. Pass criteria were also identical.

The Musical Sightreading Unit. This unit was a modified version of Capodilupo's (1992) instructional program. At the end of the unit, children were given six test melodies to play and were credited with passing if they played four of these melodies without error.

Tests to Assess Effects of Reading-Readiness Training. To assess the effects of the reading-readiness module we had designed, and to assess the differential effects that might be obtained when training was provided in two separate domains (i.e., math and language), three additional measures were included in our posttest battery and were administered to all children in the sample.

The first was a rhyming test that required children to generate rhyming words when familiar words were presented. The second was a sound categorization test (see Bradley & Bryant, 1985) that required children to listen to a sequence of four words and to choose two that sounded most alike. The reading readiness module had provided direct training for each of these skills, on the basis of Bradley and Bryant's hypothesis that these competencies facilitate reading mastery.

To obtain a measure of the effectiveness of this training module in preparing children for first formal learning of reading, a postinstruction word reading unit was designed and taught to all children in the sample. This unit was relatively brief, taking about 10 minutes to teach, and was taught to children individually upon completion of the training programs. It is described here:

The Word Reading Unit. This unit consisted of a sequence of steps designed to prepare children to read four simple words (i.e., mat, sat, pat, rat). The word "cat" was used for instructional purposes and children were first shown a picture of a cat and asked to name it; second, given practice in sounding out this word with respect to its beginning and ending sounds (e.g., "c" - "at"); third, given practice in mapping these sounds onto letters (e.g., c, at); and fourth given practice in blending the sounds into a single word when the letters were combined. Children were next presented with cards depicting a new beginning letter (m) and the same ending letters (at) and asked to read the word when the letters were combined. For this and all following criterion items, children were given assistance in identifying any letter they didn't know as well as the sound each letter makes. Pass scores were assigned on the basis of children's ability to read the new word (i.e., blend the sounds into a single utterance).

Type of Data Analysis

The central aim of our data analysis was to determine whether or not the Rightstart training prepared children for first-grade work, and whether or not it prepared a sufficient number of children to warrant its use. In other words, we were looking for educational validity rather than statistical validity and decided the appropriate form of analysis was a determination of the percentage of children in each group who were able to perform at the first-grade level (i.e., Level 1 on the developmental tests), after training, on the various tasks included in our assessment battery.

Results

Table 6.2 shows the percentage of children in each training group who performed at the first-grade level on the number knowledge test, before and after training. These data indicate that a strong majority (80%) of the children who received the Rightstart math module passed this level after training, whereas only a minority (35%–37%) of the children in the control groups demonstrated mastery. Because the Rightstart module was specifically designed to teach the knowledge assessed on this test, these results are not surprising. However, they do indicate that the readiness module did what it was supposed to do with considerable effectiveness.

Table 6.3 shows the percentage of children in each training group who performed at the first-grade level on five transfer tests. Note that no training in the specific knowledge required for any of these tests had been included in the training modules. Any reference to time dimensions, money dimensions, balance systems, birthday parties, and so on, had been conscientiously avoided when the activities included in the Rightstart training module were designed.

The results indicate that the majority of the treatment group passed the majority of the transfer tests at the first-grade level, in contrast to the two control groups where only a minority succeeded at this level. In relation to their pretest performance, this is a sizable achievement. On four of the transfer tests, the effects clearly differentiated the treatment group from the two control groups. The only transfer test on which training effects were not evident was the time-telling test.

TABLE 6.2
Percentage of Children Passing the Number Knowledge
Test at Level 1* Before and After Training

Group	Pretest (%)	Posttest (%)
Treatment ($n = 20$) (readiness module)	15	80
Control 1 ($n = 20$)** (traditional math module)	15	37
Control 2 ($n = 20$) (language module)	15	35

*Level 1 assesses knowledge typically demonstrated by the average 5- to 6-year-old.
**One child moved during the school year, reducing the size of his group to 19 on the posttest.

TABLE 6.3
Percentage of Children Passing Five Transfer
Tests at Level 1* Before and After Training

Transfer Test	Group	Pretest (%)	Posttest (%)
Time telling	Treatment	10	45
	Control 1	15	37
	Control 2	10	45
Money knowledge	Treatment	5	50
	Control 1	10	31
	Control 2	10	30
Birthday party	Treatment	5	65
	Control 1	21	42
	Control 2	15	25
Balance beam	Treatment	20	65
	Control 1	5	37
	Control 2	5	35
Conservation	Treatment	10	40
	Control 1	10	16
	Control 2	10	30

*Level 1 assesses knowledge typically demonstrated by the average 5- to 6-year-old.

Because the wording of some of the questions on this test was complicated, this test may have assessed general intelligence rather than quantitative understanding. Results of repeated measures analysis indicated a significant difference between the treatment group and the control groups on the battery of quantitative tasks included in this study; that is, the number knowledge test and the five transfer tests (F_1, 45 = 38.46, $p < .001$).

The results discussed this far assessed children's ability to perform at the dimensional level on these tasks (i.e., at the first-grade level) after training. Given the fact that a proportion of the children in the sample performed two substages below this on the pretest (i.e., at the 2-year-old level), a second analysis of this data was performed to assess the percentage of children showing an improvement of one or two substages on the posttest (i.e., moving from the 2-year-old level to the 4-year-old level; moving from the 4-year-old level to the 6-year-old level; or moving two substages from the 2-year-old level to the 6-year-old level).

Table 6.4 shows the percentage of children in each training group who demonstrated a pre- to posttraining change of one or two substages on four transfer tests. (Note: conservation of number was not included in this analysis because this test did not yield scores for three developmental levels.) When a one-substage change is considered, the results indicate that this change was greatest for the treatment group on each transfer test. When a two-substage change is considered, the results indicate that this was relatively rare but was found only for the treatment group. When the change effects were compared across trainers and across classrooms, no differences were found. It can be suggested, therefore,

TABLE 6.4
Percentage of Children Showing Pre- to Posttraining
Change on Four Transfer Tests

Transfer Test	Group	Posttest Scores 1 Substage* Higher (%)	Posttest Scores 2 Substages** Higher (%)
Time telling	Treatment	55	0
	Control 1	40	0
	Control 2	40	0
Money handling	Treatment	45	0
	Control 1	30	0
	Control 2	20	0
Birthday party	Treatment	60	15
	Control 1	40	0
	Control 2	15	0
Balance beam	Treatment	55	5
	Control 1	35	0
	Control 2	35	0

*1 substage is equivalent to 2 chronological years.
**2 substages are equivalent to 4 chronological years.

that the effects are independent of these factors and can be attributed to the training that was provided.

Table 6.5 shows the percentage of children in each training group who demonstrated mastery of three posttreatment instructional units: addition, subtraction, and musical sightreading. Note that, although success on these units is hypothesized to be dependent on a mental number-line conceptual structure, the musical sightreading unit focused children's attention on notes and keys and made no reference whatsoever to numbers and quantity. The results indicate that

TABLE 6.5
Percentage of Children Who Mastered* First-Grade Instructional
Units in Addition, Subtraction, and Musical Sightreading

Group	Addition Unit (%)	Subtraction Unit (%)	Musical Sightreading (%)
Treatment (n = 20)	75	85	75
Control 1 (n = 19)	53	42	50
Control 2 (n = 19)	42	26	47

*Mastery was scored when the child passed three-quarters or two-thirds (music only) of the criterion items.

a strong majority (75%–85%) of the treatment group demonstrated an ability to profit from each instructional unit by passing the criterion items, whereas smaller proportions of the control groups (26%–53%) demonstrated this ability.

Table 6.6 shows the percentage of children in each training group who performed at the 6-year-old level on three language tests: rhyming, sound categorization, word reading. The results indicate that the group that was trained with the reading readiness module demonstrated superior performance on each test. Although the differences between the training groups were not of the same magnitude as the differences found on the quantitative tasks, and the absolute percentage of children passing was not as high, the results indicate that the training modules produced differential effects.

Discussion

The results presented previously provided affirmative answers to the four research questions that were posed at the outset of the study. They suggested, first, that the knowledge implied in the central conceptual structure, and measured with a number test constructed for this purpose, can be taught to a group of children who gave little evidence of possessing this knowledge prior to training. Second, they suggested that the Rightstart curriculum was superior to two control treatments in enabling children to acquire this knowledge. Third, they suggested that the knowledge gained facilitated children's performance on four tasks from related domains for which no specific training was provided. Fourth, they suggested that the knowledge gained enhanced children's ability to profit from brief instruction in addition, subtraction, and musical sightreading.

Because the Rightstart module was explicitly designed to teach the central conceptual structure, it seems reasonable to conclude that children's improved performance on the posttest battery can be directly attributed to the presence of

TABLE 6.6
Percentage of Children Who Mastered* First-Grade
Instructional Unit in Reading, and Two Additional
Language Tests (Sound Categorization and Rhyming)

Group	Reading Unit (%)	Sound Categorization (%)	Rhyming (%)
Treatment			
(n = 20)	50	25	30
Control 1			
(n = 19)	37	16	37
Control 2			
(n = 20)	65	40	40

*Mastery was scored when the child passed 2/4 of the criterion items or Level 0 (Rhyme Test only).

this structure in their conceptual repertoire. In addition, on the basis of the transfer effects, it seems reasonable to conclude that this conceptual structure is indeed central to children's performance on a wide range of quantitative tasks and is a central prerequisite for first formal learning of arithmetic. Although these conclusions appear warranted, they also flow quite directly from the theoretical assumptions on which the curriculum was based. For this reason, it is worthwhile to examine other interpretations that might be offered for the findings of this study, and to consider whether the curriculum might have produced its effects for reasons other than the one just proposed.

It could be argued that the success of the program could be attributed simply to the fact that it familiarized children with the format in which numerical tests are normally presented, or to the fact that it provided them with extensive practice in counting. However, because these experiences were also provided in the traditional math training module, and children receiving this training did not demonstrate the performance gains shown by the Rightstart group, this interpretation seems unwarranted.

It could also be argued that the program's success could be attributed to the fact that it gave children enhanced general problem-solving skills that were useful on the posttest battery, or that it gave them increased confidence in their ability to perform well in a testing context. Although not wanting to dismiss the possibility that these more general elements of our program are important, this interpretation does not account for the fact that the Rightstart program did not produce superior, "across-the-board" performance on all tasks included in our posttest battery. On three language tasks, it was the reading readiness group who showed the strongest performance.

Given the pattern of strengths and weaknesses that was demonstrated by the three training groups on the posttest battery, it seems reasonable to conclude that the Rightstart program achieved its effects because it has content that enables children to develop a deeper conceptual understanding of number. This conclusion is further supported by the fact that the training group who was exposed to some, but not all, of the content implied in the conceptual structure, showed a pattern of performance on the quantitative posttests that was intermediate between the Rightstart group and the reading readiness group (who received no number training whatsoever).

When the effectiveness of the reading readiness program is considered, the results indicate that this program produced weaker effects than the Rightstart program on the sets of tasks used to assess mastery in each domain. Two explanations can be offered for this finding. First, the reading readiness program was included in the present study primarily to serve as a control for the Rightstart curriculum. It was an adapted version of a training program developed by Bradley and Bryant (1985) to teach sound categorization skills, and the version we developed may not have provided sufficient training to adequately test the hypotheses on which it was based.

Second, although it seems reasonable to assume that rhyming and sound categorization skills play an important role in reading readiness (as Bradley and Bryant suggested), these skills may not adequately specify central conceptual prerequisites for success in this domain. No attempt was made in the present study to conduct the sorts of developmental analyses for the language domain that were conducted for the quantitative domain, and that enabled us to pinpoint, rather precisely, central conceptual prerequisites for this domain. It seems possible that the greater success of the Rightstart module, when compared to the language module, can be attributed to the extensive developmental research (see Case & Griffin, 1990; Resnick, 1989, for a summary) that made precise specification of the central dimensional structure possible.

On the basis of the first-year results, we concluded that we were well on the way to creating an approach to producing an early mathematics curriculum that would be suitable for children at risk for school failure in math, and that our approach would be successful in preparing such children to master their first formal learning of arithmetic (as well as their first formal learning of musical sightreading, should the opportunity arise!).

YEAR 2 TRIAL OF THE CURRICULUM

Study 2

For the Year 2 trial of the curriculum, our first goal was to assess the need for this sort of early mathematics program focused on number concepts for populations in the United States. Although it seemed possible that children whose parents had immigrated from rural Portugal to Toronto might have the same gaps in their number knowledge as many U.S. populations, we did not feel we could take this as a "given." Thus, we decided to administer our number knowledge tests to a variety of U.S. populations that are (statistically speaking) at risk for early school failure.

On the assumption that we would be able to find a sizable number of children who had not yet developed the full structure in which we were interested, our second goal was to determine whether the instructional module we had developed would work equally well in helping such children develop this structure, at an accelerated rate. Our final aim was to improve the generality of the exercises in our program, so that they would be affectively and cognitively engaging for children with a wider range of entering competencies.

The Sample

Three inner-city schools in a central Massachusetts city were chosen as sites for the second study. These schools had the largest proportion of minority students (i.e., Blacks, Hispanics, and Southeast Asians) in the city, and children in these schools generally came from low to middle-low SES families. In the second half of the school year, all kindergarten children in these schools were given parent permission slips in their native language. From the 161 slips sent home, 112 were returned with signed parental consent to participate in the study. The number knowledge test was administered to all children with signed consent, and 55 of these children (49%) failed Level 1 of this test (i.e., they did not appear to have a well consolidated number-line structure). These children were considered to be in need of our Rightstart module and this group of 55 children constituted our training sample.

To assess the need for our readiness program in other regions of the United States, the number test was also administered to 19 children who were randomly selected from two schools in the San Francisco Bay area. These schools, one public and one private, served low SES populations of White, Black, and/or Hispanic origin. The mean age of these children was 5 years, 8 months.

As in Study 1, a rank-ordering procedure was used to assign the children in our training sample to a treatment and a control group, with the child receiving the lowest ranked score assigned to the Rightstart group (i.e., the treatment group), and the child receiving the second lowest ranked score assigned to the control group (i.e., no treatment provided), and so on. To the extent possible, each pair of children assigned to these two groups was also matched for: (a) age, (b) cultural group, (c) school, and (d) home classroom. Seven children for whom a match could not be found were eliminated from the sample. The resulting groups each contained 24 children. The mean chronological age of the treatment group was 5.7 years. The mean age of the control group was 5.10 years.

The Training

For instructional purposes, the 24 children in the treatment group were divided into six groups of four children each. These small instructional groups were evenly distributed across the three school sites. Training was provided by two research assistants who received prior training in teaching the readiness module. Each of these trainers assumed sole responsibility for training both groups of children at one of the three school sites. At the third site, each trainer taught one group of children.

As in the first study, 40 group training sessions were provided, with each session lasting approximately 20 minutes. Some children were present for every session and others, because of a high level of absenteeism from school, were absent for several training sessions. Instruction was provided in a separate room in the school, with the room used on any particular day determined by availability. The library and the cafeteria were frequent training sites. These locations, and the variability in sites used across sessions, did not provide ideal training conditions; however, they did provide conditions with frequent distractions, a reality in many inner-city schools in the United States today.

In keeping with the third goal of this study, several modifications were made to the Year 1 Rightstart module, prior to commencement of training. These modifications were informed by daily records kept by the Year 1 trainers that provided an assessment of how well each activity met the instructional objectives, and conformed to the instructional principles, for the range of children included in the program. They are summarized, in point form, here:

1. Several of the lesson plans were reordered to provide a learning sequence that seemed more natural for children and that permitted better hierarchical integration of knowledge. One example of this resequencing was the introduction of higher numbers (i.e., 6 to 10) earlier in the instructional sequence. Most of the children in the Year 1 study appeared capable of handling these numbers, and their introduction provided a broader base on which to build higher order understandings (e.g., the increment rule) earlier in the instructional program.

2. Many of the activities were rescripted to include teacher-posed questions (e.g., How did you figure that out?). These permitted more room for group discussion and, hence, increased opportunities for verbal interaction. Our hope was that this adaptation would permit children to articulate and formalize their knowledge, and to learn from each other. This adaptation seemed particularly useful for children who tended to be very quiet unless specifically called upon. It also appeared useful for the trainer, who could get a better idea of each child's current knowledge state.

3. Activities that had not seemed sufficiently multileveled and/or affectively engaging in Year 1 were adapted or deleted. In the latter instance, activities that were more game-like and that addressed several components of the knowledge structure at once were substituted.

4. Activities that had been particularly difficult for children to master in the Year 1 version (e.g., counting backward from 10) were incorporated in several versions in the "warm-up" or "closing" exercises for each day's training session. For example, in an exercise designed to prepare children to go back to their classrooms, children are assigned numbers on the basis of some salient variable (e.g., their height). They are then requested to line up at the door in a reverse order sequence, with the child with the largest number going first, and the others determining their place in the sequence and then calling out their numbers before leaving.

5. In the initial version of the module, the format of some of the competitive games (e.g., the card game "War") permitted the more capable student to call all the shots. In the adapted version, modifications were introduced that required turn-taking and that permitted greater participation for the less capable students.

Posttesting

After training, our standard battery of tests was administered to all children in the treatment and control groups. This battery included the number knowledge test and four developmental transfer tasks that were used in the first study (i.e., the balance-beam task, the birthday-party task, the time-telling task, and the money-handling task). These are described in a previous section. A fifth developmental task, a Distributive-Justice task developed by Damon (1973) to assess moral reasoning, was also included in our battery, based on our analysis, which suggested that success at the 6-year-old level was dependent on a dimensional structure. This test is described below.

Distributive Justice. In this test, children are presented with pictures of two children and told the following story: "These children helped their teacher for a number of days, making cards for sick children. When they were done, the teacher wanted to reward the children with little crackers for helping." The participants are then asked to determine which child should get the greater reward, based on the number of days the child has worked and the number of cards he or she has produced. A respondent who makes only gross comparisons of quantity, but makes no mention of number, is rated as giving a predimensional answer. Answers are scored as dimensional if the child counts and uses the information thus generated in some fashion (e.g., "She should get more crackers because she made 6 cards and he only made 4 cards").

All tests were individually administered to each child, in a single session for most children and in two sessions for children who showed fatigue part way through the first session. It is important to note that the revised module still provided no specific training for any of the transfer tests. Thus, the tasks still provided an indication of children's ability to apply the concepts they had learned in the program to new contexts.

Results

Normative Data. The normative data that were obtained from the Massachusetts sample indicated that 49% of the children tested failed the number test at the dimensional level prior to training. The data obtained from children of similar age and SES in California indicated that 68% failed the test at the same level. What these data suggest is that a substantial proportion of children did not possess, or could not yet demonstrate, the conceptual knowledge that we hypothesize to underlie success in addition and subtraction. This finding is all the more striking when one considers that the children who did not participate in the study (because parental permission was not obtained) were those who—according to classroom teachers—were most at risk for math failure. Because each cultural group was disproportionately represented in the sample, conclusions regarding the relative strengths and weaknesses of each group cannot be drawn. However, the potential utility of the Rightstart program did not appear to be restricted to any one particular cultural or linguistic group.

To identify the particular difficulties evidenced by the group of children who failed the test (i.e., the training sample), a detailed item analysis was conducted.

The percentage of children passing several specific items on the number knowledge test is presented in Table 6.7. As the data indicate, these children had little difficulty generating numbers when asked to count aloud to 10, or when presented with a small set of objects to count. However, when asked which of two numbers was bigger or smaller, which was closer in magnitude to some other target number, or how many they would have if they received four objects followed by three more, a large proportion of these children were uncertain as to how to proceed and gave inaccurate responses. Whereas the difficulties on the former two items suggest an absence of the general conceptual knowledge inherent in the mental number line structure, the latter difficulty indicates the absence of that aspect of this knowledge on which the solving of first-grade addition and subtraction problems is most directly dependent.

The Instructional Data.   Table 6.8 shows the percentage of children in each group who performed at the unidimensional level on the number test and on five transfer tests, after training (i.e., the percentage who showed evidence of a well consolidated number line structure on the posttest battery). These data indicate that a strong majority (87%) of the treatment group passed the number knowledge test, whereas only a minority (25%) of the children in the control group achieved the same level of success. Note that no child in either group had passed the number knowledge test, by the same criterion, prior to training.

A similar pattern was obtained on each transfer test. On four of these tests, the difference between the groups was substantial, with at least 50% more children passing in the treatment group when compared to the control group. On the money-handling test, the absolute percentage of children passing was not as high for the treatment group and the difference between the groups was smaller (i.e., 26%). Results of multivariance analysis indicated a significant difference between

TABLE 6.7
Performance of Research Sample on Selected
Items from Number Knowledge Pretest

Level	Item	Percentage Passing (%)
Predimensional	Can you count from 1 to 10?	91
	Can you count the triangles in this set? (total $N = 15$; triangles = 8)	77
Unidimensional*	Which number is bigger/smaller? (5 vs. 4; 7 vs. 9)	
	(8 vs. 6; 5 vs. 7)	36
	Which number is closer to 5; 6 or 2?	51
	If you had 4 chocolates, and someone gave you three more, how many would you have?	13

*This is the level illustrated in Fig. 6.1, as hypothesized as necessary for success in early math.

TABLE 6.8
Percentage of Children Passing Quantitative Tests
at Unidimensional Level, After Treatment

Test	Control Group (n = 24) (%)	Treatment Group (n = 23) (%)
Number knowledge (6/7)*	25	87
Distrib justice (2/2)	37	87
Birthday party (2/2)	42	96
Time telling (4/5)	21	83
Balance beam (2/2)	42	96
Money handling (4/6)	17	43

*Pass criterion.

the treatment group and the control group on the battery of quantitative tasks included in this study; that is, the number knowledge test and the five transfer tests (F_1, 70 = 23.46, $p < .001$).

Table 6.9 shows the percentage of children in each group who passed selected unidimensional items on the number knowledge test. Although no difference between the groups was found for one item at this level (i.e., Which number is closer to 5: 6 or 2?), on the remaining items, substantial differences were found. At least 50% more children in the treatment group demonstrated mastery of critical components of the mental number line conceptual structure (e.g., Which is bigger: 5 or 7?) and were able to determine how much they would have if they received 4 objects followed by 3 objects. When children in the treatment group failed this latter item, the answers they provided (e.g., 4 + 3 = 8) were usually reasonable and suggested that they understood the operation involved. By contrast, the answers

TABLE 6.9
Percentage of Children Passing Selected Items
on Number Knowledge Test After Treatment Period

Level	Item	Control Group (%)	Treatment Group (%)
Predimensional	Can you count the triangles in this set? (total N = 15; triangles = 8)	88	100
Unidimensional*	Which number is smaller? (8 vs. 6; 5 vs. 7)	37	92
	Which number is bigger? (5 vs. 4; 7 vs. 9)	50	100
	Which number is closer to 5: 6 or 2?	71	70
	If you had 4 chocolates, and someone gave you more, how many would you have?	29	87

TABLE 6.10
Percentage of Children Passing Quantitative Tests at
Undimensional Level, by School, After Treatment

Test	Treatment Group			Control Group		
	School A (n = 8) (%)	School B (n = 7) (%)	School C (n = 8) (%)	School A (n = 8) (%)	School B (n = 8) (%)	School C (n = 8) (%)
Number	87	86	87	37	25	13
Birthday	100	86	100	50	37	37
Time	75	86	87	12	25	25
Balance	87	100	100	50	37	37
Money	25	29	75	25	13	13
Justice	87	86	87	50	25	37
Composite Score	77	79	89	37	27	27

given by the control children often seemed like wild guesses (e.g., 13) or simple associations based on their knowledge of counting (e.g., 5).

As the data in these two tables indicate, the proportion of children passing the quantitative tasks was higher for the treatment group than was found in the Year 1 results. Because the percentage of children passing the number knowledge pretest was lower for this year's study (i.e., 0%) when compared to the Year 1 study (i.e., 15%), the strength of this year's findings can possibly be attributed to the improved curriculum that was used and the greater effectiveness of this training program.

As is shown in Table 6.10, the effects of this program were consistent across the three school sites. They were also consistent for groups of children from different cultural backgrounds (see Table 6.11). Although a small number of

TABLE 6.11
Percentage of Children Passing Quantitative Tests at
Undimensional Level, by Cultural Group, After Treatment

Test	Treatment Group		Control Group	
	Hispanic (n = 10) (%)	American (n = 9) (%)	Hispanic (n = 7) (%)	American (n = 14) (%)
Number	80	89	14	36
Birthday	90	100	43	43
Time	90	89	14	28
Balance	90	100	57	43
Money	60	44	0	28
Justice	90	78	57	21
Composite Score	83	83	31	33

Southeast Asian children also participated in our study, the size of this sample ($n = 6$) was too small to draw reliable conclusions, and these data are not reported in Table 6.11. However, the findings provide tentative evidence that the module was equally effective for this group of children as well.

GENERAL CONCLUSIONS

Taking the data that we have gathered across the last 2 years as a whole, we draw the following general conclusions.

1. Children from a wide variety of cultural backgrounds appear to be in need of some form of conceptually based readiness training in number. These problems are evident in children who are recent immigrants even when they are tested in their native language. Very often children are unable to answer such questions as whether 5 or 4 is a bigger number: a difficulty that—regardless of its origins—does not bode well for their ability to understand the conceptual basis of addition and subtraction as it is taught in schools today. Given the problems that U.S. schools already have in fostering conceptual understanding (Stigler, Lee, & Stevenson, 1990), this sort of early difficulty seems particularly unfortunate, because it increases the likelihood that school math will be treated, from the start, as a rote activity.

2. Our Rightstart mathematics module appears to be effective in teaching the knowledge it was designed to teach to a wide variety of children. Its effectiveness has now been demonstrated in two countries (Canada and the United States); in four separate schools; and with five cultural groups, from low to middle-low SES communities. It has also been shown to be effective when implemented by five different trainers.

3. It seems clear that the program does not have its effect simply by familiarizing children with the procedure for counting, or for representing numbers with numerals. Nor does it have its effect simply by engaging children in a social process with which they have had little experience up to that point in time, namely, answering test questions by an adult and justifying these answers in a "decontextualized" setting. If these were the only important aspects of the program, then one would have expected more progress to be shown by the various control groups that were used in the Year 1 study.

4. Three of the main foci of the program were (a) teaching children to respond to questions about relative magnitude in the absence of any concrete sets of objects; (b) teaching children the "increment rule," that is, the rule that dictates that the addition or subtraction of one element to a set alters the cardinal value of that set by one unit, and therefore moves the value one unit up or down on the number line; and (c) teaching children that knowledge of relative position

on the number line is useful for making determinations of relative quantity in various "real-world" tasks, when for some reason this cannot be determined more directly. Because the sorts of questions on which children showed improvement on the posttest battery all dealt with one or another of these components, it can be assumed that the program had its effect for the reason hypothesized.

5. It was hypothesized that the Rightstart program would give children a central conceptual structure that would enhance their ability to profit from instruction in formal first-grade arithmetic, as well as helping them solve a wide variety of other quantitative problems. On the basis of the transfer effects, it seems clear that the knowledge taught was central to children's performance on a range of quantitative tasks for which no specific training had been provided. The knowledge taught also appeared to facilitate mastery of brief instructional units in addition and subtraction that were taught at the end of the kindergarten year. Whether or not this knowledge will continue to enhance children's arithmetic learning as they move through the instructional programs that are typically offered in first grade American classrooms is a question that remains to be investigated. However, the extent of the transfer that has already been documented indicates that the program was effective in producing greater generalization of knowledge than is typically achieved. For this reason, the approach that was taken—teaching the central conceptual structures—may provide a means of teaching for transfer that has a much wider range of application than was tested in the present study.

ACKNOWLEDGMENTS

The Rightstart program and the studies that are reported in this chapter were made possible by a generous grant from the James S. McDonnell Foundation. The authors gratefully acknowledge this support as well as the cooperation and enthusiasm of the children and teachers who used the Rightstart program and helped shape its final form.

REFERENCES

Bradley, L., & Bryant, P. (1985). *Rhyme and reason in reading and spelling*. Ann Arbor: University of Michigan Press.

Capodilupo, A. (1992). A neo-structural analysis of children's response to instruction in the sight-reading of musical notation. In R. Case (Ed.), *The mind's staircase: Exploring the conceptual underpinnings of children's thought and knowledge* (pp. 98–115). Hillsdale, NJ: Lawrence Erlbaum Associates.

Case, R. (1975). Social class differences in intellectual development: A neo-Piagetian investigation. *Canadian Journal of Behavioral Sciences, 7*, 78–95.

Case, R. (Ed.). (1985). *Intellectual development: Birth to adulthood*. New York: Academic Press.

Case, R., & Griffin, S. (1990). Child cognitive development: The role of central conceptual structure in the development of scientific and social thought. In C. A. Haver (Ed.), *Advances in psychology: Developmental psychology* (pp. 193–230). North Holland: Elsevier.

Case, R., & Sandieson, R. (1985). Life skills training for the mentally retarded. (Final Report, Year 2). Ministry of Education under its Block Transfer grant to Ontario Institute for Studies in Education. Toronto, Ontario.

Case, R., & Sandieson, R. (1987, April). *General developmental constraints on the acquisition of special procedures (and vice versa).* Paper presented at the annual meeting of the American Educational Research Association, Baltimore, MD.

Case, R., Sandieson, R., & Dennis, S. (1986). Two cognitive developmental approaches to the design of remedial instruction. *Cognitive Development, 1,* 293–333.

Damon, W. (1973). *The child's conception of justice as related to logical thought.* Unpublished doctoral dissertation, University of California, Berkeley.

Fischer, K. W. (1980). A theory of cognitive development: The control and construction of hierarchies of skill. *Psychological Review, 87,* 477–531.

Ginsburg, H. P., & Russel, R. L. (1981). Social class and racial factors on early mathematical thinking. *Monographs of the Society for Research in Child Development, 46,* Serial No. 193.

Griffin, S., Case, R., & Sandieson, R. (1992). Synchrony and asynchrony in the acquisition of everyday mathematical knowledge: Towards a representational theory of children's intellectual growth. In R. Case (Ed.), *The mind's staircase: Exploring the conceptual underpinnings of children's thought and knowledge* (pp. 75–97). Hillsdale, NJ: Lawrence Erlbaum Associates.

Griffin, S., Case, R., & Siegler, R. (1994). Rightstart: Providing the central conceptual prerequisites for first formal learning of arithmetic to students at risk for school failure. In K. McGilly (Ed.), *Classroom lessons: Integrating cognitive theory and classroom practice* (pp. 25–49). Cambridge, MA: Branford Books.

Halford, G. S. (1982). *The development of thought.* Hillsdale, NJ: Lawrence Erlbaum Associates.

Liu, P. (1981). *An investigation of the relationship between qualitative and quantitative advances in the cognitive development of preschool children.* Unpublished doctoral dissertation, University of Toronto, Ontario Institute for Studies in Education, Toronto.

Marini, Z. A. (in press). Synchrony and asynchrony in the development of children's scientific reasoning: Re-analyzing the problem of decalages from a neo-Piagetian perspective. In R. Case (Ed.), *The mind's staircase: Exploring the conceptual underpinnings of children's thought and knowledge* (pp. 55–73). Hillsdale, NJ: Lawrence Erlbaum Associates.

National Assessment of Educational Progress. (1983). The Third National Mathematics Assessment: Results, Trends, and Issues. Denver: Educational Commission of the States.

Resnick, L. B. (1983). A developmental theory of number understanding. In H. P. Ginsburg (Ed.), *The development of mathematical understanding* (pp. 109–151). New York: Academic Press.

Resnick, L. B. (1989). Developing mathematical knowledge. *American Psychologist, 44*(2), 162–169.

Saxe, G. B., Guberman, S. R., & Geerhart, M. (1989). Social processes in early number development. *Monographs of the Society for Research in Child Development, 52,* Serial No. 216.

Siegler, R. (1976). Three aspects of cognitive development. *Cognitive Psychology, 8,* 481–520.

Siegler, R. (1978). The origins of scientific reasoning. In R. S. Siegler (Ed.), *Children's thinking: What develops?* (pp. 109–150). Hillsdale, NJ: Lawrence Erlbaum Associates.

Stevenson, H., Lee, S., & Stigler, J. (1986). Mathematics achievement of Chinese, Japanese, and American children. *Science, 231,* 693–699.

CHAPTER 7

Teaching Narrative Knowledge for Transfer in the Early School Years

Anne McKeough
University of Calgary

Knowledge transfer is widely seen as central to learning and development. It is not surprising, therefore, that the educational psychology literature contains a large number of studies that aim at producing transfer or elucidating the conditions under which it takes place. What is more surprising is that these studies have shown so little success (Cormier & Hagman, 1987).

Historically, the move from the classical learning paradigm (Skinner, 1950) to the information-processing approach brought about a shift in instructional focus from shaping specific skills, through successive approximation, to training very general metacognitive skills (Brown 1975; Pressley, 1982). Even under these new conditions, transfer proved resistant, however, as the application of metacognitive skills was typically limited to near transfer. By contrast, the sought-after far transfer, which involved moving knowledge between domains and thereby forging links through conscious strategic activity, remained elusive (Perkins & Solomon, 1987). Children's failure to engage spontaneously in what has been described as a "mindful backward search" (Solomon, 1988) eventually led researchers to turn their attention from teaching general metacognitive skills to directly teaching strategies or procedures designed to facilitate knowledge access (Bereiter & Scardamalia, 1985), transfer (Brown & Campione, 1984; Singley & Anderson, 1989), and strategy utilization (Pressley, 1990).

A similar historical progression from general to more specific knowledge structures has occurred in the area of cognitive development. Piaget's theory (Piaget, 1950) stimulated a large number of training studies, because it suggested that the structures underlying concepts such as conservation were very general ones that should be very difficult to teach but that, if taught, should produce transfer to other structurally related tasks such as seriation and transitivity. What was actually found, however, was that (a) the concept could be taught without undue difficulty, at least above the age of 5 years, and (b) when it was taught, transfer only took place to different kinds of material, but never to other tasks whose only relation was that they shared the same underlying logical structure (see Halford, 1982, for a review). Taken together with the data on decalages and low intertask correlations, this led to a view of development that held that separate skills or concepts were learned relatively independently of each other, and that transfer across domains should therefore be a rare occurrence, if it ever took place at all (Chi & Rees, 1983; Siegler, 1981).

Recently, however, a number of constructs have been proposed that allow us to look at knowledge organization in a more general way and to re-address issues related to knowledge transfer. By integrating the developmental and information processing perspectives, Case (1992) proposed that certain knowledge structures, which he labeled *central conceptual structures*, may transcend conventionally defined domains. These structures are presumed to be broadly applicable, and when taught, they are thought to produce transfer to a wide variety of tasks that share the same conceptual underpinnings, but involve different domain-specific knowledge (Case, 1992; Case & Griffin, 1990). The example he and his colleagues discuss in this volume (Chapter 6) is the concept of a quantitative dimension represented as a number line, which is thought to be acquired at about the age of 6 years under conditions of spontaneous acquisition, and which differentiates the performance of 4- and 6-year-old children on a variety of tasks as diverse as telling time, adding and subtracting numbers, handling money, determining the tilt of a balance scale, sightreading music, and making determinations of distributive justice. Griffin, Case, and Capodilupo (Chapter 6, this volume) report on studies in which 4-year-olds were trained to quantify along a single dimension, and then observed transfer of this knowledge to other tasks (also see Case & Sandieson, 1992; Griffin, Case, & Sandieson, 1992). In the light of the usual dearth of transfer, their findings are of considerable theoretical as well as practical interest. Moreover, they would appear to be complementary to the findings produced by investigators from other traditions (e.g., Brown & Campione, 1984; Singley & Anderson, 1989). There is nothing incompatible between the suggestion that general strategies for knowledge accessing exist and can be taught, and the suggestion that general conceptual structures exist that are used for making sense of new content in different task domains.

In this chapter, I extend this latter line of research into the domain of narrative. My goals are twofold: first, to document the existence of a second central conceptual structure, a *central narrative structure*, and second, to describe a program of instruction designed to facilitate the development of a storyline and its transfer to social contexts occurring outside of the classroom, involving human intentions and actions.

THE CENTRAL NARRATIVE STRUCTURE

Narrative has traditionally played a fairly central role in understanding knowledge acquisition in several disciplines outside of academic psychology. Literary theorists have sought to identify the structural components of narrative and the role of the writer and reader in assembling meaning (e.g., Culler, 1975; Levi-Strauss, 1958; Scholes & Kellogg, 1966). Anthropologists have also examined narrative, primarily in the form of folktales, in an effort to understand cultural frames of reference (e.g., Propp, 1968). In psychology, although narrative has been a traditional tool of clinicians who used it to piece together a patient's life history,[1] it was not until the cognitive revolution that it entered the arena of academic psychology.[2] Throughout the 1970s and early 1980s, cognitive research aimed at determining the structural organization of narrative and the mental structures that enable narrative comprehension (e.g., Applebee, 1978; Mandler & Goodman, 1982; Stein & Glenn, 1979).

More recently, a broader role has been assigned to narrative within cognitive psychology. Bruner (1986, 1990) suggested that narrative is one of two ways that experience is ordered and understood, the other being what he termed *paradigmatic thought.* Whereas the paradigmatic mode of thought organizes information hierarchically in categories and concepts and is suited to the scientific realm, the narrative mode "deals in human and human-like intention and action and the vicissitudes and consequences that mark their course" (p. 13). The narrative mode of thought is based upon a temporal and causal ordering of events of two sorts: those that take place in the physical world (i.e., on "the landscape of action"), and those that take place in the mental life of the characters (i.e., on "the landscape of consciousness"; Bruner, 1986). Narratives lay out the actions and thoughts of protagonists and, in so doing, provide models of the organization of human action, linking action and consequence and enabling us to interpret the intentions of others in our daily interactions (Polkinghorne, 1988).

Preschoolers' Narrative Knowledge

Research has shown that even preschoolers have a narrative schema, albeit a somewhat limited one. For example, Nelson (1981) demonstrated that 4-year-olds possess scripts for common events, such as eating at MacDonalds or going to a birthday party. These scripts are comprised of temporally ordered, stereotypic actions and events and enable children to relate events in a coherent fashion.

Similarly, work in early narrative composition has demonstrated that 4-year-olds can generate coherent stories, comprised of states, actions, and events that are temporally, causally, and referentially bound (Mandler, 1984; Stein & Glenn,

---

[1]This notion is explicated in the works of Runyan (1982), Spence (1982), and Schafer (1981).

[2]A notable exception was the work of Bartlett (1932), whose notion of story schema served as the basis for much of the work done throughout the 1970s.

1979). The following sample story, told by Lucy in response to a request to "tell a story about a happy little girl and a kind old horse," typifies 4-year-olds' narratives in that it is action/event based and reports only those actions that occur within the story world (McKeough, 1992a):

> Once upon a time there was a girl who lived on a farm with a very good horse and she always rode to the country on the horse and they had a picnic together.

Four-year-olds appear to use the same action/event schema outside of the story domain when explicitly asked to account for the actions of another person. Goldberg-Reitman (1992) asked young children to predict and account for a mother's actions when her little girl was in danger of injury. A cartoon depicting a little girl slipping off a roof was shown and read to 4-year-olds (see Fig. 7.1), and they were asked what the girl's mother would do and why. Even at this young age, the children predicted a reasonable course of action (e.g., "The mom will catch her."), and explained the mother's actions in terms of the action depicted in the cartoon (e.g., ". . . because she's falling off."). Thus, it seems clear that 4-year-olds possess an action/event schema, comprised of descriptions of states and events that map onto states and events in the physical world (see Fig. 7.2), which is used in a range of tasks, including reporting on common, real-life events, composing fictional narratives, and accounting for a mother's nurturing behavior.

In a slightly different vein, researchers who study the child's theory of mind have demonstrated that, by 4 years of age, children's knowledge of mental states has also begun to develop. For example, Wellman (1988) demonstrated that preschoolers (a) acquire mental state terms such as *forget, dream, pretend, believe, and know*; (b) appreciate the difference between mental states and objective reality (e.g., that dreaming about being chased by a dog is different than actually being chased by one); (c) understand that individuals can hold different mental states (e.g., a gift giver might know that a wrapped box contains a puzzle but the receiver might think it contains a book; and finally (d) understand that people's mental states and actions are associated (e.g., you laugh when something is funny).

It has also been demonstrated that preschoolers understand the relation between affective states and actions. For example, Bruchkowsky (1992) determined that,

A little girl   *She starts*
is up on .   *to slide*
the roof.   *down.*

FIG. 7.1. Example of mother's motive task item.

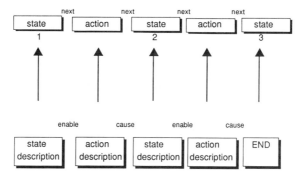

FIG. 7.2.   Action event schema.

when shown a video tape of a young girl happily playing with her dog, followed by a sequence in which the child tearfully reports that a car has hit her dog, 4-year-olds can identify the child's affective state (e.g., "sad") and explain it in terms of an action event (e.g., ". . . because the car hit him."). Further evidence of the affect–action/event link was provided by Griffin (1992). When she asked 4-year-olds to define feeling terms, such as happy and sad, they reported, for example, that "happy is getting a birthday present" and "sad is when you're crying." Thus, from this and other research (e.g., Fischer & Pipp, 1984; Fischer, Shaver, & Carnochan, 1990; Stein & Levine, 1986), it appears that preschoolers (at least those from middle-class Western "schooled" families) have, in addition to the previously described action/event schema, a fairly well established schema for relating internal cognitive and affective states to external events and actions (see Fig. 7.3).

The Narrative Knowledge of 6-Year-Olds

By the time children have passed their sixth birthday and enter school, we typically see a marked change in the use of these two knowledge structures. Unlike the 4-year-olds, who seem to use either one or the other of these structures, 6-year-olds

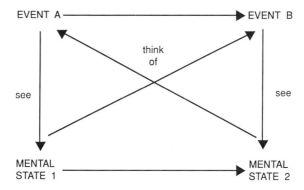

FIG. 7.3.   Internal state schema.

coordinate the two with the result that action sequences often contain reference to the mental states that underlie them or are associated with them. The following story sample composed by Amanda illustrates this point:

> Once upon a time there was a little girl. She—she was walking to go and pick some flowers. But when—but when she was picking some flowers she heard a buzzing noise and up came a big bee. She was scared and she ran home and she—and she came back and—with her big sister. . . . And she didn't know what to do, but her sister explained that bees make honey and she shouldn't be ascared.

In her story, Amanda laid out a sequence of actions (i.e., a little girl walks to pick flowers, a bee comes, she runs home, etc.). But, in addition, she made explicit reference to associated cognitive and affective states (i.e., "she was scared," "she doesn't know . . .," and ". . . she shouldn't be ascared"). By relating external events and actions to the character's internal mental states (i.e., her thoughts and feelings), Amanda produced a simple version of Bruner's (1986) dual-landscape narrative. That is, she has generated both a landscape of action (comprised of events, states, and actions) and the beginnings of a landscape of consciousness (comprised of "what the protagonist knows, feels, thinks, or believes" about the landscape of action; p. 14).

As Fig. 7.4 demonstrates, the dual-landscape notion seems to capture the flavor of the 6-year-old story structure. The story is comprised of a setting (i.e., a girl is walking to pick flowers) from which an initiating event emerges, serving to start the action rolling ("she hears a buzzing noise and up comes a big bee"). The initiating event causes affective disequilibrium (i.e., fear), graphically depicted as ☹, which sets a balance-restoring initiative or plan in motion ☀ (i.e., elicit her big sister's help). The idea yields an action response (i.e., although the little girl doesn't know what to do, her big sister explains that bees make honey), which in turn enables affective equilibrium to be reestablished ☺. Thus, a set of causal relations is represented between the external world of physical states and action, on the one hand, and the internal world of feelings and mental states (i.e., ideas or plans) on the other. We have termed the 6-year-old structure *intentional narrative* because the intentions of the characters motivate the action (e.g., I do *x* and *y* because I know, think, or feel *a* and *b*). In the intentional structure, one could say that the landscape of consciousness is both differentiated from and coordinated with the landscape of action.

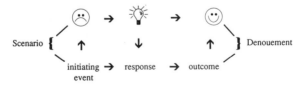

FIG. 7.4.   The intentional narrative structure at 6 years.

If this integrated intentional structure is a central one, as Case proposed, it should be used beyond the story domain. We should see intentional reasoning in the responses of the 6-year-old group on those tasks to which its component schemata were applied by the 4-year-olds. Indeed, evidence was found that 6-year-olds also used the intentional structure when answering questions pertaining to the actions and feelings of others. On the cartoon task developed by Goldberg-Reitman (1992), they explained that a mother would catch a little girl because, for example, ". . . she didn't want her to get hurt." Thus, in contrast to the 4-year-olds, whose responses remained on the landscape of action (e.g., "because she's sliding off the roof"), the 6-year-olds made additional reference to the mother's mental state or intention to account for her actions.

Similarly, on Bruchkowsky's (1991, 1992) video task, 6-year-olds explained that the girl would feel sad when the car hit the dog ". . . because she loved him" or "because she was going to miss him" and that the video made them feel "sad because I like dogs too." Recall that this reference to the "landscape of consciousness" was absent in the answers of the younger children, who explained the girl's feelings exclusively in action terms (e.g., "because the dog went on the road."). Evidence that 6-year-olds use an integrated intentional structure also came from their responses on Griffin's (1992) definition of feelings task. Here, 6-year-old children reported that "happy is when you feel happy because your mom plays with you" and "sad is when you cry because no one likes you." The central intentional structure, depicted graphically in Fig. 7.5, is comprised of the action/state description mapped onto physical-world action and states, which, in turn, are associated with internal mental states.

As can be seen, then, before entering school, children have separately constructed both a schema for relating events and action that occur in the physical world and a schema for relating mental states associated with events. Moreover, although preschoolers used one or the other of these schemata in a range of tasks, they were typically unable to use them in a coordinated fashion, as the 6-year-olds did. Case (1985) proposed that a maturationally based increase in processing capacity allows for the coordination of the two operations, forming a more complex cognitive structure. Further, although this processing capacity increase is thought to be necessary for developmental change under typical conditions, it is not considered sufficient. Experience also influences development. The children who participated in the previously described investigations were middle-class urban dwellers from "schooled" families. More specifically, they had parents who were highly literate and they had had considerable exposure to the Western literate tradition (Olson, 1986, 1987, 1988). The observed coordination of the event/action and mental state schemata in 6-year-olds described previously is thought to stem from both factors (i.e., processing capacity increase and experience) working together.

In order to test this assertion, we conducted two types of instruction studies. First, we attempted to teach a group of average-functioning 4-year-olds the

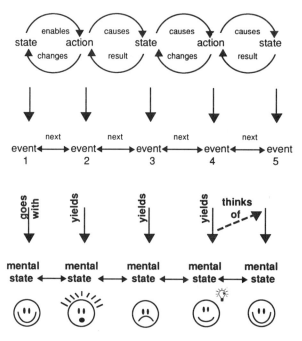

FIG. 7.5. Intentional schema.

intentional narrative structure. We reasoned that by circumventing processing capacity limitations and by offering children experience in coordinating the two component schemata we should be able to teach them to compose intentional narratives. Further, we reasoned that if the intentional structure was indeed central to a range of tasks (i.e., that the tasks were based on the same conceptual underpinnings), the newly constructed knowledge should transfer, even though the tasks differed in surface features.

Second, we worked with groups of children who were thought to have the required processing capacity but who lacked the experiential base. These were children from lower socioeconomic status (SES) neighborhoods who were identified by their teachers as being at risk academically. Their preschool linguistic and literacy experience has been shown to be different from that of their middle SES counterparts and this can put them at a disadvantage in school classrooms, where instruction is geared to middle-class norms (Goody & Watt, 1968). We reasoned that a program of instruction that aimed at teaching the intentional narrative structure would be maximally beneficial as it would be expected to produce not only criterion-related gains in the task domain of narrative (an area of great importance in the early school grades) but transfer to conceptually related tasks, as well.

TEACHING THE CENTRAL NARRATIVE STRUCTURE
FOR TRANSFER

In very general terms, the instruction program, designed to facilitate the construction of intentional narratives, initially emphasized children's existing conceptual representation. Although instruction procedures were organized in daily lessons, the rate of progress through the lessons was varied according to the conceptual needs of the individuals in the group. Thus, in cases where children's understanding seemed limited, instructors proceeded slowly and reworked concepts, as necessary for understanding. Variation in the rate at which children learn was handled by pairing less able children with more able ones, who were asked to offer story content while the less proficient children were helped to focus on the structural organization. Less proficient children also worked as the instructor's partner and were allowed more time in the various storytelling activities. Additionally, if children seemed to require less direct instruction, instructors proceeded more rapidly, using only a smattering of the activities to ensure that concepts had been mastered.

The lessons were designed so that the story topics and specific content were largely left to the child. The teacher's primary role was to offer assistance with structural organization. Using what the children generated, teachers highlighted structural organization and built on existing story concept. As a general rule, children did most of the talking. Finally, the activities in the program were intended to be fun for the children. Instructors were spontaneous and enthusiastic, patient and supportive. They not only helped children to become better storytellers, but also attempted to make storytelling an enjoyable activity that could be handled with ease (see McKeough, 1991, for a more complete discussion).

STUDY 1: TEACHING AVERAGE FUNCTIONING
4-YEAR-OLDS TO COMPOSE INTENTIONAL
NARRATIVES

Sample

The first attempt to teach the narrative structure for transfer was undertaken with a group of 15 average-functioning 4-year-olds (mean age = 4 years 10 months; see McKeough, 1992b, for a more detailed discussion of this work). These children were selected from middle-class schools in a Western Canadian urban center. At the outset of the program, all participants produced scripted event sequences but failed to generate intentional stories.

Program Overview

Instruction followed the developmental progression identified for average functioning children. That is, activities designed to build a conceptual bridge to "the landscape of consciousness" were offered in an effort to move the children from their current level of functioning to the next level in the developmental progression. The narrative instruction program designed to effect the conceptual bridging was as follows here.

Make Children Aware of Their Current Representation

Prior to attempting the developmental advance, we wished to ensure that children had a clear conception of their current narrative structure. Consequently, an external conceptual mnemonic was developed for representing narrative as a sequence of related events in "the landscape of action." The mnemonic chosen was the comic-strip frame, as this format allowed events to be depicted as discrete but related occurrences. Children's stories were depicted in line drawings that reported the flow of states, actions, and events, as is shown in Fig. 7.6.

Provide an External Conceptual Mnemonic for Bridging to the Next Level in the Developmental Hierarchy

This involved building a conceptual bridge to an intentional structure, while minimizing the load placed on the working memory. Recall that this structure is a differentiated one that includes a representation of "the landscape of consciousness," in addition to "the landscape of action." The steps in effecting the conceptual bridge are discussed here.

Present Simple, Highly Structured Intentional Stories to the Children. These stories were comprised of a problem that is immediately resolved, and contained explicit reference to two or three mental states, such as feelings or

There was a lamb that lived on grass and ate and he got fat - fat - then - and
people came to see him. And then he got a medal.

FIG. 7.6.   Action-based story with line drawings.

desires. They were taken from two sources: (a) compositions written by the researcher that centered on timely topics of immediate interest to the children (e.g., Halloween stories in late October), and (b) children's storybooks that had been simplified by removing complicating events. The states, actions, and events in the stories were depicted in comic-strip form.

Differentiate the Landscape of Consciousness from the Landscape of Action. The stories were reviewed, with children recalling the sequence of events from the line drawings. In cases where a child identified an internal mental state, it was received with enthusiasm on the part of the instructor. Its inadequate representation in the line drawings was emphasized, and an icon depicting the mental state was drawn above the appropriate frame (see Fig. 7.7). In cases where no child spontaneously identified a mental state, the instructor asked direct questions, such as, "How did he feel when that happened?" "What was his idea for solving that problem?" and "How does he feel now?" Additionally, children generated further rounds of stories, with one child telling "the problem part of the story about what the person wants" and a second child thinking of "an idea so that the person in the story will be happy again."

As can be seen from the above description, the procedure for effecting the bridge to the landscape of consciousness involved (a) pairing the action scripts with a symbol for the protagonist's mental representation, and (b) focusing on a planned manipulation of the mental representation. Moreover, throughout the instruction sequence, the icons provided an external depiction of what was believed to be the internal representation of the intentional narrative structure.

Provide Guided and Independent Practice With the New Intentional Structure

Apply the New Structure in a Familiar Context. Initially, the children were read or told familiar stories and encouraged to map the mental state icons onto the action/event sequences. They were also given an opportunity to practice mapping one "landscape" onto the other under guided conditions across different story content.

Broaden the Range of Intentional States. Children were read stories about characters who held various mental states (see Table 7.1 for examples) and asked to compose stories wherein the characters held similar mental states.

Provide Opportunities for Independent Practice. With the icons in view across the page, each child was asked to compose an entire story. Additionally, the icons were drawn on index cards and children were encouraged to use them during their regular classroom instruction and at home to tell stories to family members.

Once there was a little boy and he had no one to play with but 'cept hid trucks only
to play with, 'cause he was very sad. So he asked his mom, "Could someone be my
friend?"

And his mom said, "O.K."

And there was this little boy and - was - was - he comed over to the house and he
got a toy to play with. And he said to his mom, "Could he stay over night?"

And so, "O.K."

And then he went when it was bed time. They went to school and then when the
mom and dad picked them up they got - had - got a game and they went for a drive
and they lived happily ever after.

FIG. 7.7. Intentional story with line drawings and mental state icons.

Gradually Remove Cueing Support
When New Structure Is Consolidated

In the latter portion of the instruction sequence, the event/action sequence depictions were presented intermittently and then removed, leaving only the "landscape of consciousness" icons. Finally, these were removed and children were asked to tell their stories in the absence of cueing support.

Results

After 15 instruction sessions, the performance level of the children taught according to these developmental methods was found to differ significantly from that of children who were assigned to a control condition ($n = 14$), the process approach

TABLE 7.1
Stories Exemplifying Range of Possible Mental States

Patty

Once there was a little girl named Patty. She had a baby brother who was always taking her toys and breaking them. Every time she went in her room to get something to play with, he was there—wrecking it. Patty felt very angry at her little brother. She told her dad about how he was always taking her things and her dad put a hook on her door that was too high for her little brother to reach. Patty could hook it every time she left her room so her little brother couldn't get in. She felt happy now that her toys were safe.

Ms. Pinkie

There was a little piggy named Ms. Pinkie who lived in a barnyard on a farm. Other animals lived there too. Some were nice but some were mean. When she had to walk across the barnyard to get a drink of water, sometimes they chased her and sometimes they pushed her down. Ms. Pinkie was scared of the mean animals. One day she was really thirsty so she had to walk across the yard to the water trough. She was scared but she went anyway. When they came up to her she said in a loud tough voice, "Leave me alone, you bullies!!!" And then she just walked away. They did leave her alone and now she's not scared any more.

TABLE 7.2

Sample Pre- and Postinstruction Stories of the Control
and Experimental Subjects From Study 1

Story prompt: Tell me a story about someone about your age who has a problem they want to solve,
you know, make all better.

Experimental subject:

Pretest: Once upon a time a little girl . . . once upon a time there was a little girl . . . and she
             liked to play down stairs. The end.

Posttest: Once upon a time there was a little boy and he wanted to see the pandas at the zoo. But
             his mom said no. So - so - so then he built up his own car and he drive to there. All
             done.

Control subject:

Pretest: A little girl had a problem. A little girl had a problem and that's all . . . cause she wants
             a dog.

Posttest: When Rudolph had a red nose . . . his father put a black nose on him.

Story prompt: Tell me a story about a happy little girl and a kind old horse.

Experimental subject:

Pretest: The horses was riding and it run away from the girl cause he bites the rope and it cut
             off.

Posttest: There was a horse and a happy girl and the girl was riding on the horse. And she falled
             off it and the horse was going faster. She told it to not go faster. Then she broke her leg
             and she went to the doctor but she tell the horsie to slow down and (he) was walking.

Control subject:

Pretest: The little girl was a cowboy. She was a girl and she sit down on the horse and she rode
             with the horse . . . She rode with the horse and the cowboys came. And that's the end.

Posttest: A girl went to a store where there was animals and her mom bought her a . . . a horse
             and she ride it all day

---

advocated by Donald Graves (1983).[3] Whereas the pre- and postinstruction stories
of children taught according to the control approach showed no significant
improvement, those of the experimental group moved up one level on the
developmental scoring scale from action-based to intentional narratives. The pre-
and postinstruction stories presented in Table 7.2 serve to illustrate this point.

   Although these findings are compelling pedagogically, they did not address
the issue of knowledge transfer across task domains. Moreover, they do not allow
us to conclude with certainty that a change in a central representational structure

---

[3]The process approach was selected as the control method because it is similar to the experimental
approach in mode of presentation (e.g., both are dialogic and child-centered) but differs on critical
features. More specifically, the control methodology focuses on children's experiences with literature
and develops their mode of expressing these experiences through exposure to the practices of expert
writers (e.g., conferencing, revising, and publishing), whereas the experimental methodology focuses
on the semantic structure of narrative and offers students a developmentally relevant mnemonic that
serves as a conceptual bridge between their spontaneous level of achievement and the developmentally
adjacent level. Thus, the two approaches differ in terms of (a) the goal of instruction (expert
performance vs. developmental recapitulation) and (b) the focus of instruction (teaching process and
strategies vs. teaching structure).

(and not simply a change in storytelling rules) effected the change in story production.

Consequently, we added several additional posttests to assessed knowledge transfer, specifically, the three tasks discussed previously that were thought to share conceptual underpinnings with the training task, namely, Goldberg-Reitman's cartoon tasks, Bruchkowsky's video task, and Griffin's definition-of-feelings task. Because of the conceptual similarity among the tasks, it was assumed that if the training successfully advanced children's conceptions of narrative from the preintentional to the intentional level, a comparative increase should also be observed for the transfer tasks. Conversely, if no change was effected in the intentional representation as a result of the story training, children would be expected to remain at a preintentional level on the transfer tasks. Scoring criteria for determining developmental level for each of the four tasks is presented in Fig. 7.8.

When the children were presented with these social tasks after receiving the narrative composition training outlined above, it was found that, on the average, those who had received the developmental instruction used intentional reasoning to solve the problem 70% of the time, compared to 29% for the control group.

This finding that the intentional narrative instruction was successful, not just in teaching specific content but also in producing general transfer had clear practical as well as theoretical implications. Theoretically, it lent considerable support for the central narrative structure construct. Practically, it positioned us to address the more critical problem of teaching academically at-risk children.

STUDY 2: TEACHING ACADEMICALLY AT-RISK KINDERGARTEN CHILDREN TO COMPOSE INTENTIONAL NARRATIVES[4]

Subjects

Eleven children from "high needs" schools, in a large urban center in Western Canada, participated. These schools have a greater than average incidence of academic failure, mid-year transfer, and single-parent families headed by females. All schools were located in lower SES neighborhoods. Participants were enrolled in Early Childhood Services Programs and included six girls and seven boys. The mean age of the students was 5 years and 10 months.

---

[4]This work was conducted by Lise Godbout as part of her Master of Science thesis research (Godbout, 1992). The primary purpose of Godbout's work was to determine if each central conceptual structure had a unique set of cognitive operations. To this end we tested the hypothesis that training in each of two central conceptual structures (i.e., narrative and number) would produce knowledge transfer to tasks within the conceptual domain but not beyond it. Because it is beyond the scope of the present chapter to discuss these comparative findings, only the portion of Godbout's work pertaining to narrative instruction will be summarized. Very briefly, however, our predictions were supported. Training and transfer effects were identified within each of the instructed central conceptual structures, but no significant improvement was noted outside of the instructed conceptual domain.

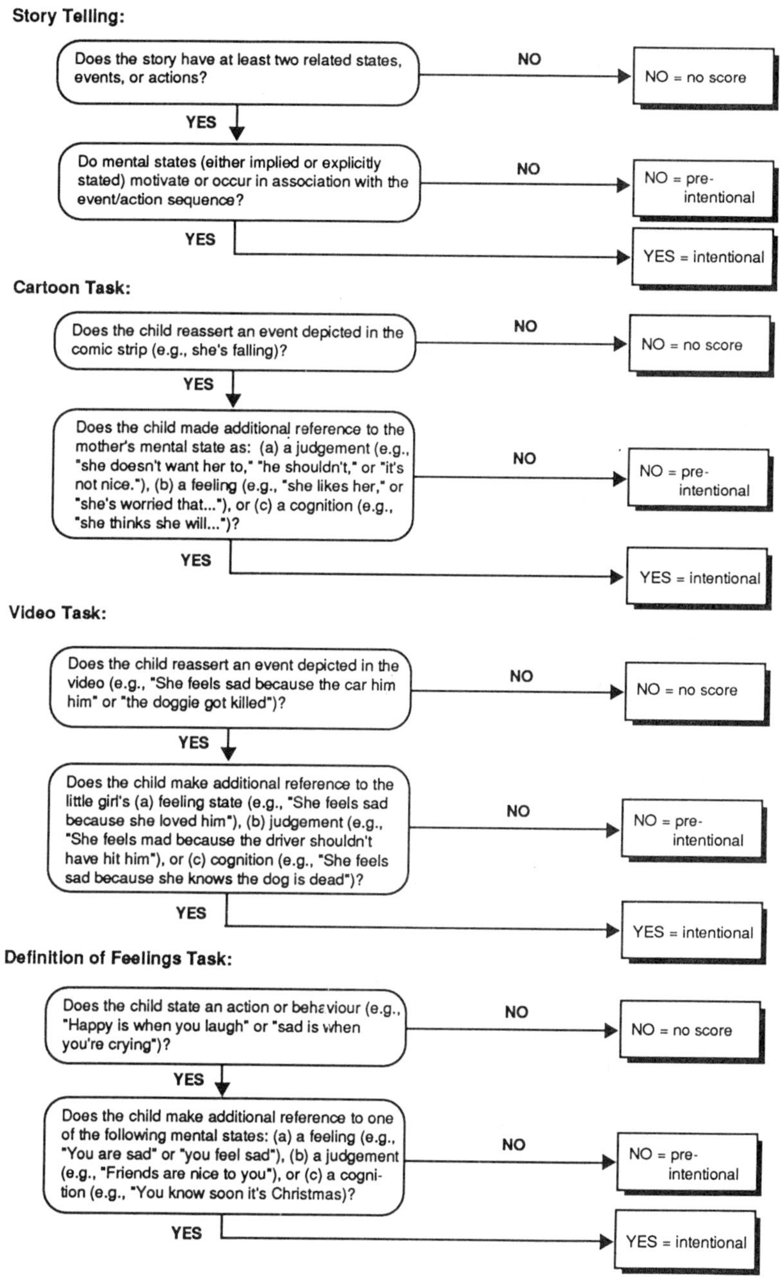

Story Telling:

Does the story have at least two related states, events, or actions? — **NO** → NO = no score

YES ↓

Do mental states (either implied or explicitly stated) motivate or occur in association with the event/action sequence? — **NO** → NO = pre-intentional

YES → YES = intentional

Cartoon Task:

Does the child reassert an event depicted in the comic strip (e.g., she's falling)? — **NO** → NO = no score

YES ↓

Does the child made additional reference to the mother's mental state as: (a) a judgement (e.g., "she doesn't want her to," "he shouldn't," or "it's not nice."), (b) a feeling (e.g., "she likes her," or "she's worried that..."), or (c) a cognition (e.g., "she thinks she will...")? — **NO** → NO = pre-intentional

YES → YES = intentional

Video Task:

Does the child reassert an event depicted in the video (e.g., "She feels sad because the car him him" or "the doggie got killed")? — **NO** → NO = no score

YES ↓

Does the child make additional reference to the little girl's (a) feeling state (e.g., "She feels sad because she loved him"), (b) judgement (e.g., "She feels mad because the driver shouldn't have hit him"), or (c) cognition (e.g., "She feels sad because she knows the dog is dead")? — **NO** → NO = pre-intentional

YES → YES = intentional

Definition of Feelings Task:

Does the child state an action or behaviour (e.g., "Happy is when you laugh" or "sad is when you're crying")? — **NO** → NO = no score

YES ↓

Does the child make additional reference to one of the following mental states: (a) a feeling (e.g., "You are sad" or "you feel sad"), (b) a judgement (e.g., "Friends are nice to you"), or (c) a cognition (e.g., "You know soon it's Christmas")? — **NO** → NO = pre-intentional

YES → YES = intentional

FIG. 7.8. Scoring criteria for the four intentional tasks.

A two-step participant selection procedure was instituted. First, teachers identified learners at risk for academic failure in the targeted instruction area. Teachers were asked to exclude those children whose performance deficit was due to neurological impairment, mental handicap, minimal second language proficiency, and very severe behavior problems. They were asked to include those children they considered as slow learners, learning disabled, experientially limited, or culturally different. Second, children were pretested on the training task (i.e., narrative composition) as well as on the three transfer tasks (i.e., Goldberg-Reitman's cartoon task, Bruchkowsky's video task, and Griffin's definition-of-feelings task). These selection procedures were instituted to ensure that the selected sample was operating at a preintentional level (more typical of 4-year-olds) prior to instruction.

Program Overview

As with the previously described narrative instruction, the goal of this program was to facilitate children's construction of intentional narratives. In this sequence of sessions, we followed the same general procedure for effecting the transition from action-based stories, starting with activities to solidify the children's existing representation. However, in addition to depicting the stories in line drawings (to capture the flow of action), we also focused on the representational nature of narrative. We reasoned that our aim of helping children construct a representation of characters' internal mental states would be facilitated by first discussing actions and events as represented entities.

With this goal in mind, we drew upon the child's theory of mind literature (e.g., Astington, Olson, & Harris, 1988; Perner, 1991), wherein children's early representational capacities are studied. We devoted the first half of the instruction sequence to facilitating the construction of an understanding of mental representation, focusing on integrating the following elements of this concept: (a) people hold representations of what they see in the world; (b) representations of objects, actions, and events can change across time and conditions; and (c) people can hold alternative representations, for a variety of reasons. Conditions under which representations might vary were introduced sequentially, as follows: (a) a point of reference has an effect on how an object is represented, (b) additional information presented over the course of time and events changes our understanding, (c) misinformation can cause an object or event to be misrepresented (appearance/reality distinction; Flavell, 1986); and (d) lack of information can cause a misrepresentation (false belief; Gopnick & Astington, 1988).

These concepts were presented in suspenseful, game-like situations, using various items presented in a similar task format. The conceptual mnemonic used to depict the notion of a mental representation was a thinking cloud (⌒⌒). It was introduced to the children by explaining that we think about things when we're pretending. Pretend events were depicted as "thought of" events within a thinking cloud (e.g., she pretended to be the pilot of an airplane).

Additionally, in a guessing game, children were given thinking cloud crowns (see Fig. 7.9) and asked what they thought was in a smarties box (this task was borrowed from Gopnick & Astington, 1988, who used the smarties box to store colored pencils). They selected a picture from an array of cards depicting familiar objects (including smarties and pencils) and placed it in a slot in the crown, displaying their thought to peers. As might be expected, the children selected the picture of smarties. When the box was opened, and the children saw that the box actually contained pencils, they were asked to place the pencil card on top of the smarties card to show that now they knew there were pencils in the box. As is no doubt clear, the goal of this activity was to help the children gain awareness of their representational capacities, that is, that they commonly represent objects and that these representations are subject to change. Attempts were made to contextualize all tasks in the children's daily experience.

The second portion of the instruction program deviated from the original sequence considerably less. Stories were presented as a given storyteller's representation of events (i.e., what they think might happen) evolving from some initiating event that was offered as a story prompt. Two children composed stories in response to the same prompt. These event sequences were depicted in line drawings following a comic-strip format, in order to keep a readable record of the representations. Following the procedures outlined in the first study, the plot structure, comprised of a problem, a plan, and a resolution, was introduced and emotions (e.g., sad ☹ or happy ☺) and ideas or plans (☼) were also depicted in the thinking cloud. Toward the end of the instruction sequence, the conceptual mnemonics were phased out and children were asked to generate problem/plan/resolution stories with no conceptual supports. The instruction program took, on average, 32 sessions. Children were seen an average of 4 days per week, for approximately 20 to 30 minutes.

Results

As was the case in the first study, a strong training effect was found. That is, children's performance on the story measure improved markedly over the period of instruction. As well, a transfer effect was found for two of the three tasks,

FIG. 7.9. Thinking cloud crown.

namely, for the mother's motives task and for the peer-empathy video. Contrary to predictions, there was no significant difference in pre- and postinstruction performance on the definition-of-feelings task, although the direction of the effects was similar to the other transfer tasks.

DISCUSSION

Whereas the findings of the first study conducted with average children are noteworthy in light of the limited transfer usually found, those of the second study, which used academically at-risk children, are even more compelling. This group has not typically responded readily to efforts aimed at bringing their level of academic functioning in line with their middle SES counterparts. The present instruction effort not only succeeded on this count, at least in the short term, but additionally produced knowledge transfer. Thus, the results clearly demonstrated that curricula designed to foster the construction of central conceptual knowledge not only improved performance on the training tasks, but also produced transfer to other tasks that differ in surface but share conceptual underpinnings. The following examples from the assessment protocols serve to illustrate these outcomes.

In the pretest condition of the storytelling task, Leanne's stories were very limited, as illustrated by the following generated in response to a request to tell a story about a kind old horse who had a problem he wanted to solve:

> A girl—and a boy—and a kind old horse. They got mad at each other. That the end.

This story contains only a problem, and is typical of a 4-year-old level of production (McKeough, 1992a). As previously discussed, children at this conceptual level understand mental states. However, they do not typically coordinate this schema with an event sequence schema, such that feelings are transformed across time.

This latter cognitive capability is typical of 6-year-olds and is evident in Leanne's posttest story:

> Once upon a time there was a girl. She was playing with her toys and—um—she asked her mom if she could go outside—to play in the snow. But her mom said no. And then she was very sad. And—and she had to play. So she she asked her mom if she could go outside and she said yes. She jumped in the snow and she was having fun and she had an idea and she jumped in the snow and she feel happy.

In this story, Leanne lays out a problematic event (i.e., a girl asks to go outside to play but is refused), its associated mental state (she feels sad), her response to the problem (she asks again), the outcome (she is permitted to go and has fun), and the feeling associated with the outcome ("she feeled happy"). It is clear that Leanne has constructed an intentional story, that is, one that begins to link the landscapes of action and consciousness.

Additionally, the results of the second study showed that the intentional knowledge structure was spontaneously used in other tasks, including a task that measured children's knowledge of a mother's motives and one that assessed understanding of peers' feelings. On the mother's motives task, preinstruction children's responses were largely action based (e.g., Angie explained that a mother would rescue her daughter from drowning because "she was under the water") whereas her postinstruction responses stipulated the mother's mental state that motivated her action (e.g., "because she didn't want her to die).

Similarly, on the peer-empathy task, most children replaced action-based responses with intentional ones. For example, prior to instruction, Matthew stated that the girl in the video was "sad because her dog got runned over," whereas after instruction he explained that "she was sad because she'll miss her dog." Although no significant difference was found between the pre- and posttest performance on the definition-of-feelings task, it should be noted that performance on this task was not different, but merely resulted in less dramatic changes. Slightly less than half of the children demonstrated the shift to intentional responses. By way of explanation for this result, it might be that this task is not presented in a narrative format and so transfer is cued less directly.

CONCLUSIONS, IMPLICATIONS, AND QUESTIONS

At the outset of this chapter I identified two goals. The first was to present empirical evidence that supported the existence of a central narrative structure, and the second was to show that the central narrative structure can be taught, and when taught will transfer to conceptually related task domains. In what follows, these are discussed in relation to the conclusions that can be drawn from the work, the implications it holds for theory and practice, and directions of future research.

The Central Narrative Structure

The studies reported in this chapter demonstrate that children's performance on school-related tasks (such as story composition and word definition) and on everyday social reasoning tasks (such as those relating to a mother's motivation and peers' feelings) is similar and can be described by a narrative structure that transforms developmentally. More specifically, a shift in children's thinking from an action orientation to an intentional one, between 4 and 6 years of age, was documented in each of these task domains. Although these studies were conducted on separate groups of children, other work (e.g., Case, Griffin, McKeough, & Okamoto, 1992; Case, Okamoto, Henderson, & McKeough, 1993; Godbout, 1992; McKeough, 1993) has shown that when these tasks are presented to one group of children, the majority (i.e., from 63% to 70%) perform at the same conceptual level on all tasks, whereas the vast majority (i.e., from 97% to 99%) show performance variance of no more than one substage.

What are the implications of these findings? One general implication is that narrative knowledge plays a central role in numerous task domains. Recently, a good deal has been written on this topic. Narrative knowledge has been implicated in domains as diverse as history (Polkinghorne, 1988), legal practice (Jackson, 1990), economic theory (McCloskey, 1990), and moral development (Tappan & Packer, 1991). Although such wide-ranging applications of narrative will no doubt serve to strengthen our understanding of its organizing potential (Nash, 1990; Polkinghorne, 1988), it is important to articulate the nature of the narrative under discussion, in terms of both content themes and structure, so that our understanding of narrative itself will not be obfuscated.

By identifying the structural components of narrative and their interrelations, as exemplified in the work reported in this chapter, we can test the descriptive utility of the narrative structure and the limits of its applicability. In more recent work this narrative structure has been used to map out developmental changes in aggressive boys' understanding of human intention (McKeough, Yates, & Marini, 1994), showing that their functioning is developmentally delayed in comparison to a group of behaviorally normal boys. The necessity of combining this structural analysis with an analysis of content themes has been highlighted by Howard (1994) in a 3-year follow-up study of this group. Her analysis of the behaviorally aggressive boys' narratives not only demonstrated that the developmental delay was maintained, but that the boys' reasoning also differed qualitatively. More specifically, the attempted resolutions in the stories composed by the aggressive boys were less prosocial than those articulated by the normal comparison group. The complementary nature of structural and thematic content analyses allows the perturbations in aggressive boys' reasoning about human action, and its probable relation to their personal lives, to be captured more fully. Although this study represents only a first attempt in our research program to integrate structural and content analyses, this line of work clearly merits further study.

Another line of work worthy of investigation involves linguistically related aspects of narrative. Narrative competence obviously involves more than a well developed understanding of the motives and factors underlying human action. For example, the use of figurative language has traditionally been considered central to competence in narrative (Scholes & Kellogg, 1966). Thus, it seems reasonable to assume that any understanding of narrative, its development, and its application must involve an analysis of associated linguistic competence. A first step has been taken in this regard by Mah (1993), who studied two examples of figurative language, metaphor and humor, both characteristic of more advanced adolescent narrative (Case, Bleiker, Henderson, Krohn, & Bushey, 1993). Although more work is clearly needed, Mah's work represents a first step in identifying a central linguistic structure. Future research into the interplay of linguistic and social knowledge in narrative is also required.

Instruction and Knowledge Transfer

The second goal of this chapter related to instruction: To show that teaching children to compose more advanced stories would produce equivalent gains in conceptually related domains. The results of two instruction studies reported in the chapter demonstrated that the learning transferred.

The implications of this work are twofold. First, it offers a means of testing the theoretical formulations upon which the studies were built. Second, the work offers programs of instruction that have potential practical utility for average-functioning students as well as to those who are at risk academically. More specifically, the findings lent support to the notion that the central narrative structure can be taught by circumventing processing capacity limitations (as was the case in the first study involving average-functioning 4-year-olds) and by providing equalizing experiences with the narrative structure (as was the case in the second study involving academically at-risk 5- to 6-year-olds).

Although the gains noted from pre- to posttesting are noteworthy, this work lacks a detailed analysis of the way in which the youngsters altered their understanding of narrative as a result of the instruction activities. In order to gain a clearer understanding of the changes and how they occurred, we are currently conducting what Siegler and Jenkins (1989) referred to as a "microgenetic" analysis of response to instruction. This involves examining learning dialogues, on a moment-by-moment basis, in an attempt to document subtle signs that the child is constructing a more advanced concept of narrative. With this analysis in hand, we will be in a better position to address issues related to individual differences in children's knowledge construction.

In conclusion, the 4 to 6 shift has traditionally been a point where investigators have found it necessary to focus on "readiness" skills and delay direct instruction until this readiness was present. The present findings demonstrate that we can, in fact, help children to cross the 4 to 6 barrier in the narrative domain and can enhance generalization of this knowledge to tasks that share no common surface features but that share an underlying conceptualization. Although it is clear that a good deal of work remains, it would appear that we have moved one step closer to describing the structural organization of knowledge and its developmental changes, and to developing complementary cognitive curricula that aim at training a central conceptual understanding of intermediate generality with a wide, yet delimited, application to scholastic tasks.

ACKNOWLEDGMENTS

I am most grateful for the assistance of Deborah Fairhurst, Lise Godbout, Cathy Harwood, and Sue Humphry, who conducted much of the instruction, and for the help of the school administrators, teachers, and students who participated in the study. The financial support of the Social Sciences and Humanities Research Council is also gratefully acknowledged. A final word of heartfelt thanks goes to Robbie Case, who has unfailingly offered support and guidance.

REFERENCES

Applebee, A. (1978). *The child's concept of story.* Chicago, IL: The University of Chicago Press.

Astington, J., Olson, D., & Harris, P. (Eds.). (1988). *The child's developing theory of mind.* Cambridge, MA: Cambridge University Press.

Bartlett, F. C. (1932). *Remembering.* London: Cambridge University Press.

Bereiter, C., & Scardamalia, M. (1985). Cognitive coping strategies and the problem of "inert" knowledge. In S. Chipman, J. W. Segal, & R. Glasser (Eds.), *Thinking and learning skills: Current research and open questions* (Vol. 2, pp. 65–80). Hillsdale, NJ: Lawrence Erlbaum Associates.

Brown, A. L. (1975). The development of memory: Knowing, knowing about knowing, and knowing how to know. In H. W. Reese (Ed.), *Advances in child development and behavior* (Vol. 10, pp. 104–152). New York: Academic Press.

Brown, A. L., & Campione, J. C. (1984). Three faces of transfer: Implications for early competence, individual differences, and instruction. In M. Lamb, A. L. Brown, & B. Rogoff (Eds.), *Advances in developmental psychology* (Vol. 3, pp. 143–192). Hillsdale, NJ: Lawrence Erlbaum Associates.

Bruchkowsky, M. (1991). The development of empathy in school-aged children. *Exceptionality Education Canada, 1*(4), 77–101.

Bruchkowsky, M. (1992). The development of empathic understanding in early and middle childhood. In R. Case (Ed.), *The mind's staircase: Exploring the conceptual underpinnings of children's thought and knowledge* (pp. 153–170). Hillsdale, NJ: Lawrence Erlbaum Associates.

Bruner, J. (1986). *Actual minds, possible worlds.* Cambridge, MA: Harvard University Press.

Bruner, J. (1990). *Acts of meaning.* Cambridge, MA. Harvard University Press.

Case, R. (1985). *Intellectual development: Birth to adulthood.* New York: Academic Press.

Case, R. (Ed.). (1992). *The mind's staircase: Exploring the conceptual underpinnings of children's thought and knowledge.* Hillsdale, NJ: Lawrence Erlbaum Associates.

Case, R., Bleiker, C., Henderson, B., Krohn, C., & Bushey, B. (1993). The development of central conceptual structures in adolescence. In R. Case (Ed.), *The role of central conceptual structures in the development of children's numerical, literary, and spatial thought* (pp. 104–128). Final report submitted to the Spencer Foundation.

Case, R., & Griffin, S. (1990). Child cognitive development: The role of central conceptual structures in the development of scientific and social thought. *Developmental psychology: Cognitive, perceptuo-motor, and neuropsychological perspectives* (pp. 193–230). North Holland: Elsevier.

Case, R., Griffin, S., McKeough, A., & Okamoto, Y. (1992). Parallels in the development of children's social, numerical, and spatial thought. In R. Case (Ed.), *The mind's staircase: Stages in the development of human intelligence* (pp. 269–284). Hillsdale, NJ: Lawrence Erlbaum Associates.

Case, R., Okamoto, Y., Henderson, B., & McKeough, A. (1993). Individual variability and consistency in cognitive development: New evidence for the existence of central conceptual structures. *Contributions to Human Development, 23*, 71–100.

Case, R., & Sandieson, R. (1992). New data on learning and its transfer: The role of central numerical structures in the development of children's scientific, social, and scholastic thought. In R. Case (Ed.), *The mind's staircase: Exploring the conceptual underpinnings of children's thought and knowledge* (pp. 117–132). Hillsdale, NJ: Lawrence Erlbaum Associates.

Chi, M. T. H., & Rees, E. T. (1983). A learning framework for development. In M. T. H. Chi (Ed.), *Trends in memory development* (pp. 71–107). New York: Karger.

Cormier, S. M., & Hagman, J. D. (1987). *Transfer of learning: Contemporary research and application.* New York: Academic Press.

Culler, J. (1975). *Structuralist poetics: Structuralism, linguistics, and the study of literature.* Ithaca, NY: Cornell University Press.

Fischer, K. W., & Pipp, S. L. (1984). Development of the structures of unconscious thought. In K. Bowers & D. Meichenbaum (Eds.), *The unconscious reconsidered* (pp. 88–148). New York: Wiley.

Fischer, K. W., Shaver, P. R., & Carnochan, P. (1990). How emotions develop and how they organize development. *Cognition and Emotion, 4*(2), 81–127.

Flavell, J. H. (1986). The development of children's knowledge about the appearance–reality distinction. *American Psychologist, 41,* 418–425.

Godbout, L. (1992). *Teaching the central intentional structure for transfer.* Unpublished master's thesis, The University of Calgary, Alberta, Canada.

Goldberg-Reitman, J. (1992). Young girl's conception of their mother's role: A neo-structural analysis. In R. Case (Ed.), *The mind's staircase: Stages in the development of human intelligence* (pp. 135–152). Hillsdale, NJ: Lawrence Erlbaum Associates.

Goody, J., & Watt, I. (1962). The consequences of literacy. *Contemporary studies in society and history, 5,* 304–345.

Gopnick, A., & Astington, J. (1988). Children's understanding of representational change and its relation to the understanding of false belief and the appearance–reality distinction. *Child Development, 59,* 26–37.

Graves, D. H. (1983). *Writing: Teachers and children at work.* London: Heinmann Educational Books.

Griffin, S. (1992). Young children's awareness of their inner worlds: A neo-structural analysis of the development of interpersonal intelligence. In R. Case (Ed.), *The mind's staircase: Exploring the conceptual underpinnings of children's thought and knowledge* (pp. 189–206). Hillsdale, NJ: Lawrence Erlbaum Associates.

Griffin, S., Case, R., & Sandieson, R. (1992). Synchrony and asynchrony in the development of children's everyday mathematical knowledge. In R. Case (Ed.), *The mind's staircase: Exploring the conceptual underpinnings of children's thought and knowledge* (pp. 75–97). Hillsdale, NJ: Lawrence Erlbaum Associates.

Halford, G. (1982). *The development of thought.* Hillsdale, NJ: Lawrence Erlbaum Associates.

Howard, M. (1994). *Structural and thematic analyses of the narratives of behaviourally aggressive boys.* Unpublished master's thesis, The University of Calgary, Alberta, Canada.

Jackson, B. S. (1990). Narrative theories and legal discourse. In C. Nash (Ed.), *Narrative in culture: The uses of story telling in the sciences, philosophy, and literature* (pp. 23–50). New York: Routledge.

Levi-Strauss, C. (1958). *Structural anthropology* (C. Jacobson & B. G. Schoepf, Trans.). New York: Basic Books.

Mah, J. (1993). *Developmental change in children's understanding of figurative language.* Unpublished master's thesis, The University of Calgary, Alberta, Canada.

Mandler, J. M. (1984). *Stories, scripts and scenes: Aspects of story schema.* Hillsdale, NJ: Lawrence Erlbaum Associates.

Mandler, J. M., & Goodman, N. (1982). On the psychological validity of story structure. *Journal of Verbal Learning and Verbal Behavior, 21,* 507–523.

McCloskey, D. N. (1990). Story telling in economics. In C. Nash (Ed.), *Narrative in culture: The uses of story telling in the sciences, philosophy, and literature* (pp. 5–22). New York: Routledge.

McKeough, A. (1991). Neo-Piagetian theory goes to school: Program development and program delivery. *Exceptionality Education Canada, 1*(4), 1–16.

McKeough, A. (1992a). The structural foundations of children's narrative and its development. In R. Case (Ed.), *The mind's staircase: Stages in the development of human intelligence* (pp. 171–188). Hillsdale, NJ: Lawrence Erlbaum Associates.

McKeough A. (1992b). Testing for the presence of a central social structure: Use of the transfer paradigm. In R. Case (Ed.), *The mind's staircase: Exploring the conceptual underpinnings of children's thought and knowledge* (pp. 207–225). Hillsdale, NJ: Lawrence Erlbaum Associates.

McKeough, A., Yates, T., & Marini, A. (1994). Intentional reasoning: A developmental study of behaviorally aggressive and normal boys. *Development and Psychopathology, 6,* 285–304.

Nash, C. (Ed.). (1990). *Narrative in culture: The uses of story telling in the sciences, philosophy, and literature* (pp. 5–22). New York: Routledge.

Nelson, K. (1981). Social cognition in a script framework. In J. H. Flavell & L. Ross (Eds.), *Social cognitive development: Frontiers and possible futures* (pp. 97–118). Cambridge, England: Cambridge University Press.

Olson, D. (1986). The cognitive consequences of literacy. *Canadian Psychology, 27*(2), 109–121.

Olson, D. (Ed.). (1987). Understanding literacy. Special issue of *Interchange*, 18(1/2).

Olson, D. (1988). Mind and media: The epistemic functions of literacy. *Journal of Communication, 38*(3), 27–36.

Perkins, D., & Solomon, G. (1987). Transfer and teaching thinking. In D. Perkins, J. Lockhead, & J. Bishop (Eds.), *Thinking: The second international conference.* Hillsdale, NJ: Lawrence Erlbaum Associates.

Perner, J. (1991). *Understanding the representational mind.* Cambridge, MA: MIT Press.

Piaget, J. (1950). *The psychology of intelligence.* London: Routledge & Kegan Paul.

Polkinghorne, D. E. (1988). *Narrative knowing and the human sciences.* Albany: State University of New York Press.

Pressley, M. (1982). Elaboration and memory development. *Child Development, 53,* 296–309.

Pressley, M. (1990). *Cognitive strategy instruction that really improves children's academic performance.* Cambridge, MA: Brookline Books.

Propp, V. (1968). *The morphology of the folktale* (L. Scott, Trans.). Austin: University of Texas Press.

Runyan, W. M. (1982). *Life histories and psychobiographies.* New York: Oxford University Press.

Schafer, R. (1981). Narration in psychoanalytic dialogue. In W. J. T. Mitchell (Ed.), *On narrative* (pp. 25–49). Chicago: The University of Chicago Press.

Scholes, R., & Kellogg, R. (1966). *The nature of narrative.* London: Oxford University Press.

Siegler, R. S. (1981). Developmental sequences within and between concepts. *Monographs of the Society for Research in Child Development, 81* (Serial No. 189).

Siegler, R. S., & Jenkins, E. (1989). *How children discover new strategies.* Hillsdale, NJ: Lawrence Erlbaum Associates.

Singley, M. K., & Anderson, J. R. (1989). *The transfer of cognitive skill.* Boston: Harvard University Press.

Skinner, B. F. (1950). Are theories of learning necessary? *Psychological Bulletin, 57,* 193–261.

Solomon, G. (1988, April). *Two roads to transfer: Two roads of transfer.* Paper presented at AERA annual meeting, New Orleans, LA.

Spence, D. P. (1982). *Narrative truth and historical truth: Meaning and interpretation in psychoanalysis.* New York: W. W. Norton.

Stein, N. L., & Glenn, C. (1979). An analysis of story comprehension. In R. Freedle (Ed.), *New directions in discourse processing* (Vol. 2, pp. 53–120). Norwood, NJ: Ablex.

Stein, N. L., & Levine, L. (1987). Thinking about feelings: The development and organization of emotional knowledge. In R. E. Snow & M. Farr (Eds.), *Aptitude, learning, and instruction: Cognition, conation, and affect* (Vol. 3, pp. 165–197). Hillsdale, NJ: Lawrence Erlbaum Associates.

Tappan, M. B., & Packer, M. J. (Eds.). (1991). Narrative and storytelling: Implications for understanding moral development. *New Directions in Child Development, 54.* San Francisco: Jossey Bass.

Wellman, H. (1988). First steps in the child's theorizing about the mind. In J. Astington, P. Harris, & D. R. Olson (Eds.), *Developing theories of mind* (pp. 64–92). Cambridge: Cambridge University Press.

CHAPTER 8

A Transactional Strategies Instruction Christmas Carol

Michael Pressley
University at Albany, State University of New York

in collaboration with

Pamela B. El-Dinary
Rachel Brown
University of Maryland

Ted Schuder
Janet L. Bergman
Marcia York
Montgomery County, MD, Public Schools

Irene W. Gaskins
Benchmark School, Media, PA

The Faculties and Administration of Benchmark School
and the Montgomery County, MD, SAIL/SIA Programs

Every year, I try to write something during the December–January respite from teaching. I composed this chapter during the 1991 holiday break. For Christmas 1991, the prose came easier than it did a few Christmases back. In 1986, I faced the task of writing a chapter on reading comprehension strategies instruction, with the particular assignment to specify what was known about teaching reading comprehension strategies in elementary classrooms. This proved to be an impossible holiday assignment.

What is summarized here is how I journeyed from Christmas 1986 to Christmas 1991, in search of a new model of comprehension strategies instruction. Much changed for me during this journey. I came to understand better the limitations of a literature I long had held in high regard. I recognized that methodologies that had served me well for years were not serving me as well as alternative methodologies might—that the experimental methods I so embraced were not much good for creating a theory about complex classroom practices.

So I learned and applied new methodologies, with the result a new perspective on how comprehension strategies instruction might be done well.

I call my new perspective *transactional instruction of reading comprehension strategies* (Pressley, El-Dinary, Gaskins, et al., 1992) because (a) it involves teachers and students interpreting text, with this search for meaning resembling the reader–text transactions described by reader response theorists such as Rosenblatt (1978), and (b) what happens during reading instruction is determined both by teachers and students, with the reactions and interpretations of the participants in reading group determining the direction of the lesson rather than some preset script or teacher plan (see Bell, 1968, for discussion of transactions in this sense). The instruction is transactional in a third sense as well. The interpretations of texts constructed by the teachers and students during reading groups committed to transactional strategies instruction are different from interpretations that would be generated by any one member of the group, either teacher or student. There is a group mind in reading group, what some organizational psychologists refer to as a transactive mind (e.g., Wegner, 1987).

It was a long trip from Christmas 1986 to the transactional strategies instruction perspective. I made some important personal discoveries on the way. For example, the most compelling comprehension strategies instruction probably is being designed in schools by people who have both knowledge of the research and theoretical literature and the realities of classrooms, rather than by the university-based reading research community. The educators have extensive knowledge about how to design effective instruction and the potential impacts of such instruction. The field is not as aware of their work as they are aware of the university-based research because school-based educators do not set as their priority the generation of scholarly descriptions of their settings and interventions. Writing articles and chapters is something that university-based people do. My 5 years of contact with this community has made clear that a credible theory of comprehension strategies instruction requires collaboration between educators who do the instruction and university-based researchers who are motivated and able to document it. The educators who have worked with me have provided many insider perspectives not captured previously in the formal scientific literature, perspectives not known previously by many members of the university-based educational researcher community. Just as university-based research inspired these educators to modify their instruction, the resulting instruction and the challenges in understanding it led me to change dramatically my style of research. I once was an experimenter studying issues of reading comprehension as determined by the university-based research community; I am now a methodological eclectic, studying comprehension instruction as it happens in schools that are doing a good job of developing young readers who understand what they read. My 5-year sojourn will begin to make sense with a review of Christmas 1986.

A CHRISTMAS PAST: 1986[1]

On the face of it, I was well qualified for the task of writing a chapter on teaching of comprehension strategies to children, having produced my fair share of investigations pertaining to comprehension strategies teaching. My very first piece of published research was an investigation of imagery strategy instruction in Grade 3 reading instruction (Pressley, 1976). In 1986, I was in the midst of a study of reciprocal teaching of comprehension strategies that would eventually appear as Lysynchuk, Pressley, and Vye (1990). In addition to producing research myself, my student colleagues and I were reviewing exhaustively the experimental research pertaining to comprehension strategies instruction with elementary-age students, work that would eventuate in two major integrative articles (Lysynchuk, Pressley, d'Ailly, Smith, & Cake, 1989; Pressley, Johnson, Symons, McGoldrick, & Kurita, 1990). All of this hands-on research and scholarly consideration of the literature should have put me in a position to write at length about what was then known about doing comprehension strategies teaching in the elementary grades. What it did, however, was make me painfully aware of how little we actually did know in 1986, despite years of experiments evaluating comprehension strategies instruction, research that filled the pages of the very best archival journals in education.

What was wrong? Why did I spend countless hours pacing my home office and fretting during the 1986 holiday season? What became apparent somewhere between the post-Christmas exam party at the faculty club and *Auld Lang Syne* on Dick Clark's "Rockin' New Year's Eve Party" was that the research designs employed to study comprehension instruction could not possibly inform about actual classroom instruction: There were many studies in which single strategies were taught by experimenters, rather than teachers, often to single children or to groups of children brought together only for the study. Most comprehension strategies instruction research efforts involved extremely brief instruction, ranging from minutes to a few sessions spread over a few days. In short, much of the instruction that had been done as part of comprehension strategies instruction research was not much like the teaching that goes on in school. If that had been the only problem with the comprehension strategies research, I might not have felt so bad, as I watched others enjoy the carolers and festivity that is Christmas.

The middle and late 1980s involved extensive consideration of the nature of good thinking and the role that strategies might play in sophisticated cognition. John Borkowski, Wolfgang Schneider, and I had produced a framework (e.g., Pressley, Borkowski, & Schneider, 1987) making the case that good thinking

---

[1]Some of the studies considered over Christmas 1986 were available then in prepublication form and thus, I refer here to the publications that appeared later because they are more accessible than the prepublication technical reports.

involves complex coordination of a repertoire of strategies with other types of knowledge. The good thinker knows when and where to use strategies and other forms of knowledge and is motivated to do so according to the model that we had developed, which eventually came to be known as the "good information processor" model (Pressley, Borkowski, & Schneider, 1989). Our perspective was a particular instantiation of the generally accepted perspective in the middle to late 1980s that sophisticated thinking involves cognitive, metacognitive, and motivational components in interaction, with authors such as Ann Brown, Scott Paris, David Perkins, and others offering variations on this general theme. The richness of these frameworks contrasted with the conceptualization behind most strategy instructional research studies.

As I considered most of the comprehension strategies instruction available in 1986, it was clear that much of it was motivated by a variation of Flavell's production deficiency hypothesis (e.g., Flavell, 1970)—because students do not use comprehension strategies on their own, teach them to use comprehension strategies and comprehension will improve. From the good information-processing perspective, it was obvious why instruction so conceived failed to produce strategy use that transferred, a common lament about strategy instruction in the 1980s (see Brown, Bransford, Ferrara, & Campione, 1983). There was little teaching of repertoires of strategies in this body of research, scant attention to coordination of strategies with other knowledge, rare concern with metacognition that regulates use of strategies, and infrequent acknowledgment that motivation to use strategies might matter at all. What these studies illuminated was whether carrying out strategy X affected reading comprehension given some severe constraints: (a) if the situation were such that execution of strategy X was assured (i.e., metacognitive awareness to use strategy X was not required nor was it necessary for the student to be motivated to carry out the strategy given the strength of the instructional control exerted in the study), and (b) there was no need to coordinate use of strategy X with other strategies. My hopes for producing a chapter about strategies instruction for the classroom evaporated as I came to these realizations.

There were a few studies, however, that were a bit more uplifting. These had been carried out over a longer term and involved instruction of a repertoire of strategies, often by real classroom teachers. There was at least one success story at the Grade 3 level (subsequently published as Duffy et al., 1987) and two at the Grade 7–8 level (Bereiter & Bird, 1985; Palincsar & Brown, 1984), so that I was able to entertain the possibility that complex reading strategies instruction might be effective for a reasonably large proportion of the grade-school years.

Although uplifted, my spirits did not soar. As I got into these studies, I realized that based on the written descriptions of the research, no one could possibly define what had actually happened in the classrooms in these investigations. Although some of the mechanisms were specified (e.g., direct explanation of Grade 3 reading skills recast as strategies in Duffy et al., 1987; "scaffolding" of instruction in Palincsar & Brown, 1984), it was very difficult to imagine even what single lessons might look like, let alone how such instruction could be implemented over months, a school year, or several years. Thus, although I felt good that some researchers were producing evidence of effective comprehension strategies instruction in schools, I felt bad about the lack of craft knowledge emanating from this literature.

The problem was that Duffy et al. (1987), Palincsar and Brown (1984), and Bereiter and Bird (1985) were true experiments:

1. Reports of true experiments are better at specifying experimental designs and data-based outcomes than at providing detailed information about the interventions studied.

2. More problematic, however, was that I sensed that in achieving experimental control, these studies had created skeletons of effective strategy instruction. Remember that I was convinced at a theoretical level that effective strategy instruction interventions would have to promote development of strategic repertoires, metacognition about strategies, motivation to use strategies, and an extensive base of knowledge about important academic contents that could be used in conjunction with strategies. When I read Duffy et al., Palincsar and Brown, and Bereiter and Bird, I could find the strategy instruction and the metacognitive embellishment. There was less attention to motivation and almost no mention of the development of an extensive knowledge base. My guess was that really effective strategies instruction would have to be fuller than the experimental prototypes developed by Duffy et al., Palincsar and Brown, and Bird and Bereiter—that strategies, metacognition, motivation, and nonstrategic knowledge would all have to be addressed in potent strategies instruction in actual classrooms.

3. In order to conduct true experiments, the instruction was never more than an academic year, which was longer term than in the single strategy experiments but short term relative to the time line used to evaluate most real-school curricula. Acquisitions as complex as strategic repertoires are taught over years of schooling, not months.

I did learn one more thing from reading the comprehension strategies literature during Christmas 1986. I had suspected for many years that there was little instructional value in providing teachers with strategies lesson kits, a common practice in education. Scott Paris and his colleagues (e.g., Paris & Oka, 1986) gave such an approach to comprehension instruction an extremely sensitive test. They tested whether boxed kits of strategy instruction lessons might make a difference in Grade 3 and Grade 5 classrooms. Their kit included lessons to be implemented more than 20 weeks or so. There were high quality posters depicting the strategies to be learned, posters based on powerful metaphors for strategy use (e.g., the reading detective who searched for clues during reading was depicted in one such poster). The lessons were carefully thought out, reflecting the strategies validated in the many true experiments on instruction of individual strategies. Lessons also captured other processes validated in laboratory studies of reading conducted during the 1970s and 1980s (e.g., comprehension monitoring was encouraged by lessons in the Paris kit). There were workbooks with exercises sensibly tied to the lessons.

What was most impressive about the Paris research was that so many respondents were included in the study that the power was unbelievably high for detecting even very small effects—a large number of classrooms received kits and a large number of classrooms served as comparison-condition participants. Still, there was no detectable effect of the strategies kits on standardized reading comprehension. The comprehension measures affected by the lessons tapped exercises practiced as part of the lessons (but not practiced in control classrooms). Thus, there were significant differences favoring strategy-instructed classrooms on a cloze task much like cloze tasks practiced in the boxed curriculum and on comprehension monitoring exercises like comprehension monitoring exercises practiced in the curriculum. Even these differences were small (about a half standard deviation or less), however. I felt confident after studying the Paris work that strategies-instruction kits were not the way to go. (Several years later I obtained a copy of the kit used in the Paris' studies. The materials were very high quality and thus, I feel even more strongly now that the Paris work gave the kit approach a fair shot, with little evidence of impact of such kits on student achievement.) Thus, Christmas 1986 was not totally a loss, for I became certain that one approach that was receiving a lot of consideration in the middle 1980s (i.e., curriculum kits aimed at enhancing reading comprehension) was not the way to go.

When I finally had sifted through all of the data on teaching of reading comprehension strategies, I decided not to write the chapter that was invited, informing the editor who had issued the invitation that a chapter on comprehension strategies instruction in classrooms was premature based on the state of the science in early 1987. I was also determined to figure out how to do more telling research that might provide information about strategy instruction that would definitely be useful to educators. Fortunately, I had access to people who were able to help me get some ideas about what really good strategy instruction in classrooms might look like. Much of the next 2 years was spent on the road.

ON THE ROAD: 1987–1988

Having conducted a great deal of basic research on strategies instruction, my path had crossed those of many researchers and practitioners who were attempting to study or implement strategy instruction in schools. Many of these folks had invited me to visit their settings. In 1987, I took up some of these invitations, visiting many researchers and practitioners who were doing strategy instruction in school: Donald Deshler, Jean Schumaker, and their colleagues entertained me at Kansas; Gerry Duffy took me to Wainright School in East Lansing, where he was teaching preservice teachers his direct explanation approach; and Carol Sue Englert and Taffy Raphael provided a tutorial on their writing strategies instruction. I had long discussions with Steve Graham and Karen Harris about their strategy instruction interventions. I met with Margo Mastropieri and Tom Scruggs at Purdue and was provided firsthand knowledge of their classroom mnemonics interventions that were being applied with real-school curricula (see Mastropieri & Scruggs, 1991). There also were many visits to schools where lone teachers were trying strategy instruction in their classrooms and to schools where entire faculties had dedicated themselves to trying some form of strategy instruction. There were also the videotapes. Strategy instructors seem to love to make videotapes, tapes that many of them graciously passed along to me. I found myself spending hours watching strategy instruction, watching the famous, such as Annemarie Palincsar, doing reciprocal teaching, and many more extremely capable teachers who are not famous at all except in the eyes of their lucky students.

All of the trips and the hours with the videorecorder paid off. I began to get a well grounded understanding of what good strategy instruction in schools might be like.

The Beginnings of Transactional Strategies Instruction: Pressley, Goodchild, Fleet, Zajchowski, and Evans (1989)

During Christmas 1987, I planned an article based on my newly found knowledge of strategy instruction. It was not a bad first draft, but that Christmas season concluded with the knowledge that I had only a draft. It would be improved immensely in spring 1988 by three study-skills counselors serving the University of Western Ontario student community (Fiona Goodchild, Joan Fleet, & Richard Zajchowski), who had years of experience teaching strategies to secondary and postsecondary students, and one senior professor (Ellis D. Evans of the University of Washington), who had done more than his share of visiting classrooms where effective cognitively oriented instruction occurs.

For the most part, the article that emerged from the negotiations with the study-skills counselors and Ellis Evans (Pressley, Goodchild, et al., 1989) was a compilation of impressions, with references to the extant research literature to the extent it seemed consistent with the impressions. Two perspectives were concatenated in that piece: The first was a view that good strategy instruction is very hard to do, a perspective built up from many conversations with researchers, teachers, and teacher-researchers who had extensive personal experiences with strategy instruction. The second was of what good strategies instruction looks like, a vision built up for me through my visits to strategies-instruction settings and for my associates through their professional contacts with educational units doing strategies instruction.

Why is good strategy instruction hard to do? Some of the more important reasons are the following:

1. Teachers have received little formal training in information processing. Thus, much of strategy instruction as described by cognitive psychologists and cognitively oriented curriculum developers in information processing terms is foreign to much of the teacher corps.

2. There are a number of strategies to learn, with each one achieving particular, limited goals.

3. There are individual differences in children, so that some strategies work only with particular children. For example, many imagery strategies are difficult for primary-grades children, perhaps because of limited short-term memory capacity in primary students. Prior knowledge activation strategies are only effective when students have task-relevant prior knowledge.

4. The lack of evaluation data for many strategies makes it difficult for educators to make informed choices concerning strategies instruction. The evaluation data that are available are often published in journals that are not available or comprehensible to many teachers.

Although it was not mentioned in the 1989 article, I would add now, that educator selection of strategy interventions is made more difficult by the commercialization of strategies instruction. The many publishing outfits that now produce strategies-instruction products all make claims that are optimistic about the efficacy of the strategies instruction they can provide, optimism that is rarely based on relevant research. In summary, it is difficult for teachers to find high quality information about strategies instruction, with the need for quite a bit of information given the diversity of strategies required across the curriculum and with students varying in competencies and preferences.

Even so, it was apparent to me in 1987 and 1988 that some educators had figured out how to provide high quality strategies instruction to students despite the obstacles, although it was also apparent that successful strategies instruction involved a demanding form of teaching. The Pressley, Goodchild, et al. (1989) article claimed that good strategies instruction involves teaching a very few strategies at a time and teaching them well. In that paper, my co-authors and I argued for extensive direct explanation and modeling of strategies, followed by extensive teacher-guided practice of strategies. Good strategies instruction was portrayed as long term, with provision of extensive information about where and when to use strategies and practice using strategies in different situations. Good strategies teachers were described as helping students to determine how the strategies they were learning might be applied across the curriculum. Pressley, Goodchild, et al. (1989) concluded that good strategies teachers make extensive efforts to motivate student use of strategies and, in particular, try to make obvious to students the performance gains produced by use of the strategies being learned. Good strategies teachers encourage their students to believe they can become good readers, writers, and problem solvers by applying strategies to their academic tasks.

The completion of the Pressley, Goodchild, et al. (1989) article simultaneously and paradoxically produced great relief and great anxiety. I was relieved because at Christmas 1986 I had begun to wonder if experimenters might have been just playing an academic game with strategies instruction, and reading comprehension instruction in particular. I sincerely wondered if strategies interventions might produce detectable effects only when studied in experiments tightly controlled to isolate the effects of the strategies; I seriously entertained the possibility that if strategies instruction were deployed in the much less controlled world of school, that strategies instructional effects often would evaporate or be overshadowed by the effects of other factors.

As I traveled in 1987 and 1988 and then wrote Pressley, Goodchild, et al. (1989), it was clear to me that strategies instruction could be deployed in real school settings, and there were more than a few educators and educational researchers who were firmly convinced that strategies instruction could make an important difference in real schools. For the first time, I was sure there was a real-school purpose to the strategies instructional research to which I had dedicated my career. The interventions that had been my intellectual pleasure since graduate school really did have potential for positively affecting the academic lives of children in school. Thus, I was relieved.

Even so, my anxiety soared as I completed the Pressley, Goodchild, et al. article. For someone who was completely steeped in experimental methodology and the intellectual conservatism associated with that tradition, the Pressley, Goodchild, et al. article was a radical departure. It was the first time in my professional life that I had written what was an impressionistic document. My data were many informal observations and many conversations, albeit complemented by published research studies and descriptions of some of the interventions I had visited. The conclusions offered by the Pressley, Goodchild, et al. article went well beyond anything that could have been defended on the basis of the published research on strategies instruction. The empiricist in me made me sweat—I had to get some hard data to validate the impressions in the Pressley, Goodchild, et al. article. The sweat was especially voluminous, for I was convinced that true experimental validation of the instructional model or models that emerged from the Pressley, Goodchild, et al. (1989) article was simply out of the question. I knew after 2 years of travel that good strategies instruction in school takes place over years. I also knew enough about experimental educational psychology to know that high quality cognitive-process-oriented experiments in schools cannot be conducted over years. The sweat did not end as I recognized that even if I could muster the resources to conduct true experiments, I really would not know how to craft a strategies instructional curriculum for delivery in multiple-year-school environments!! This was a crisis point in my life as a researcher. Perhaps that is what made me open to the events that occurred on a trip to Kansas. . . .

A Trip to Kansas: My Introduction
to Qualitative Methods

About that time, I journeyed back to the University of Kansas as a consultant on one of their projects. Whatever help I provided to them was more than repaid by the help they gave me in coming to terms with my dilemma—to produce some harder data evaluating the ideas presented in Pressley, Goodchild, et al. (1989). Some of the Kansas graduate students were especially vocal during the day's discussions. Frank Kline (now at the University of Wichita) and Mary Brownell (now at the University of Florida) had gained familiarity with qualitative methods through Lincoln and Guba's (1985) text and some other readings that were part of a course offered at Kansas. At the time, I knew little about qualitative methods and had never heard of Lincoln and Guba!! The students convinced me that in constructing Pressley, Goodchild, et al. (1989) as I had, I had done informally what qualitative methodologists prescribed: I went to various settings, attempted to make sense of the behaviors in the setting, checked my observations with the inhabitants of the setting, and then moved on to another setting to do some additional observation and refinement. In the end, I composed a paper and then had it "member checked" (a Lincoln & Guba, 1985, term), in that some of the educators who had been visited, interviewed, and/or observed, read and re-acted to the paper, with their input used to revise the conclusions. Additional member checking came from my co-authors, for three of them were in-the-trenches strategies instructors.

My methodologically based anxiety about the Pressley, Goodchild, et al. article went down with this discussion, with this reduction in anxiety motivating me to find out more about qualitative methodology. I purchased a copy of Lincoln and Guba's *Naturalisitc Inquiry* at the Kansas bookstore and read continuously on the trip back and for the next several days. I was beginning to understand what was needed to build a credible empirical case for my emerging model of strategies instruction. Qualitative analyses promised to provide an important window on strategies instruction that would validate my impressions to date and permit development of even more sophisticated understanding about strategies instruction. Once again, I would be in the right place at the right time in order to act on this desire to begin qualitative analyses of sophisticated strategies instruction.

WEEKLY COMMUTES TO BENCHMARK SCHOOL:
1989–1990

In summer 1989, I moved from the University of Western Ontario to the University of Maryland. I knew the move was coming for about a year in advance and had made a point of cultivating at long distance some relationships with school personnel in Maryland, Virginia, Delaware, and Pennsylvania, educators who had contacted me over the years regarding strategies instruction. I wanted to locate some schools that arguably were doing good strategies instruction.

My good fortune was that there were a number of schools within 150 miles of my new home that were doing credible strategies instruction. Some could even provide evidence that the interventions they were deploying were effective! In many ways I felt like I had landed in a gold mine, for there were many potential research sites for studying teaching of strategies in actual schools. I knew that I had better start with one school, however, for the task of beginning a new research program, using methods I had never tried before, was daunting.

Perhaps the best known of these settings was Benchmark School in Media, Pennsylvania, outside of Philadelphia. Irene Gaskins and her colleagues had been doing strategy instruction of various sorts for a number of years in the context of a school dedicated to serving high ability, underachieving students. Benchmark was particularly interesting to me because of the emphasis on reading instruction there. A visit in late fall 1988 convinced me that if there was any school anywhere that was doing extensive strategy instruction, Benchmark was it. As a result of that trip, I felt more confident about the Pressley, Goodchild, et al. article, which was the basis of the talk I gave at the school. The faculty let me know that they resonated to the description of strategy instruction I provided and felt that Benchmark was consistent with it.

During Christmas 1988, my last Christmas in Ontario, I would think about Benchmark, hoping that it would be part of Christmas future when I settled in Maryland: I was attracted to Benchmark in particular because the case in its favor as an effective institution was strong: Most of their clients entered after 2 years of school failure, with the presenting symptom often failure to read at all after 2 years in school. No one could doubt that the children coming to them were at extreme risk for long-term school failure. Even so, most of their students learn to read and exit after 4 years on average. When they return to regular schooling, the typical Benchmark alumnus performs at an average or above-average level. Virtually all former Benchmark students graduate from high school; many go to college.

I was ecstatic when Irene Gaskins, the director, opened Benchmark's doors to me, agreeing that a research collaboration would make sense. For all of the 1989–1990 school year, I commuted one day a week on average to Media. Those treks on Interstate 95 were some of the most worthwhile miles I have ever put on an automobile. Irene, her Benchmark teachers, and I worked on three projects together that year. All of them were informative about what strategy instruction can look like when done well.

A Teacher Interview Study

The first study was an interview of all 31 academic teachers at Benchmark (Pressley, Gaskins, Cunicelli, et al., 1991). The interview was designed around the issues identified in Pressley, Goodchild, et al. (1989). Specifically, each of the teachers was asked about 150 questions about how they taught strategies. Questions were structured so that teachers had to provide "objective" responses to each question, although teachers were permitted to add whatever remarks they wished during the face-to-face interview, which took up to 5 hours for teachers who were especially committed to elaborating their answers! Not surprisingly, the longer a teacher had served at the school, the more elaborations were offered. Even though there were differences in the amount of commentary, what was much more striking were the similarities in responses. The teachers at Benchmark have a common perspective about the usefulness of strategy instruction and how to teach strategies.

What did the teachers say? First, they consider strategy teaching to be important and useful for students. In general, the Benchmark faculty believes that strategy instruction makes learning more fun for students and teaching more fun for teachers.

The teachers reported that they explain strategies to students and extensively model strategy use. They reported that re-explanations are common in light of student difficulties in carrying out and applying strategies being taught. Students extensively practice use of strategies, with teachers providing guidance as needed. The teachers reported having students practice the strategies across the curriculum and school day (e.g., for reading strategies, in classes other than reading). The teachers reported providing extensive metacognitive information to students, including information about where and when to use the strategies and the utility of the strategies being taught. The teachers specified how they explicitly tried to teach students to transfer strategies to new academic settings and tasks. The teachers were emphatic that only a few new strategies a year could be taught with this intensity, with the teachers clearly believing that students build up a repertoire of strategies over years of instruction.

The teachers provided detailed information about how strategy instruction changed from initial presentation of a strategy to later instruction: At first, explanations about the strategy are extensive. Teachers reported that explanations and modeling of strategies declined as students practiced strategies, but experienced teachers indicated they continue to explain and model the strategies long after a strategy is introduced. In general, what the more experienced teachers said was that they did not stop modeling and explaining. Rather, when Benchmark students start to become proficient in using a strategy, the students are then required to apply and adapt the strategy to new and more demanding situations. The re-explanations and modeling provided to students are reported as depending on the needs of the students, although the teachers recognized that often it was difficult to know when students were experiencing difficulties learning and applying strategies. The teachers recognized that the road to proficient use of strategies was filled with difficulties, but that it was imperative that there be a fair amount of success along the way and plenty of reinforcement of student efforts and accomplishments.

The teachers were sold on strategies as the heart of reading instruction and integrated with the rest of the curriculum. The Benchmark teachers were enthused about problem-solving and writing strategies as well. They believed that the particular strategies taught to a student, however, should be tailored to the needs of the student.

For the most part, I felt very good about the Benchmark faculty interviews. Their reports were generally consistent with my perceptions of how good strategy instruction occurs, as reflected in Pressley, Goodchild, et al. (1989). My enthusiasm for the teacher reports and confidence in them was heightened by one additional aspect of the study. I sent many of the questions that were given to the Benchmark faculty to nine nationally recognized experts in strategy instruction, senior scientists and educators who had years of hands-on experience with strategy instruction. (The items were reworded slightly to reflect that the experts were to provide information about how a good strategies teacher should behave rather than how a Benchmark teacher behaves.) These nine experts provided practically identical responses (i.e., there was little variability between experts). Moreover, their responses were strikingly similar to the Benchmark teachers' responses, with correlations of .65 or higher, depending on the subscale. The only really striking difference between the experts and the teachers was that the experts believed in more dramatic fading and reduction of explanations and modeling as student practice with strategies proceeded than did the more experienced Benchmark teachers.

I was elated as I analyzed the teacher and expert data and wrote them up. When all of the interview data were considered, there was substantial evidence in favor of the claims about strategy instruction made by Pressley, Goodchild, et al. (1989). The Benchmark study included substantial support for the conclusion that good strategy instruction involves teaching only a few new strategies at a time using extensive explanation and modeling. There was clear support for providing extensive feedback about student performance using strategies as well as re-explanations and re-instruction tailored to student difficulties. The Benchmark teachers were sensitive to the need to teach students to use the strategies across a range of situations (i.e., transfer is not automatic). The teachers also provided multiple indicators that they encouraged students to become habitually reflective and planful.

The many elaborations provided by Benchmark teachers also began to put flesh on the skeleton of general conclusions about the nature of strategy instruction. I felt that even more flesh was needed, however, and thus, for the first time in my career, I conducted a case study. As that project proceeded, I was even more elated! (By the way, the Benchmark interview data were analyzed and written up over Christmas 1989, making that a wonderful holiday season, far merrier than Christmas 1986; there was much less anxiety than when I constructed the first draft of the Pressley, Goodchild, et al., 1989, article over Christmas 1987.)

An Ethnographic Case Study

During much of spring semester 1990, I spent 1 day a week in a classroom supervised by Debra Wile and her co-teacher, Jackie Sheridan. During each visit I watched writing, reading, and social studies instruction, typically seeing about 2½ hours of teaching during each visit. Wile and Sheridan were introducing text-structure-analysis strategies to their 10-year-old students during this semester. In particular, the students were taught how to make semantic maps of texts specifying descriptive relationships in texts, causes and effects, and temporal sequences. Students also were taught how to construct such semantic maps in advance of writing essays that contained descriptions, cause-and-effect sequences, and events in temporal order.

I constructed field notes each day, which were "member checked" (Lincoln & Guba, 1985) for accuracy (i.e., the two classroom teachers confirmed that the notes captured their teaching). The observations in the field notes were amalgamated and consolidated using a variation of the method of constant comparison (e.g., Strauss & Corbin, 1990). The conclusions about instruction that emanated from these analyses were checked by the classroom teachers and another person who was visiting Wile and Sheridan's classroom frequently as part of the larger program of research on classroom learning conducted by Benchmark School (see Gaskins & Elliot, 1991). The final result was an ethnography published as Pressley, Gaskins, Wile, Cunicelli, and Sheridan (1991).

What I observed was that the focal strategies were covered during writing, reading, and social studies. The regular curriculum content did not stop for strategies instruction. Rather the students worked with the regular content, applying the text-analysis strategies to content reading and in advance of generating essays over content. What was especially striking was how writing occurred not just during writing period but throughout the day, how reading and reading strategies instruction occurred all day, and how reading and writing strategies instruction was completely complementary to what went on in social studies—that is, the semantic mapping activities practiced during reading and writing were used to structure the social studies content lessons. Through the several months of observation, the students had many opportunities to generate semantic maps of text, to watch teachers and other students generate their own maps, and to produce essays from semantic maps they had created.

When strategy lessons occurred, they proceeded from teacher-led discussions, explanations, and modeling of strategy use to scaffolded attempts by the students to apply the strategies. Sometimes "a lesson" occurred during a single session on one day; sometimes the lesson extended over several days. The teachers scaffolded use of the new strategies in a number of ways. Thus, during reading lessons, use of the strategies was prompted frequently, with teachers sometimes co-producing maps with students, especially if students experienced difficulties producing their own maps. When students worked individually, the teachers circulated and provided gentle hints about how mapping strategies might be applied to current assignments. Although the teachers never completely stopped scaffolding instruction, by the end of the period of observation, students were much more capable of using the strategies than they had been earlier in the term. Thus, by the end of the semester, the teachers were giving students fairly long pieces and asking them to construct semantic maps, with the students completing these assignments with very little external support.

In teaching the focal strategies, Ms. Wile and Ms. Sheridan did not neglect the other strategies that had been taught to these students. Rather, teachers explained and modeled coordination of the new strategies with other strategies. For example, this class was thoroughly familiar with the most important strategies supporting comprehension (e.g., anticipating the content of text, relating text to prior knowledge, seeking clarification when meaning is unclear, summarization), with these strategies cued frequently by teachers and used often by students as they applied the new strategies.

I was especially impressed that students were encouraged to come to their own interpretations of texts as they applied strategies. The teachers sent the clear message throughout the term that the semantic maps generated by different students for a text would differ. The students were encouraged to make personal associations to text that summarized their unique understandings of the content. Becoming sophisticated interpreters of text, rather than students who simply learned the surface message, was consistently encouraged in this classroom.

What was most amazing to me was how all aspects of the school day were complementary. Homework required application of strategies. The teacher would feign errors in comprehension (or occasionally actually made an error) so she could model fix-it strategies. Discussions about how and when to use strategies occurred frequently and naturally. The benefits of strategy use were never showcased but rather slipped into the conversations and the lessons. Both Wile and Sheridan modeled flexible use of strategies and expectations of individual differences in strategy applications and preferences. They encouraged their students to be flexible thinkers both explicitly and by their own fluid outlook on tackling academic tasks. Review of strategies simply happened as part of ongoing activities. There was never a "review period" for strategy application, although there were review periods over content before exams. All of this took place in a well organized, happy classroom environment. The teachers liked their students and the students liked their teachers, with the students recognizing that Debra and Jackie were on their side, real advocates for their cognitive development.

A semester in Ms. Wile and Ms. Sheridan's classroom firmed up my growing commitment to the view that good strategy instruction is long term, involves consistent explanation and modeling of strategies, extensive teacher guidance of student practice with strategies, and encouragement of flexible thinking. In this classroom, the goal was development of sophisticated, extensive repertoires of strategies, with students coming to understand that "how" they tackled tasks mattered. The good strategy instruction I watched that semester was completely integrated with content.

Analyses of Dialogue During Lessons

When I arrived in the fall of 1989 at Benchmark, Irene Gaskins and her colleagues were in the midst of analyzing the structure of Benchmark strategy lessons. In particular, they were interested in the structure of the dialogues in Benchmark classrooms, convinced it was very different from the structure of conventional classroom discourse. In typical classrooms, there is a high proportion of cycles of one form: The teacher initiates a question, the student responds, and the teacher evaluates the response (IRE cycles; e.g., Cazden, 1988; Mehan, 1979). Irene Gaskins' experience in Benchmark classrooms made clear to her that Benchmark strategy lessons were certainly not of this form, a desideratum given the low level of real student involvement and commitment during IRE cycles.

Irene and her colleagues graciously invited me to join in their exploration, and I offered what help I could. Mostly, I provided technical assistance and did so willingly, given the opportunity to have a front-row seat during analyses of extremely interesting lessons. The eventual result was a paper co-authored by Gaskins, Anderson, Pressley, Cunicelli, and Satlow (1993).

Although hundreds of lessons at Benchmark had been recorded, it was necessary to come up with some reasonable sampling procedure, for the analysis of even a single lesson was formidable given the detail that Irene and her colleagues wanted in their descriptions. The Benchmark research team settled on six teachers, watching an entire "unit" of instruction on some new strategy (e.g., what I had watched over the semester in Ms. Wile and Ms. Sheridan's classroom was a unit on text-analysis strategies). For each of the six teachers, one entire lesson near the beginning of the unit was analyzed, one in the middle of the unit, and one near the end of the unit.

What was documented in these lessons? Eight "moves" were observed consistently: (a) the strategic process and curriculum content objectives were specified early in a lesson; (b) information was presented about why the strategies being instructed were important; (c) students received information about when and where to apply the strategies they were learning; (d) students were taught what to do in order to carry out strategies; (e) teachers modeled the strategies being instructed; (f) teachers shared their own personal experiences about how strategies benefited them; and (g) students were provided opportunities for teacher-guided practice of strategies. All eight of these moves occurred in one-third of the lessons. Another 44% of the lessons included 7 of the 8 moves. At least half of the 8 moves were present in all but 2 of the 18 lessons that were analyzed. The least frequent move was provision of information about when to use the strategy under instruction, detected in 55% of the lessons. The next least frequent move, modeling of the strategy, occurred in 78% of the lessons.

Particularly important to Gaskins and her colleagues, it proved easy to demonstrate that Benchmark lessons were not IRE cycles. Rather, the teachers engaged in extended interactive dialogues with their students 88% of the time, in what Gaskins et al. (1993) referred to as process-content cycles. In such a cycle, the teacher uses content as a vehicle for discussing the thinking-learning process. When a teacher responds to a student's input to a discussion, the concern is not with the content of the student's remarks but with encouraging the student to think additionally about the information and to continue to apply strategic processing to dig deeper. The overarching goal is understanding the content through the applications of the strategies the student is learning and knows.

How process and content are intertwined is illustrated by this example of industry by the Puritans in colonial Plymouth. The teacher is trying to encourage the students to identify big themes in the lesson and to focus their attention on those themes, rather than worrying about details. Because the processes being emphasized in the lesson are applied to content, this is a process-content cycle.

Teacher: What do you have to think about as you look at the notes I am putting on the board or as you look at your own notes? . . . Tom?

Tom: See if you have the right information.

Teacher: That's one thing to do, but more importantly, what do I think? Do I just rattle off a bunch of points totally unconnected? Rocky—forests—rivers—settlers. No. What do I want to do when I see rocky in my book? What goes on in the brain as soon as you look at the word rocky? If I am taking notes I might put something like rocky down, but there is a lot that goes on behind my putting that down on a piece of paper. I spent 5 minutes thinking about it maybe before I put rocky down.

.

.

.

Teacher: I don't get it. It was rocky ground. Oh, big news.

Student: Well, then they can't farm because of the rockiness. So it affects their way of life.

Teacher: I'm going to add that in there. Do you think I should add that in my notes?

There were many cycles like this in the lessons that were analyzed, with the teacher modeling and cuing students to use strategic processes with the content being covered in the lesson.

In addition to the focal strategy, each teacher, on average, cued eight other strategies across his or her three lessons. The nonfocal strategies that were cued most frequently were asking for clarification, visualizing, surveying, relating content to background knowledge, and having materials open to the correct page at the beginning of the lesson. There was clear orchestration of strategies in these lessons.

Summary

Three different methodologies were applied at Benchmark School: teacher interviewing, traditional case study, and discourse analysis. All three methods yielded a picture of long-term strategy instruction involving extensive direct explanation and modeling, with guided student practice of strategies in the context of the ongoing content curriculum. The Benchmark year was incredibly important, however, in that, for the first time in my career, I systematically worked with qualitative methodologies—and three of them at that—applying them to strategy instruction data. The increases in my personal understanding of strategy instruction and how it can occur in classrooms were enormous during that year. I had acquired a new set of lenses for looking at something I had been viewing in another way for years. I was also coming to understand that qualitative methods could provide information that is extremely important to the educator community—detailed information about how to do strategies instruction, information not provided in typical experimental evaluations of strategies instruction. I packed up my new set of lenses and headed for another school environment in which strategy instruction was occurring and benefiting students.

THE MONTGOMERY COUNTY SIA
AND SAIL PROGRAMS: 1990–1991

I first came into contact with the Montgomery County strategy instruction programs when their developers (Ted Schuder, Jan Bergman, Marcia York) invited me to a briefing in early 1990. Two of my students who were interested in qualitative analyses of strategies instruction accompanied me to the meeting. One was Pamela El-Dinary, who had come to Maryland after completing a master's degree at the University of Georgia and who had received a rigorous introduction to qualitative methods while at Athens. Rachel Brown had been working on problems of comprehension for some time as part of her graduate work at the University of Maryland Reading Center. Both felt, as I did, that the Montgomery County programs had high potential for analysis, principally because the programs were carefully thought out and driven by a clear understanding of the existing strategies-instruction literature, including knowledge of the most current theories and research. In addition, the county had documented rather striking changes in the comprehension performances of students receiving the strategies instruction devised by the Montgomery County team, with students in these programs outperforming comparable students not receiving such instruction on standardized measures of comprehension administered to all students in the county.

Montgomery County was operating two interesting programs when we entered the scene. One was dubbed "Students Achieving Independent Learning," or SAIL for short. This program was developed explicitly to boost the reading achievement of at-risk students in Grades 1 to 6 and was being administered in Chapter 1 classrooms.

SAIL students are taught to read for meaning rather than simply to decode text. They are also taught to adjust their reading depending on their purpose, the type and difficulty of the text being read, and their personal interest and previous knowledge of the topic of the text. SAIL students are also taught other strategies including to (a) anticipate the content of text based on picture and context clues; (b) evaluate their expectations and to adjust them in light of text content; (c) generate questions as they read; (d) respond aesthetically to text, including the generation of personal interpretations and evaluations of text; (e) visualize the content of text; (f) summarize content periodically; (g) seek clarification when confused by treating miscomprehension as a problem to be solved; and (h) attend selectively to important and interesting parts of text. In short, students are urged to read actively and to make associations between their prior knowledge and text as they construct predictions about text, read for meaning, monitor their understanding of what they are reading, and construct representations summarizing the meaning of text, including verbal summaries and images. Although all of this sounds like hard work, a main feature of SAIL is that teachers constantly make it clear that reading is fun and one reason that cognitive strategies are important is that they permit entry to a source of great pleasure.

The Summer Institute for Achievement (identified as SIA for short) involves many of the SAIL teachers, providing reading and mathematics instruction to at-risk students during a summer session (e.g., more than 3,000 students in summer 1991). The reading instruction is much like SAIL in that the same strategies are emphasized and the teaching methods are similar. A crucial difference, given the 4-week time frame of SIA, of course, is that the strategies introduced slowly in the SAIL program are introduced rapidly during SIA. One strategy is emphasized during each of the 4 weeks of the program—for example, prediction is highlighted in the first week, although students are exposed to and encouraged to use the other SAIL comprehension strategies. As with the SAIL program, the county has collected quasi-experimental data indicating significant achievement advantages for students who attend SIA summer sessions.

Consistent with the emphasis on reading as a pleasurable activity, SAIL and SIA instruction occur in reading groups that involve reading of high quality, interesting texts and exchange of ideas about what the texts might mean. The main approach to strategy instruction in these groups is a variant of direct explanation (Duffy & Roehler, 1987). Teachers model, coach, and provide opportunities for students to practice reading strategies in pairs or small groups, as well as independently. This explicit instruction goes on in SAIL classrooms while students are in the process of constructing and evaluating interpretations of text.

A Sample SAIL Lesson With Commentary

Exactly what goes on during a SAIL lesson can be appreciated by considering a sample lesson, generated in May 1990 in a Grade 2 reading group taught by Lynne Coy-Ogan. This group of children had been nonreaders when they entered Grade 2. Eight months later they were active participants in the reading group, which on this day took up Maurice Sendak's *Where the Wild Things Are.*

The seven students in this reading group were experiencing *Wild Things* as the last of several books in a unit on Sendak and thus, the students brought to the lesson a rich background about the author and his approaches to writing. Ms. Coy-Ogan began the lesson like all SAIL reading groups begin, by reminding the students to apply their SAIL strategies and by being the first member of the group to do some reading aloud. As she read aloud, Ms. Coy-Ogan thought aloud to permit students exposure to how she approached the text. She began:

> "That night Max wore his wool suit and made mischief of one kind and another."
> . . . I can visualize Max. He's in this monster suit and he's chasing after his dog with a fork in his hand [a response cued by the picture accompanying the text]. I think he's really starting to act crazy [a personal interpretation of the text by Ms. Coy-Ogan]. I wonder what made Max act like that . . . [cuing students to think beyond the surface structure of the text to the deeper meaning]. I bet he was getting a little bored and wanted to go on an adventure. I think that's my prediction [prediction is one of the strategies SAIL students are taught to apply early in the reading of any text].

After this introduction to the story, Ms. Coy-Ogan turned the reading over to students, who read aloud and used strategies, with the teacher prompting additional use of strategies when appropriate and providing minilessons pertaining to strategy use as needed and appropriate. Here is an example of one such minilesson, which was offered after a student elected to skip over an unknown word encountered in the reading:

> OK, we have some problem-solving strategies we can use [pointing to a bulletin board display summarizing the problem-solving approaches that can be used as part of word attack]. When we get to a word, we can guess and substitute; we can ignore and read on; we can reread the sentence; we can look back in the story for clues; or we can use the picture clues.

Throughout the lesson, Ms. Coy-Ogan takes advantage of opportunities to explain and model strategies and gently to prompt students to use strategies.

Throughout this process, use of the strategies promoted student interpretations of the text. Consider this sequence later in the lesson:

Marie: I think he's not dreaming anymore.

Ms. Coy-Ogan: You don't think he's dreaming anymore. How come? That's changing your prediction.

Marie: Because he would wake up if somebody growled or something, maybe.

Ms. Coy-Ogan: A loud noise might wake him up. It certainly would startle me up. What do you think, Ellen? You're shaking your head.

Ellen: I think Marie is right about that.

Ms. Coy-Ogan: Do you have any background knowledge that helped you make that prediction?

And so it went for the entire story, with Ms. Coy-Ogan encouraging students to make predictions while they read, seek clarifications when meaning was obscure, visualize, summarize, generate questions about the text, and deal constructively with unfamiliar vocabulary. All who have viewed the videotape of this lesson agree that there is active construction of meaning during these lessons and diverse student interpretations of various parts of the text. The lessons involve friendly interactions between teachers and students about the text and a great deal of discussion about potential meanings of the text.

The Theory Behind SAIL

The big idea in the SAIL program is that years of participating in such reading groups will result in students coming to own the strategies practiced and encouraged in the group context. Of course, this is a prediction derived from Vygotskian theory (e.g., Vygotsky, 1978) that intraperson cognitive processes can be developed through interpersonal processing—that how one thinks now reflects previous interactions involving group thinking and problem solving. The designers of SAIL worked very hard to design instruction that would maximize the likelihood of internalization of active and coherent reasoning processes.

A key ingredient in this process is that students are taught to think aloud, consistent with Meichenbaum's (1977) theory that self-verbalization can promote self-regulation of cognitive processes, which in turn was informed by Soviet theorists such as Luria (e.g., 1961, 1982) and Vygotsky (e.g., 1962, 1978). Thinking aloud during application of reading strategies should promote student control of attention, the contents of their thoughts, and use of strategies (see Meichenbaum, 1977; Pressley, 1979). In addition, thinking aloud gives the teacher and other members of the group access to a student's thought processes, so that members of the reading group are continually modeling active thinking about text for their peers. This is critical, because such mental modeling is known to affect those exposed to it (Bandura, 1986; Duffy, Roehler, & Herrmann, 1988).

From my initial contact with the SAIL program, including the opportunity to observe a number of lessons, it was clear that instruction was proceeding along pretty much as the developers had intended. Direct explanation and modeling of the SAIL strategies were apparent. So was student participation in reading group. Even so, Pamela El-Dinary, Rachel Brown, and I believed that some systematic observation might reveal subtleties not intended by, or apparent to, the program developers or the causal observer. Thus, with the assistance and support of Ted Schuder and his Montgomery County colleagues, Pam El-Dinary and I set out to document what happens during SAIL and SIA reading groups. Our first analysis was an ethnography (Strauss & Corbin, 1990) of three SIA classrooms during the summer 1990 SIA.

Ethnographic Study of the 1990 Summer Institute for Achievement

Over the course of the 4 weeks of the 1990 SIA, El-Dinary visited three classrooms, each six times, observing on each occasion all of the teaching during the 2½-hour morning session (SIA only met during the morning hours). The three teachers who ran the sections studied by El-Dinary were experienced in the SAIL program. El-Dinary spent each day making field notes that summarized what went on in the classes. She sorted her notes to develop categories that summarized what went on in these classrooms. She then took her notes and preliminary categories back to the teachers for their verification. Another researcher (me) also developed categories summarizing the components of teaching based on El-Dinary's original notes. Eventually, El-Dinary and I got together and compared our categorizations, finally agreeing on a set of classifications that captured the instructional behaviors in the SIA classes. Those close to the program, including the participating teachers, concurred with our categorical synopsis of the program.

In general, El-Dinary observed a program consistent with the goals and expectations of its developers, although there were rich consistencies in the instruction that were made apparent by the ethnography. What did El-Dinary see (summarized in substantially greater detail by El-Dinary, Pressley, & Schuder, 1992)?:

- There was explicit explanation of one or more strategies in every class, sometimes new strategies and sometimes review of strategies covered previously.
- The information-processing vocabulary used in lessons was sophisticated. For example, the term *strategy* was used often and specific strategies were referenced using names common in the cognitive-processing literature (e.g., visualization, summarization). Such vocabulary was used habitually, almost nonchalantly by teachers and students alike.

- Most lessons included teacher modeling of one or more strategies, typically by teachers thinking aloud as they performed an academic task (e.g., reading part of a story).

- Students were often required to model and explain the strategies they were using.

- Teacher guidance of student use of strategies was prominent. This included hints and cues to use strategies as well as elaborations of student reactions to content. Often the prompts were in the forms of questions that led students to continue strategic processing (i.e., much as was observed in the Benchmark classrooms).

- Throughout instruction, the utility of strategies was emphasized, including information about when and where it would be profitable to apply the strategies being learned. The positive effects of strategy use on student performance were consistently pointed out to students (i.e., when a student experienced a strategy-mediated success, the teacher made apparent to the student the linkage between the success and use of strategies).

- Teachers emphasized flexibility both in their actions and in their words. There were frequent discussions about how different students might use strategies differently to accomplish the same task. Students were encouraged to notice and embrace the diversity of images, summaries, and interpretations produced by the members of the class.

- Teachers consistently sent the message that student thought processes mattered a great deal.

In summary, El-Dinary observed mental modeling and direct explanation of strategies as Duffy and his colleagues have recommended (e.g., Duffy & Roehler, 1987; Duffy et al., 1988). Both the teachers and students talked aloud about their thinking processes, sharing interpretations of text in a relaxed and pleasant atmosphere. The teachers encouraged students to coordinate the use of comprehension strategies such as predicting, self-questioning, seeking clarification, and summarizing as a means of coming to understand text. It was apparent to El-Dinary that the students liked what was going on, with converging evidence of this being that the students were there on an entirely voluntary basis and attendance was generally good. In many ways, much of 1990–1991 involved activities that simply corroborated El-Dinary's observations.

More Study of Montgomery County Instruction: 1990–1991

During spring 1991, I spent a great deal of time observing SAIL classrooms in one school, visiting classes in Grades 1 through 4, with the students ranging from first- to third-year SAIL students. In general, what I observed in the daily lessons was consistent with the instructional model summarized by El-Dinary et al. (1992), although an analysis reported by Pressley et al. (1994) provided insights not possible from El-Dinary's previous work with SIA.

Variations in SAIL as a Function of Grade/Experience of Students. If the theory behind SAIL is correct, that with experience students internalize the SAIL strategies, then with each additional year of SAIL, there should be decreasing need for explanation and modeling of strategies or teacher prompting of strategy use. In fact, that is what I observed during my visits. Thus, in Grade 1 SAIL classes, there was a great deal of modeling, explanation, and coaching of strategies. Moreover, the strategies lessons were much more narrowly focused, often with a great deal of attention to one strategy. For example, I witnessed a lesson in which students were encouraged to make predictions throughout a story, with the purpose of the lesson being to practice predictions. This was a lesson filled with teacher prompts that elicited predictions (e.g., What might happen?). Although there was some teacher modeling and prompting of other strategies (e.g., teacher modeling of prior knowledge associations, teacher modeling of clarification seeking), the lesson began with predictions and ended with students evaluating whether their initial predictions had been confirmed by the story.

Grade 2 lessons were most like the SAIL lesson described earlier, with overt, coordinated use of all of the strategies encouraged by the SAIL program. A lesson conducted in March 1991 by Miss Kathy Green was typical. The students were reading the 11th chapter in a trade book they had been covering as part of reading group. Miss Green began the lesson by informing the students that her goal in reading the chapter was to know the information in it, to be able to summarize the chapter at the end of the reading. She briefly reviewed the SAIL strategies with students by having them indicate which strategies they might apply to the text in order to meet such a goal.

Before the reading began, Miss Green spread out in front of the students a set of cards that summarized the SAIL strategies, one card per SAIL strategy. She quickly but systematically went over each strategy before the lesson began. Then, she began reading the chapter, first predicting what might be in the chapter based on what she knew from previous chapters. Miss Green then elicited student predictions and reminded students to be looking for information in the text that was relevant to their predictions.

Miss Green was the first to read aloud, thinking aloud as she went through the text, relating her reactions to the text to her students. Sometimes students chipped in with their responses. As she read, Miss Green reminded herself explicitly that getting the meaning of the text was the most important thing to do while reading. After several pages of reading aloud to the students, Miss Green turned reading over to a student. After the student finished reading a page, Miss Green asked, "What are you thinking?" After the student provided his response, Miss Green asked if other students had other reactions to the text. Miss Green then thought aloud, modeling her own feelings about the content.

As each student completed some reading, the student reported his or her thinking. Miss Green commented on students' use of strategies, such as when a student applied background knowledge to make a prediction about the content of upcoming text. She also pointed out parts of text that might be visualized profitably and modeled, summarizing from time to time.

In contrast to Grade 1, where students were getting familiar with the particular strategies, Miss Green's Grade 2 students knew the strategies and were provided lessons in which the teacher emphasized coordinated application of the different techniques in order to understand the text. Miss Green's lessons were especially interesting to watch, as were the other Grade 2 lessons, because the use of the strategies was so overt and explicit. Whenever I want to show someone how a teacher might encourage coordinated use of strategies, I play a tape of a Grade 2 lesson. Students who are just a bit older do not need nearly as much prompting, so that there is less to see on the videotapes of lessons in the higher grades.

For example, consider a prototypical Grade 4 lesson conducted by Ms. Kim Powell. Most of Ms. Powell's students had received 3 years of SAIL instruction and were thoroughly familiar with the comprehension strategies comprising SAIL. For the lesson in question, the students were beginning a new novel. Ms. Powell began the lesson by prompting students to look at the cover of the book. The students then made a written prediction about what might happen in the book, a prediction that could be updated at the end of each day's reading of the book. Several of these predictions were discussed by the class before the reading began.

As is always true of a SAIL lesson, Ms. Powell was the first to read, thinking aloud about the meaning of the text as she read. Thus, when there was a mention of "Georgetown" in the reading, Ms. Powell wondered aloud if that was the Georgetown in Washington, DC, a meaningful reflection to the students because their school was located in suburban Washington. When Ms. Powell came upon "August" in the reading, she reacted that that must be the name of a person given the context. She offered this prediction tentatively, making obvious the possibility that this assumption might be changed depending on the content of the text that followed. After several minutes of reading, Ms. Powell turned the reading over to the students.

From time to time, Ms. Powell prompted students to summarize what they had been reading. Students indicated on their own when they needed clarification, with other students often filling in gaps for their peers. When unfamiliar words were encountered, the students automatically applied the problem-solving strategies taught in the SAIL program. The students often made interpretive responses to the text and provided spontaneous reflections on how events in the text related to their own lives.

In short, for the most part, the Grade 4 students were doing the SAIL comprehension and interpretation strategies on their own. The wall cards summarizing the strategies that were so prominent in the Grade 1 and Grade 2 lessons were never referred to during the Grade 4 lesson. In fact, the Grade 4 lesson was in a part of the room far removed from the wall cards, whereas lessons in Grade 1 and Grade 2 classrooms always occurred in the corner of the room displaying wall cards. These Grade 4 students did not need the wall cards to engage in processing aimed at comprehending, interpreting, and enjoying the reading. Nonetheless, I was struck that there was still some teacher cuing of the SAIL strategies and processes encouraged by SAIL, although this prompting was much less obvious than in the lessons with the younger students. What was certainly obvious from the observations summarized by Pressley, Faculty and Administration of Summit Hall School, et al. (1994) was that the explicitness of teacher explanations and promptings varies with student experience with the SAIL procedures, an outcome consistent the Vygotskian perspective informing the development of SAIL instruction, that processes that are initially interpersonal and overt become intrapersonal and covert.

Potential Effects and Shortcomings of SAIL. I was interested in much more than possible differences in SAIL instruction as a function of the maturity and experience of students, however, as I watched SAIL classrooms in the spring of 1991. I suspected that SAIL was having many effects on students, some positive and some negative. My strong feelings were that if my colleagues and I were to have any chance of understanding this intervention, it was necessary to determine what effects the intervention might produce. In addition, it was clear to me that not everyone involved with SAIL was satisfied with all features of the program. I thought that there might be aspects of the intervention that could be rethought before attempting formal summative evaluation of the procedure.

I started the project by attending a focus group with teachers. Most of the teachers knew me well by this point. We had established long before that I was interested in what really went on in their classrooms and that I was not evaluating them, but only trying to understand the nature of the SAIL instructional program. They trusted me. I explained to them that my current concern was with the potential effects of the program and potential shortcomings with it. I also explained that they were the only window I had on program effects and difficulties, so that it was essential they provide honest information both during the focus group and throughout the coming semester. The focus group meeting started with a renewed commitment from the teachers to provide their most candid input to my study.

Then, for the next hour the teachers provided an enormous amount of information about what the program seemed to be doing for their students, when it was working, and when it was not. My pen could hardly keep up with their output. At the end of the session, I let them know that I would be systematically observing their classrooms in the next few months as part of this project, followed by individual interviews of them. I made clear to them that I viewed them as co-investigators in the process of understanding program effects and problems.

Then began a long period of observation, visiting classrooms and taking fieldnotes whenever I detected anything that might suggest a program effect (e.g., that the children seemed to be enthused about participating in reading group) or a program difficulty (e.g., noticing that some children were having difficulty participating in the readings because they could not decode). Then I went over field notes, attempting to identify categories of effects and problems (i.e., used a variant of the method of constant comparison; Strauss & Corbin, 1990). I also consulted informally with the teachers concerning the categories of potential effects that were emerging. More than once, the teachers explained to me that "what I was actually seeing" was different from "what I thought I was seeing." The teachers were also masterful at suggesting category labels that would make sense to the teachers, critical because teachers eventually would be interviewed about these potential effects and shortcomings. The teachers were both informants and co-investigators.

After the focus group, many observations, and many informal interviews, I had a long list of potential effects and potential shortcomings of the program. I then devised a questionnaire tapping potential effects and hassles. Before administering it to all of the teachers, I asked several teachers, as well as the program developers, for their help in improving the instrument—for example, by making the wording clearer for teachers and by checking for possible omissions and misstatements.

The final questionnaire was constructed so that every question required a numerical "objective" response (e.g., agree completely, agree a little . . . completely disagree) but also permitted open ended responses. That is, the teachers were informed that they could and should provide any additional information that might be pertinent to coming to terms with potential program effects and weaknesses. Teachers were given the entire questionnaire to take home and do at their leisure. When they returned the questionnaire, it was as part of a 1-hour interview in which I went over every question, with each teacher permitted to make clarifications and elaborations during this interview.

There were three important types of information generated by this observation-and-interview exercise. First, the SAIL program was clearly acceptable to these experienced SAIL teachers. All teachers offered multiple comments reflecting their enthusiastic acceptance of the program.

Second, the teachers perceived a wide range of positive effects of the program on their students. These included the following:

1. improved oral reading;
2. improved comprehension and interpretation of text;
3. improved understanding that comprehension of text is under the control of the reader;
4. better writing;
5. more higher order thinking;
6. greater use of background knowledge and prior experiences;
7. greater attention to the meaning of the text;
8. more intertextual comparisons;

9. greater involvement in reading group;

10. greater student excitement about reading;

11. more reading of more difficult books as part of outside reading;

12. greater student enjoyment of reading instruction;

13. greater student comfort with reading instruction;

14. improved academic self-esteem;

15. reduced disciplinary problems during reading instruction;

16. more and better teacher-to-student and student-to-student communication; and

17. greater student engagement during reading group than with traditional instruction.

The diversity of outcomes suggested by this list contrasts greatly with the limited range of outcomes tapped in previous research on the effects of comprehension instruction. Most of the experimental studies of the 1970s and 1980s focused on objective memory and comprehension of text. Rarely were the interactions in reading group considered; rarely was the affect of students taken into account; and rarely was student engagement in reading both during group and outside of group considered. What the SAIL interview study suggested was that if complete understanding of reading comprehension instruction is to be achieved, a much broader range of indicators must be tapped than has been the case to date.

This observation-and-interview study also provided insights into the weaker aspects of the SAIL intervention. The teachers were not at all reticent to express reservations about the program. For example, the primary teachers were extremely concerned about the appropriateness of SAIL for nonreaders, believing that SAIL instruction needed to be meshed with traditional decoding instruction. Another concern was with generalization of the SAIL strategies. Although teachers reported they perceived some generalization of strategies, there were frequent mentions of concern about the extent of generalization. In addition, the Grade 1 and Grade 2 teachers in particular felt it difficult to find materials that meshed with the SAIL emphasis on comprehension. Moreover, a number of teachers expressed concerns about grading given the SAIL emphasis on improvement of individual performances rather than on rank-ordering of student performances.

Perhaps more positively, the teachers were also able to dismiss some other potential concerns, one that I had considered possible as I watched SAIL instruction. For example, I wondered if SAIL would be considered compatible with whole language, an important consideration given the widespread acceptance of whole language by language arts teachers in the 1990s. The SAIL teachers felt strongly that SAIL and whole language were compatible. One said it as follows: "SAIL is whole language with a strategy emphasis," with this teacher impressed with the emphasis on reading of real literature and on meaning-getting as the main goal of reading. I also wondered how difficult it was for students to become accustomed to participating in SAIL instruction. This was not a concern for many teachers. I thought the interpretive discussions might disrupt the flow of reading. The majority of the SAIL teachers did not believe that use of strategies or construction and discussion of interpretations was disruptive, although 4 of the 14 participating teachers shared my concern.

Thus, what the SAIL teachers told me was that SAIL was a good program in their eyes but one that required some fine tuning, in particular with respect to decoding instruction for nonreaders and generalization of strategies by all readers. Most of the other concerns were minor ones, however. For example, teachers were finding ways to generate reading grades even though grading was more challenging with SAIL than with conventional instruction.

Summary

There were many similarities in the instruction offered in the SIA and SAIL programs and at Benchmark School. Both involve long-term teaching, with a few new strategies introduced at a time. The small group is the principle vehicle of instruction in both, with strategies taught so as to increase interpretive discussion of the meaning of text. In both, there is concern that students acquire understanding of when and where to use the strategies they are learning and are motivated to use the strategies, with motivation stemming in part from understanding of strategy effects on skilled reading. In both, the goal is internalization of strategies through long-term participation in groups involved in sophisticated strategy use and application. The prediction, visualization, question generation, clarification, and summarization strategies at the heart of the SAIL and SIA interventions are also prominent in the Benchmark curriculum. Montgomery County is coping with coordination of decoding and comprehension instruction as this chapter is being written; Benchmark has solved the decoding problem by developing a word attack program ("Word ID"; see Gaskins & Elliot, 1991) that is integrated with other instruction. The points of convergence between the Benchmark and SAIL/SIA programs have pointed the way to a model of comprehension strategies instruction that I now refer to as "transactional strategies instruction," a model that is consistent with my 1989 perspective (Pressley, Goodchild, et al., 1989), although more complex and better informed than the model proposed several years ago. I close this personal journey with an overview of my current thinking about transactional strategies instruction.

CHRISTMAS PRESENT: A TRANSACTIONAL MODEL OF TEACHING READING COMPREHENSIONS STRATEGIES

I have spent most of Christmas break 1991 constructing this chapter, with this holiday filled with joy, for I was reviewing excitement and confidence built up over the past 5 years: I was excited but not very confident when I wrote Pressley, Goodchild, et al. (1989); I was more excited and increasingly confident as I analyzed the first Benchmark data (Pressley, Gaskins, Cunicelli, et al., 1991); and my positive feelings and certainty of perspective increased dramatically as I lived much of my life in a SAIL school in the spring of 1991 (Pressley, Schuder, SAIL Faculty and Administration, Bergman, & El-Dinary, 1992). Christmas 1991 was a Christmas filled with wonderful nostalgia about a terrific 5-year journey—a journey first stimulated by that terrible Christmas of 1986.

What Is Transactional Strategies Instruction?

So what have I learned about teaching comprehension strategies to elementary students? Transactional instruction of cognitive strategies is an integral part of the regular school curriculum, typically taught in the context of reading stories, science, or social studies. Strategies are introduced a few at a time to students through direct explanation and modeling of the steps comprising the strategy. Additional explanations and modeling are provided as needed, with need determined by teachers monitoring student practice of strategies with real school tasks (e.g., reading material they must learn as part of the curriculum). Such instruction is scaffolded (Wood, Bruner, & Ross, 1976) in that enough is provided so that students do not falter but not so much that they depend entirely on teacher support. Teacher input and control is reduced as the student becomes more adept at using the strategies.

Students are taught to relate text to their prior knowledge and personal experiences using the strategies and in doing so to generate personally meaningful interpretations of text. These interpretations are shared as part of reading group, with an emphasis on diversity of interpretations. There is explicit recognition by all in the reading group that diverse purposes, backgrounds, and interests produce diverse uses of strategies and interpretations of text. Transactional strategies instruction teachers endorse and model flexible use of strategies and flexible thinking in all aspects of academic functioning, consistently sending the message to their students that good thinking is uniquely reflective and planful. The result is a reading group that creates interpretations of text through the involvement of all participants. Because the students are reading worthwhile texts, a great deal of incidental learning of important content occurs, so that reading instruction serves to increase the general knowledge of students. General knowledge created in this way should be deeply meaningful because it is acquired through interpretive discussions that are highly engaging for students.

As in most elementary schools, language arts takes up most of the morning in classrooms committed to transactional instruction of comprehension strategies. Writing strategy instruction occurs and often can be related to reading comprehension strategies, such as when Ms. Wile and Ms. Sheridan taught their students to use text-analysis strategies as frames for preparing outlines of expository essays. There is seatwork and homework in transactional strategies instruction classrooms. Such homework often can be accomplished by applying the strategies learned in class. Students are taught strategies for preparing for exams and taking them. Teaching involves thorough and frequent review both of strategies and content.

Strategies instruction proceeds at different paces, depending on the readiness of the students, so that Grade 1 students experience lessons emphasizing one of the strategies more than others. Older students are provided more extensive instruction about coordinating strategies as well as practice doing so. After a while, instruction is little more than gentle prompts to use strategies, although the reading group's processing of text is rich with sophisticated interpretations, reflecting strategic processing that students now carry on with little external direction from the teacher. Transactional strategies instruction is teachers and students coming together to generate understandings of text, a creation process largely orchestrated by the teacher at first, who eventually cedes most of the control to students who become capable of directing their own reading and interpretation of text.

Transactional strategies instruction is long term, with the theory being that sophisticated thinking processes are developed through long-term interactions with others, that eventually one internalizes the group processes. That is, the predictive, clarifying, interpretive, visualizing, and summarizing activities of the group eventually are adapted and adopted by the individual members of the group and applied by the individual members as they read on their own. What is involved here are many transactions with students, in which strategies are explained, modeled, re-explained, and modeled again as students and teachers work through important content in the curriculum. As such, transactional strategies instruction is completely consistent with Vygotsky's (1978) model of mental development, which had as its most important tenet that interpersonal thought processes eventually become intrapersonal thought processes.

Transactional strategies instruction teachers motivate students to use strategies and to try hard in school, largely by making certain students understand the advantages associated with use of strategies. Teachers reinforce student improvement and completion of academic tasks rather than reinforcing students for being "best" or "first" (i.e., task involvement rather than ego involvement is emphasized in transactional strategies instruction classrooms; Nicholls, 1989)—I have not witnessed a single episode in a transactional strategies instruction classroom where there was salient rank ordering of students, with reinforcement for the students on top. Comprehension strategies are applied to readings that are interesting, so that students see an obvious benefit of learning to read with high comprehension—access to a wonderful world only open to the reader. Participation in reading group and class discussion is painless, with alternative interpretations embraced. The consistent message is that each student's contribution is valuable.

This approach to instruction contrasts with the single strategy instruction that was studied during much of the 1970s and 1980s and with short-term instruction of a number of strategies, an approach that now is popular in many education settings as a logical application of the reading comprehension strategies research of the 1970s and 1980s (see Pressley, El-Dinary, & Brown, 1992, for discussion).

These latter two approaches are consistent with a skills model of instruction—if all of the discrete skills (strategies) are taught, somehow—and it is never specified how—the learner will figure out how to use the skills together (Duffy, 1989). I am not confident that most students do so, however. This pessimistic expectation is reinforced by the many transfer failures following single strategy instruction that have been reported (see Brown et al., 1983) and the failures of rapid teaching of many strategies to affect reading comprehension in general (e.g., Paris & Oka, 1986).

The transactional strategies instruction perspective is completely different from the teaching of single skills, different in ways that I believe have dramatic effects on academic motivation. What is being taught here is how to read whole texts, coordinating strategies and background knowledge in order to do so. The teacher is a model of what a good reader does to get meaning from text. The teacher is not trying to develop students who know strategies, but rather is trying to develop readers. An important part of transactional strategies instruction is that with success in getting meaning from authentic and interesting texts, students will come to think of themselves as readers—that is, their identity will be transformed from that of "someone who cannot read" to being a "reader," which is important because such an identity transformation has powerful motivational implications (see Lave & Wenger, 1991). Students who conceive of themselves as readers are much more likely to read extensively than students who view themselves as having difficulty reading, a critical point because continued, rapid growth of reading competency depends on substantial, voluntary reading (Stanovich, 1986). A primary goal of transactional strategies instruction is to get students to believe they are readers who can become better readers through their own efforts. See Pressley, El-Dinary, Marks, Brown, and Stein (1992) for an extensive discussion of the motivational advantages of transactional strategies instruction.

How Did the Transactional Strategies Instruction Model Come About?

Educators implicitly constructed the transactional strategies instruction model, which was then formalized by informal and formal collaborative investigations between educators and researchers. The educators invented transactional strategies instruction by taking their knowledge of the experimental and theoretical literatures of the 1970s and 1980s and combining it with their grounded understandings about the realities of classroom life. By the time I saw instruction at Benchmark and in Montgomery County and at other sites (i.e., the ones informing the analysis published in Pressley et al., 1989), the educators involved had had several years to "get it right." The abstract discussions of cognition and instruction that I had studied so carefully in the scientific literature pertaining to strategy instruction came to life for me with my first visits to Kansas strategy instructional classrooms, Duffy's project at Wainright School, Benchmark School, and the Montgomery County SAIL/SIA programs, among others.

Even though I had tried to make observations and come to conclusions about transactional strategies instruction with a mental "clean slate," some of my most deeply held convictions in 1986 (see Pressley, Borkowski, & Schneider, 1987, 1989) were reinforced during my 5-year journey. I came to believe ever more strongly that effective strategies instructors teach strategies, enhance metacognition about strategies, promote motivation to learn strategies and try hard in school, and extend students' content knowledge.

As I concluded this chapter at the close of Christmas season 1991, I was reminded of a feeling I often have at the end of Christmas. Throughout every December I read W. H. Auden's, *For the Time Being: A Christmas Oratorio*, each night reflecting on a page or so of the Christmas journey the poem summarizes. The ending, which I reached the night before completing this chapter, is a lament by the narrator about how once again, people failed this year to understand Christmas completely, although they had a glimpse of something of the vision that is Christmas. As I concluded this chapter on December 31, that was how I felt. Somehow, I was on a long journey, and I had seen something of the possibility of transactional strategies instruction and understand it somewhat, yet there was much that I did not understand. The conclusion of the *Christmas Oratorio* would be tragic, if it were not so clear that there will be Christmas next year and another chance to understand its meaning. So it is with transactional strategies instruction. I have some visions about Christmases future.

CHRISTMASES FUTURE

Research on transactional strategies instruction is proceeding along a number of fronts. As I wrote this chapter, Pamela El-Dinary, Ted Schuder, and I were struggling with another set of data collected from three teachers during their first year of SAIL. Hopefully, these data will help us understand better the challenges of becoming a transactional strategies instruction teacher, especially because we extended Pam's study with some first-year SAIL teachers who were attempting to mesh SAIL and decoding instruction. Based on what I know at this point about these analyses, next Christmas I expect to be writing about how challenging it is for teachers during their first year of transactional strategies instruction. I also expect that my colleagues and I will devote substantial effort in the next year or so to determine if training might be developed that would permit teachers to understand better and more quickly the nature of transactional strategies instruction and how to do it.

Rachel Brown is working hard on a quasi-experimental study of the interactions in SAIL reading groups and traditional groups and how the information exchanged in these two types of reading groups affects the representations of text developed by members of the group. The differences between interactions in SAIL reading groups and traditional reading groups were striking, with those differences much as Gaskins and her colleagues at Benchmark (Gaskins et al., 1993) have hypothesized—few IRE cycles in SAIL classes and many in traditional classes. Preliminary evaluations of Brown's data have confirmed that the differences in interaction in the two types of reading groups produce differences in children's understanding of the stories that are read as part of group (see Brown & Pressley, 1994). A variety of comprehension measures, standardized and nonstandard, were administered in this investigation, with all analyses to date consistent with the conclusion that transactional strategies instruction produces striking changes in comprehension.

On the one hand, I have come to understand that true experiments on long-term transactional strategies instruction are extremely unlikely. First, it seems clear that teachers never could be assigned randomly to transactional strategies instruction and traditional instruction: It probably takes several years to become a transactional strategies instructions teacher, and even if we do devise more efficient training, extremely great commitment is required to carry out transactional strategies instruction. Those who stay the course and become strategies instruction teachers have told us that they do not want to go back to traditional instruction and thus, randomly assigning strategies-instruction-trained teachers to strategies instruction versus traditional instruction is out of the question. Although it might be possible to assign students randomly to transactional instruction classes and traditional classes (with different teachers teaching the strategies-instruction and the traditional classes), it seems unlikely such an assignment could be held intact for more than 1 year. For a number of reasons, schools need flexibility to move students around. This need for year-to-year flexibility in student assignment is problematic for an experimental evaluation of transactional strategies instruction, because the theory is that comprehension strategies competence develops over several years of transactional strategies instruction.

On the other hand, I am certainly far from satisfied with the information currently available as supportive of the efficacy of transactional strategies instruction. Although it is encouraging that so many Benchmark alums do well and that standardized comprehension scores are better in SAIL classrooms than in otherwise comparable classrooms, I will feel better when there are several controlled studies that assess the impact of SAIL on many of the variables the SAIL teachers believe are affected by transactional strategies instruction. The costs of well controlled quasi-experiments in which the potentially diverse effects of transactional strategies instruction are evaluated seem reasonable to me. Rachel Brown's current work and the previous analyses conducted by the county suggest that it is possible to match SAIL classrooms and other classrooms, and I am looking forward to conducting additional quasi-experiments that are carefully planned to capture a large range of potential effects of transactional strategies instruction. For the present, the study Rachel Brown is now analyzing is the best validating data in existence; fortunately, the outcomes in that work are unambiguous. Grade 2 SAIL students, who were low-achieving at the start of the study, comprehend better after a year of strategies instruction than do otherwise comparable control students receiving high quality, conventional language-arts instruction (Brown & Pressley, 1994).

I also look forward to conducting and reading more true experiments evaluating individual strategies. Every strategy that my colleagues and I have identified as now being taught as part of transactional strategies instruction was previously studied in single experiments. Single experiments seem to provide a sign to education professionals that a procedure is worth a try in their setting. I suspect that there are many interesting strategies that will be suggested by new theories of thinking and instruction; I also suspect that study of them in single experiments will once again be a good first step toward eventual dissemination and integration in real-school educational interventions.

In closing, I believe that the data on comprehension strategies instruction that are available now are substantially richer than the data that were available for Christmas 1986. My view is that there was not much to celebrate then with respect to comprehension strategies instruction compared to the celebration that is possible during Christmas 1991. Many research possibilities are either underway or in the planning, ones almost certain to make writing during future Christmas seasons even brighter. This Carol will be continued, for like Scrooge, I feel revitalized by the journey I have been on, one in which I was transformed from someone who did only experiments to someone who attempts to understand education using a wider range of methodologies. I am grateful for the experiences of Christmas Past and Christmas Present and for the vision of a Christmas Future.

REFERENCES

Bandura, A. (1986). *Social foundations of thought and action: A social cognitive theory.* Englewood Cliffs, NJ: Prentice-Hall.

Bell, R. Q. (1968). A reinterpretation of the direction of effects in studies of socialization. *Psychological Review, 75*, 81–95.

Bereiter, C., & Bird, M. (1985). Use of thinking aloud in identification and teaching of reading comprehension strategies. *Cognition and Instruction, 2*, 91–130.

Brown, A. L., Bransford, J. P., Ferrara, R. A., & Campione, J. C. (1983). Learning, remembering, and understanding. In P. H. Mussen (Series Ed.) & J. H. Flavell & E. M. Markman (Vol. Eds.), *Handbook of child psychology: Vol. 3. Cognitive development* (pp. 177–206). New York: Wiley.

Brown, R., & Pressley, M. (1994). Self-regulated reading and getting meaning from text: The transactional strategies instruction model and its ongoing evaluation. In D. Schunk & B. Zimmerman (Eds.), *Self-regulation of learning and performance: Issues and educational applications* (pp. 155–179). Hillsdale, NJ: Lawrence Erlbaum Associates.

Cazden, C. B. (1988). *Classroom discourse.* Portsmouth, NH: Heinemann.

Duffy, G. G., & Roehler, L. R. (1987). *Improving classroom reading instruction: A decision-making approach* (2nd ed.). New York: Random House.

Duffy, G. G., Roehler, L., & Hermann, G. (1988). Modeling mental processes helps poor readers become strategic readers. *Reading Teacher, 41*, 762–767.

Duffy, G. G., Roehler, L. R., Sivan, E., Rackliffe, G., Book, C., Meloth, M., Vavrus, L. G., Wesselman, R., Putnam, J., & Bassiri, D. (1987). Effects of explaining the reasoning associated with using reading strategies. *Reading Research Quarterly, 22,* 347–368.

El-Dinary, P. B., Pressley, M., & Schuder, T. (1992). *An ethnographic study of transactional strategies instruction* (Technical report). College Park: University of Maryland, National Reading Research Center.

Flavell, J. H. (1970). Developmental studies of mediated memory. In H. W. Reese & L. P. Lipsitt (Eds.), *Advances in child development and behavior* (Vol. 5, pp. 181–211). New York: Academic Press.

Gaskins, I. W., Anderson, R. C., Pressley, M., Cunicelli, E. A., & Satlow, E. (1993). The moves strategy instruction teachers make. *Elementary School Journal, 93,* 277–304.

Gaskins, I. W., & Elliot, T. T. (1991). *The Benchmark model for teaching thinking strategies: A manual for teachers.* Cambridge, MA: Brookline Books.

Lave, J., & Wenger, E. (1991). *Situated learning: Legitimate peripheral participation.* Cambridge, England: Cambridge University Press.

Lincoln, Y. S., & Guba, E. G. (1985). *Naturalistic inquiry.* Beverly Hills, CA: Sage.

Luria, A. R. (1961). *The role of speech in the regulation of normal and abnormal behavior.* New York: Pergamon.

Luria, A. R. (1982). *Language and cognition.* New York: Wiley.

Lysynchuk, L. M., Pressley, M., D'Ailly, H., Smith, M., & Cake, H. (1989). A methodological analysis of experimental evaluations of comprehension strategy instruction. *Reading Research Quarterly, 24,* 458–470.

Lysynchuk, L. M., Pressley, M., & Vye, N. J. (1990). Reciprocal teaching improves standardized reading comprehension performance in poor grade-school comprehenders. *Elementary School Journal, 90,* 469–484.

Mastropieri, M. A., & Scruggs, T. E. (1991). *Teaching students ways to remember: Strategies for learning mnemonically.* Cambridge, MA: Brookline Books.

Mehan, H. (1979). *Learning lessons: Social organization in the classroom.* Cambridge, MA: Harvard University Press.

Meichenbaum, D. M. (1977). *Cognitive behavior modification.* New York: Plenum.

Nicholls, J. G. (1989). *The competitive ethos and democratic education.* Cambridge, MA: Harvard University Press.

Palincsar, A. S., & Brown, A. L. (1984). Reciprocal teaching of comprehension-fostering and comprehension-monitoring activities. *Cognition and Instruction, 1,* 117–175.

Paris, S. G., & Oka, E. R. (1986). Children's reading strategies, metacognition, and motivation. *Developmental Review, 6,* 25–56.

Pressley, G. M. (1976). Mental imagery helps eight-year-olds remember what they read. *Journal of Educational Psychology, 68,* 355–359.

Pressley, M. (1979). Increasing children's self-control through cognitive interventions. *Review of Educational Research, 49,* 319–370.

Pressley, M., Borkowski, J. G., & Schneider, W. (1987). Cognitive strategies: Good strategy users coordinate metacognition and knowledge. In R. Vasta & G. Whitehurst (Eds.), *Annals of child development* (Vol. 4, pp. 89–129). Greenwich, CT: JAI Press.

Pressley, M., Borkowski, J. G., & Schneider, W. (1989). Good information processing: What it is and what education can do to promote it. *International Journal of Educational Research, 13,* 857–867.

Pressley, M., El-Dinary, P. B., & Brown, R. (1992). Is good reading comprehension possible? In M. Pressley, K. R. Harris, & J. T. Guthrie (Eds.), *Promoting academic competence and literacy: Cognitive research and instructional innovation* (pp. 91–127). San Diego: Academic Press.

Pressley, M., El-Dinary, P. B., Gaskins, I. W., Schuder, T., Bergman, J. L., Almasi, J., & Brown, R. (1992). Beyond direct explanation: Transactional instruction of reading comprehension strategies. *Elementary School Journal, 92,* 513–555.

Pressley, M., El-Dinary, P. B., Marks, M. B., Brown, R., & Stein, S. (1992). Good strategy instruction is motivating and interesting. In K. A. Renninger, S. Hidi, & A. Krapp (Eds.), *The role of interest in learning and development* (pp. 333–358). Hillsdale, NJ: Lawrence Erlbaum Associates.

Pressley, M., Faculty and Administration of Summit Hall School, Almasi, J., Schuder, T., Bergman, J., Hite, S., El-Dinary, P. B., & Brown, R. (1994). Transactional instruction of comprehension strategies: The Montgomery County MD SAIL program. *Reading and Writing Quarterly, 10,* 5–19.

Pressley, M., Gaskins, I. W., Cunicelli, E. A., Burdick, N. J., Schaub-Matt, M., Lee, D. S., & Powell, N. (1991). Strategy instruction at Benchmark School: A faculty interview study. *Learning Disability Quarterly, 14,* 19–48.

Pressley, M., Gaskins, I. W., Wile, D., Cunicelli, E. A., & Sheridan, J. (1991). Teaching literacy strategies across the curriculum: A case study at Benchmark School. In J. Zutell & S. McCormick (Eds.), *Learner factors/teacher factors: Issues and literacy research and instruction* (pp. 219–228). Chicago: National Reading Conference.

Pressley, M., Goodchild, F., Fleet, J., Zajchowski, R., & Evans, E. D. (1989). The challenges of classroom strategy instruction. *Elementary School Journal, 89,* 301–342.

Pressley, M., Johnson, C. J., Symons, S., McGoldrick, J. A., & Kurita, J. (1990). Strategies that improve memory and comprehension of what is read. *Elementary School Journal, 90,* 3–32.

Pressley, M., Schuder, T., SAIL Faculty and Administration, Bergman, J. L., El-Dinary, P. B. (1992). A researcher-educator collaborative interview study of transactional comprehension strategies instruction. *Journal of Educational Psychology, 84,* 231–246.

Rosenblatt, L. M. (1978). *The reader, the text, the poem: The transactional theory of the literary work.* Carbondale: Southern Illinois University Press.

Stanovich, K. E. (1986). Matthew effects in reading: Some consequences of individual differences in the acquisition of literacy. *Reading Research Quarterly, 21,* 360–406.

Strauss, A., & Corbin, J. (1990). *Basics of qualitative research.* Newbury Park, CA: Sage.

Vygotsky, L. S. (1962). *Thought and speech.* Cambridge, MA: MIT Press.

Vygotsky, L. S. (1978). *Mind in society.* Cambridge, MA: Harvard University Press.

Wegner, D. M. (1987). Transactive memory: A contemporary analysis of the group mind. In B. Mullen & G. Goethals (Eds.), *Theories of group behavior* (pp. 185–208). New York: Springer-Verlag.

Wood, P., Bruner, J., & Ross, G. (1976). The role of tutoring in problem solving. *Journal of Child Psychology and Psychiatry, 17,* 89–100.

CHAPTER 9

Exceptional Learners and Teaching for Transfer

Judy L. Lupart
University of Calgary

One of the primary goals of education is to assist students in developing their learning potential to the maximal degree. An important assumption is that learning accomplished within the classroom will prepare the student to function independently and successfully in out-of-school contexts and particularly later in adult life. The role of the teacher is to provide instructional experiences that will not only facilitate learning but also facilitate the transfer of acquired knowledge and skills beyond the initial learning context to new circumstances and for differing purposes. This emphasis has been particularly evidenced in the recent literature on teaching for transfer, and it is generally affirmed that the study of transfer of learning has important theoretical and pedagogical implications (Butterfield & Nelson, 1989; Cormier & Hagman, 1987; Singley & Anderson, 1989).

Gagne and White (1978) proposed that learning and transfer involves a complex interaction between the learner, the original task, and the transfer task. As can be seen by a brief perusal of the chapters in this text, much of the recent research on transfer has been concentrated on the latter two components. Generally speaking, research has been focused on the in-depth analysis of teaching and/or training tasks, the degree of transfer to both similar and novel contexts, and the establishment of principles regarding effective transfer of learning. The central issues for this line of research have been earmarked by Cormier and Hagman (1987) as "(a) how transfer should be measured, (b) how training for transfer differs from training for rapid acquisition, (c) how direction and magnitude of transfer are determined, and (d) whether different principles of transfer apply to motor, cognitive, and metacognitive elements" (p. 1). Studies relevant to these issues have significantly advanced the general understanding of learning and transfer in youngsters of average intellectual ability. Nevertheless, no theory of transfer can be considered adequate without giving consideration to the interactive effects of the full range of learner characteristics and differences.

In an attempt to present a more comprehensive picture of these interactive effects in transfer of learning, the focus of this chapter is on the first component, the learner and the exceptional learner in particular. Specifically, the purpose of the present chapter is to review what is known about the development of self-regulation in atypical learners, a key aspect of the recent transfer and generalization literature.

The rationale for taking this perspective is prompted by two important field-based considerations. First, studies on transfer have consistently shown that the student's self-regulation of cognitive and metacognitive strategies is the essential factor in facilitating learning and transfer, regardless of learner characteristics or limitations. Studies on transfer with learning disabled, mentally retarded, or gifted students can extend the parameters of understanding about self-regulation development (Jenkins, 1979). Knowing more about the diversity of learner characteristics and the ways in which these characteristics can facilitate or impede the development of an individual's self-regulation ability is an important prerequisite for effective instruction. Second, recent instructional research has highlighted the key role that teachers play in facilitating transfer in children. The teacher's knowledge of transfer-promoting instructional procedures and their ability to create suitable instructional environments in the classroom are equally important factors in ensuring that students are afforded the maximal assistance in developing self-regulatory abilities. Classroom instructional applications may be strengthened by combining what is known about learning and transfer from the current literatures on both regular and exceptional learners. Moreover, current predominant movements such as school reform, school restructuring, effective schools, and inclusive education suggest an immediate urgency to merge the most powerful and effective school practices into a unified system of service delivery that better meets the needs of all students (Lipsky & Gartner, 1989; Stainback, Stainback, & Bunch, 1989).

DEVELOPMENT OF SELF-REGULATION
IN ATYPICAL LEARNERS

Recent work on transfer and learning has documented the central importance of promoting self-regulation in learners and its positive effects on academic achievement and transfer to other contexts both in and out of school contexts (Pressley, Harris, & Guthrie, 1992; Whitman, 1990; Zimmerman & Schunk, 1989). Zimmerman (1989) pointed out that although there are several theoretical perspectives for studying self-regulated learning, they all share a proactive view of the learner in which proponents "seek to explain and describe how a particular learner will learn and achieve despite apparent limitations in mental ability (as traditionally assessed), social environmental background, or in quality of schooling" (p. 4). Features common to all self-regulation theories include: (a) the purposive use of specific processes, strategies, or responses by students to improve their academic achievement; (b) a self-oriented feedback loop during learning; (c) a description of how and why students choose to use a particular self-regulated process, strategy, or response; and (d) an interest in examining why students do not self-regulate during all learning experiences (pp. 4–5). Research efforts in this area have had a profound impact on the ways we view learning potential, particularly as it relates to student exceptionality. The following sections will highlight the important new directions this work has instigated. Themes included here are: (a) dynamic versus static views of the learner; (b) all students can and need to learn to self-regulate; (c) how exceptional learners are different from other learners; and (d) motivation and positive attitudes foster self-regulated learning.

Dynamic Versus Static Views of the Learner

Intelligence tests have been fundamental to the categorization and instructional segregation of exceptional learners. Their use in schools has been based on the assumption that IQ differences reflect variations in students' ability to learn and to transfer learning (Campione, Brown, Ferrara, Jones, & Steinberg, 1985). Accordingly, the concept of intelligence and its assessment has dominated both theory construction and educational practice as it relates to the diagnosis of mental retardation, learning disability, and giftedness (Day & Borkowski, 1987). The basic assumption is that measured mental ability on standardized tests is broadly associated with academic achievement potential and remains relatively stable over one's lifetime. Thus, low scores may be causally associated with permanent structural limitations or defects that are presumed to be essentially unchangeable. Accordingly, instruction can be tailored to accommodate presumed ability limitations. However, such static approaches to learning assessment tap only what an individual knows, providing a snapshot of isolated, decontextualized learning acquired by the individual. As Brown, Bransford, Ferrara, and Campione (1983) astutely suggested, although static measures of acquired learning tell us something about a person's level of expertise in a specified area, they offer very little information about what an individual can learn and how he goes about regulating his own learning.

In contrast, dynamic approaches assume that learning is not something that resides solely within the individual. Individuals are not passive recipients of the knowledge, skills, and strategies they have been exposed to. Rather, the child is seen to be an active, self-regulating learner who is intrinsically motivated through self-discovery and successful learning experiences. Dynamic approaches are focused on what an individual can learn by examining how learning resources are self-regulated in and across learning situations. This shift in focus brings us much closer to the actual teaching and learning situation where the interactive effects of learner abilities and instructional procedures are in constant, dynamic fluctuation.

Brown et al. (1983) asserted that both static and dynamic approaches to transfer are important to a comprehensive understanding of instructional effects and intelligence. Constructive theories of intelligence require *both* the specification of "the processes involved in intellectual functioning *and* the extent to which individuals differ with regard to those processes" (Campione, Brown, & Ferrara, 1982, p. 395). Recent divergent, in-depth examinations of intelligence and mental retardation (Campione et al., 1982), giftedness (Sternberg & Davidson, 1986), and the dimensions and diagnosis of learning disability (Kavale, Forness, & Bender, 1987) have been important in establishing a broadly based understanding of the scope and variety of characteristics that distinguish these subgroups in terms of their associated intellectual competence. Nevertheless, these and the associated voluminous literatures have created substantial inconsistencies and confusion among the educators who work with these students, particularly in the areas of diagnosis and educational practice (Day & Borkowski, 1987). One way to bring balance to both theoretical and practical concerns, and concomitantly advance our understanding of these three areas of exceptionality, is to consider the convergent analysis of research that focuses on the dynamic assessment of self-regulation and learning potential in exceptional children (Butterfield & Ferretti, 1987). In this regard, Day and Borkowski (1987) and Campione and Brown (1978) and Campione et al. (1982) noted the importance of distinguishing the biologically linked components of intelligence, such as memory and perception (referred to as the *architectural system*), and the environmentally influenced *executive system* that regulates learning propensity, and the interactive effects of the two systems. Day and Borkowski (1987) noted that the executive system is directly associated with strategic, adaptive learning that accrues from instruction and formalized training. The very fact that exceptional learners, mentally disabled or gifted, vary considerably within these traditionally defined subgroups, using almost any indicator of success from academic achievement to job satisfaction, suggests that category-based assumptions and quantitative indexes of mental ability need to be balanced with assessments of how an individual learns and how self-regulated learning can be promoted. For educators, the distinction is particularly relevant and powerful: Their guiding concern is not whether a student having difficulty in the classroom is mentally handicapped or learning disabled, but if the learning environment they have created maximizes the student's self-regulated learning. Knowing something about the learning limitations and abilities of students at the extremes can generate a better understanding of how this mix fosters intelligent behavior.

All Students Can and Need to Learn to Self-Regulate

There has been a virtual sea of research activity carried out in the past two decades aimed at charting the course of self-regulation development and the instructional conditions that promote this development. Early efforts were focused on the training of schoollike tasks and assessing the degree and distance of transfer effects. A tetrahedral model of learning and transfer, initially proposed by Jenkins (1979) and later adapted by Brown et al. (1983) provided a useful framework for this work. This "learner-in-context" perspective (Lupart, 1989) assumes the collective and interactive influence of four factors central to any learning situation: (a) characteristics of the learner (e.g., IQ, motivation); (b) learning activities (e.g., subordinate and superordinate cognitions, Butterfield & Ferretti, 1987); (c) nature of the materials (e.g., conceptual difficulty, sequencing); and (d) criterial tasks (e.g., the measures used to assess learning effectiveness). The systematic analysis of these interactive effects with exceptional learner subgroups has yielded a solid foundation for the generation of the current complex models of transfer and self-regulation.

For example, studies with educable mentally retarded (EMR) students (Belmont & Butterfield, 1977; Brown, Campione, & Murphy, 1977) have shown that intensive, explicit instruction results in improved strategic memory performance and that such training effects are maintained long after initial training. However, when these students are exposed to novel tasks in which the same trained strategies would be useful, they fail to utilize them. This finding led researchers to a reexamination of instructional procedures, and ultimately to the notion that generalization of training might best be focused on general metacognitive skills applicable to a wide variety of problem-solving and schoollike tasks. Thus, training emphasis was given to improving the EMR students' ability to orchestrate and control their own attempts at using performance-enhancing strategies such as self-interrogation. However, initial research attempts utilizing this approach (Brown, Campione, & Barclay, 1979) resulted in limited success in promoting generalization in EMR students. Nevertheless, continued research, analysis, and manipulation of the key variables of the tetrahedron and instructional conditions eventually resulted in increased transfer on schoollike tasks and promulgated further research efforts in self-control and self-management processes as key factors in the transfer and generalization of learning (Brown, Campione, & Day, 1981; Campione, Brown, & Bryant, 1985). Building from these early studies in one area of exceptionality, and synthesizing transfer research from other areas of exceptionality and differing levels of student expertise, researchers have been able to piece together a comprehensive picture of the key characteristics that distinguish more and less successful learners (Borkowski, Schneider, & Pressley, 1989; Brown & Campione, 1986a; Brown et al., 1981; Campione, Brown, & Bryant, 1985; Campione, Brown, Ferrara, Jones, & Steinberg, 1985; Jackson & Butterfield, 1986; Sugden & Newall, 1987). Most important is the consistent finding that although students differ substantially in terms of the *architectural systems* that limit or enhance overall learning propensity, *executive systems* can be markedly improved through effective instructional intervention to promote intelligent behavior and school achievement.

As researchers learn more about the performance-enhancing and self-regulatory aspects of learning, more comprehensive and sophisticated models of these important processes have been generated (Borkowski & Muthukrishna, 1992; Borkowski et al., 1989; Borkowski & Turner, 1990). While these and other developing models continue to be refined by new research, it remains essential for educators to approach intervention and instruction with the view that students can learn, use, and ultimately self-regulate learning and that the independent utilization of newly learned strategies and metacognitive routines underscores an individual's ability to make transfer to new learning situations. Learning and transfer are interdependent processes in the sense that both what is learned and how it is learned influence whether or not previous learning is transferred and/or generalized in different or novel learning situations. The comparative study of individual differences among children with exceptional learning needs (Borkowski & Day, 1987; Campione et al., 1982) is aimed at delineating the extent to which these students experience particular problems or success with learning and/or transfer, and to specify those sources of comparative differences that are most prominent. As a result of these efforts, our current understanding of the learning characteristics typical of different exceptional groups has been substantially broadened and deepened.

How Exceptional Learners Are Different From Other Learners

A recognition that exceptional students have unique learning needs has underscored the provision of special education in the majority of Canadian and U.S. schools. However, recent school reform initiatives, particularly inclusive education, have placed increasing emphasis on meeting the needs of all students in the regular classroom (Andrews & Lupart, 1993; Lipsky & Gartner, 1989; Stainback et al., 1989). Consequently, it will be increasingly important for all educators to become familiar with the knowledge base that has guided special education in the past. Research carried out over the past 2 decades has served to delineate important architectural and executive system characteristics of mentally handicapped, learning disabled, and gifted learners, which are outlined in the following segments.

Students Who Are Mentally Retarded. Butterfield and Ferretti (1987) outlined five key factors emerging from the recent developmental and comparative research that collectively suggest that children assessed as having less intelligence are seen as follows:

1. to have smaller memory capacities or less efficient working memory;
2. to have smaller and less elaborately organized knowledge bases;
3. to use fewer, simpler, and more passive processing strategies;
4. to have less metacognitive understanding of their own cognitive systems and how the functioning of these systems depends on the environment; and
5. to use less complete and flexible processes for controlling their thinking. (pp. 195–196)

Recognizing the consistent pattern of access inflexibility demonstrated by these individuals, Brown and Campione (1986b) raised two key points that might guide training and transfer efforts: (a) the significance of the change, in the sense that the learning truly contributes to the improved functioning of the individual on important academic and everyday life tasks; and (b) the durability of the learning, in the sense that an individual continues to demonstrate competence in applying new learning over an extended period of time. For students who are mentally handicapped, self-regulation training will require extensive, prolonged instructional intervention using multiple tasks and materials in multiple contexts, explanations about the utility of using a trained strategy or executive procedure, and guided instruction in general self-management skills (Day & Hall, 1988). Mapping out the precise interactive factors of knowledge base, strategic and executive functioning, formalized versus everyday learning, and ways to promote flexible access are important investigative inroads to a complete understanding of the development of self-regulation in mentally handicapped children (Campione et al., 1982).

Students Who Are Gifted. At the other extreme of the intelligence continuum, gifted students have typically been viewed as being exceptionally competent in all learning-related dimensions. Not surprisingly, research on transfer with highly able students has shown them to be particularly adept at self-managing their learning and, consequently, more capable of profiting from a given learning situation than less able students do. In situations were instruction is incomplete they have the resources to fill in the gaps because they know more about themselves as learners. Campione, Brown, and Bryant (1985) identified a number of executive routines, such as planning, monitoring their own learning progress, appropriate deployment of effort, and knowing how and when to seek advice, that contribute to their learning competence and their self-understanding of how they are learning. When faced with new learning situations, they effectively integrate past learning to the present situation and anticipate the utility of doing so for future learning situations. These collective characteristics figure prominently in comparative research, which documents the fact that gifted students typically learn more quickly, transfer learning more broadly and spontaneously, and maintain knowledge or strategy use over longer periods of time than average and less able learners, even when respondents are initially equated on pretest performance and mental age (Campione, Brown, Ferrara, et al., 1985; Ferrara, Brown, & Campione, 1986; Ferretti & Butterfield, 1992).

Guided by an interest in what distinguishes able learners in everyday class-rooms, Meichenbaum and Biemillar (1992) found that these students excelled in the same dimensions that have been observed in expert studies; they typically were observed to:

1. access and employ declarative, procedural, and elaborative knowledge
2. evidence metacognitive behaviors (defining or labeling tasks, planning, monitoring, and evaluating)
3. emit more preparatory, deliberate, and sustained scripted behaviors
4. be motivated to achieve . . .
5. have others (teachers and peers) interact with them in ways that nurture, exercise, and reinforce their metacognitive skills. (p. 16)

General learning characteristics aside, it cannot be assumed that all individuals who score high on IQ tests will become high achieving, self-regulating learners. The current literature (i.e., Lupart, 1992; Richert, 1991; Rimm, 1991) has revealed an alarming number of subgroups of gifted students who are at risk for a variety of reasons ranging from underachievement and cultural background to more serious school-related factors such as inappropriate identification practices that systematically favor students who achieve high academic ratings. Moreover, research studies on gifted learners and transfer (Muir-Broaddus & Coyle, 1991) have shown that qualitative differences in strategy use and transfer are reliably associated with student performance and achievement.

A plausible resolution of these inconsistencies has been suggested by Jackson and Butterfield (1986) who proposed a view of giftedness as an attribute of performance as opposed to the traditional view of giftedness as an attribute of a person. Hence, "gifted performances are instances of excellent performance on any task that has practical value or theoretical interest" (p. 155). This perspective is meant to offset the limitations inherent in research that is framed by a view of giftedness as a trait and the concomitant belief that giftedness is stable across situations and over long periods of time. They assert that an examination of the literature concerning cognitive efficiency, knowledge, strategy use, and metacognition yields some useful hypotheses about cognitive performances responsible for gifted performance and provides a testable framework for future research directions. Specifically, Jackson and Butterfield (1986) proposed that "we do not know whether (or in what contexts) some of these processing components are more important than others, how the developmental origins of each might differ, or how the components interact with one another during problem solving" (p. 177). Moving toward a view of giftedness as an attribute of performance would be compatible with the work of many leading researchers (Campione, Brown, Ferrara, et al., 1985; Ferrara et al., 1986; Meichenbaum & Biemiller, 1992) and appears to be a promising direction for advancing a more complete understanding of self-regulation development.

Students Who Are Learning Disabled. The learning disability field had been recently riddled with controversy concerning the theoretical utility of reductionist versus constructivist approaches toward learning characteristics and transfer. The constructivist view of the child as an active, self-regulating learner who is intrinsically motivated through self-discovery has been contrasted with the reductionist view, which depicts the child as a passive recipient of knowledge who acquires new information in isolated, decontextualized bits that have been hierarchically sequenced from basic elementary information processing to advanced, complex problem solving (Poplin, 1988). The latter perspective has been criticized on the grounds that it runs counter to recent advances in transfer theory highlighting the self-regulatory basis of human learning and development, and consequently has outlived its utility as a dominant framework for learning disability research. Others (Harris & Pressley, 1991; Resnick, 1987) have argued against this kind of false dichotomizing, emphasizing instead the critical need for an integration of instructivist and constructivist views for any meaningful advancement of theories of transfer. A balance of carefully assessed educational interventions that maximize the child's ability to construct accurate knowledge and to self-manage powerful learning acquisition procedures would appear most promising. Accordingly, Jackson and Butterfield (1986) and Butterfield and Ferretti (1987) suggested that the most judicious future research direction would be to generally view intelligence as a property of performance in which "the study of all manners of expertise . . . and its instruction would become a part of the study of intelligent action, so that the range of skills that we could aspire to teach to special children would be wonderfully expanded" (p. 228).

The learning difficulties of children who are categorized as learning disabled can be distinguished from other students' on the basis of typical patterns of school performance (Sugden, 1989). First, they do not reach the same level of achievement as their same-age peers in certain academic subject areas, predominantly mathematics and reading. Second, they do not present the typical learning pattern of rapid acquisition at first with a gradual slowing as learning progresses. Instead, students with learning difficulties will show very slow initial learning, with a subsequent increase in learning rate. Finally, these students often fail to generalize or transfer learning to new situations. Significant advances in the field of learning disability have been made through the systematic study of these students in a wide variety of learning and transfer research studies. These advances are due to an important and fundamental shift in focus from the determination of performance differences and limitations to an emphasis on the instructional conditions that facilitate performance improvement (Brown & Campione, 1986a). Research emphasis shifted from the search for the global "deficit" areas underlying all cognitive processing to the notion that performance may be situation specific and might change substantially depending on the interactive effects of task demands and student ability. For example, on the basis of their research with learning disabled students, Sugden and Newall (1987) surmised that there may be limits to the transfer that can be generated to a particular class of events, and tasks requiring different cognitive skill focus. In other words, the specific strategy taught was transferable and generalizable to tasks within the same class of events, which depended primarily on that particular cognitive skill, even for more difficult tasks. Studies such as these have made an important contribution to the general transfer literature in documenting and mapping out the instructional conditions necessary to achieve successful performance and transfer in numerous cognitive processing and subject area domains. Moreover, Brown and Campione (1986) suggested that on the basis of the past 15 years of research on reading comprehension, there is sufficient understanding of the components and processes necessary for effective performance to pinpoint the particular difficulties of a given child and to translate this knowledge into instructional or remedial intervention.

Using their model of "Components of Good Information Processing," Borkowski et al. (1989) suggested that the three primary factors associated with the information processing and transfer problems of learning disabled students are: neurological impairments; deficiencies in general world knowledge; and negative beliefs, attitudes, and styles that limit self-efficacy. The proportionate influence and critical degree of difficulty of each of these factors as defining attributes of learning disability is at best speculative and controversial at present. Even though this brings educators much closer to an educationally relevant diagnosis of a child's learning problems, the focus and presentation of instruction needs to be thoroughly assessed for age relevance, concreteness versus abstraction, and, most importantly, teacher-directed versus student-centered learning. As Borkowski et al. suggested, we may not be able to produce "good" information processors out of LD students, but ample evidence suggests that they can certainly become "better" information processors through effective teacher assessment and instructional mediation. Indeed, Harris and Pressley (1991) noted that several studies in self-instructional strategy development have been successful in improving the reading comprehension, written language, and mathematical problem-solving skills for students with learning disabilities.

Motivation and Positive Attitudes Foster Self-Regulated Learning

It is becoming increasingly evident that self-regulatory development is dependent on dimensions beyond knowledge acquisition, strategic and executive performance, and intellectual ability. The combination of the learner's beliefs and attitudes about himself, attributional beliefs, and characteristic learning styles have been found to interact significantly with an individual's self-esteem development and other motivational components considered necessary for school achievement and the actualization of learning potential (Borkowski et al., 1989; Borkowski & Turner, 1990; Carr, 1990; Covington, 1987; Ellis, Lenz, & Sabornie, 1987a, 1987b; Zimmerman, 1989). Negative self-held beliefs about innate abilities, dysfunctional attributional beliefs about their self-control over academic achievement, and a lack of effort and persistence on tasks that require cognitive effort contribute significantly to an ability to generalize in learners of all ability levels. These kinds of self-perceptions and attributional beliefs "are deeply embedded within cultural and familial contexts and are often reinforced by parents' and teachers' interpretations of the causes of academic successes and failures" (Borkowski et al., 1989, p. 178). For students having a long history of failure in school (i.e., learning disabled and mentally retarded), initial learning problems and related slow development of self-regulatory abilities, may be significantly compounded by teachers who may have inappropriate expectations. As noted by Covington (1987): "To demand too much of any child, either retarded or gifted, relative to his or her developing skills and abilities is to invite a disruption of the processes that led to a willingness to learn, to strive, and to persist" (pp. 199–200). Contemporary studies with low-achieving youngsters (Borkowski & Turner, 1990; Carr & Borkowski, 1989; Cullen, 1985; Reid & Borkowski, 1987) have shown that children vary considerably in the ways that they cope with classroom failure, and that instructional interventions that combine both new strategy learning and attributional retraining are important precursors to significant performance gains that are maintained and generalized to other classroom activities. On the basis of a comprehensive review of preliminary work in this area, Borkowski and Turner (1990) concluded that executive processes and attributional beliefs are the critical, bidirectional interactive components that promote generalized problem-solving across domains. Moreover, they asserted that "these attributional beliefs are both the *consequences* of repeated strategy use (and corresponding feedback conditions) and the *causes* of problem seeking, strategy selection, and monitoring behaviors. In this sense, attributions arise from lower level skills but inspire higher level executive processes" (p. 173). Although the intricacies of how positive self-esteem, an internal locus of control, and effort-related attributional beliefs about school-related success and failure are just beginning to be explored, early indications are that these "motivational factors play key roles in 'spontaneous' strategy use by providing incentives necessary for deploying strategies, especially on challenging transfer tasks that are at the extremes of a domain, or perhaps in different domains" (p. 169). As researchers continue their work in unraveling these important transsituational characteristics, educators must be encouraged to incorporate these findings into their instructional interventions in regular and special education classrooms.

CONCLUSION

The past two decades of research in teaching for transfer have significantly advanced educational theory and practice. Associated research with exceptional learners has extended the scope and depth of transfer theories, and it has directed the attention of general transfer theorists to the important dimension of learner differences and the interactive effects this dimension plays in the teaching of any new information, strategy, or process. Research with students who are mentally handicapped, learning disabled, and gifted has revealed that despite fundamental differences in innate abilities that substantially delimit or enhance student learning, self-regulation—the critical element to improved performance potential—is a viable teaching goal for each of these exceptional learner subgroups. Moreover, the research in systematic instructional intervention that was necessary to achieve this result, particularly for mildly and moderately handicapped students, has generated new ways of thinking about assessment and instructional intervention that have potential utility for all students. By incorporating current transfer and teaching models and practices into inclusive classrooms, the eventual transition of schools from separate systems of regular and special education into a unified system of education may be substantially and effectively facilitated.

REFERENCES

Andrews, J., & Lupart, J. L. (1993). *The inclusive classroom: Educating exceptional children.* Scarborough, Ontario: Nelson.

Belmont, J. M., & Butterfield, E. C. (1977). The instructional approach to developmental cognitive research. In R. V. Kail, Jr., & J. W. Hagen (Eds.), *Perspectives on the development of memory and cognition* (pp. 437–481). Hillsdale, NJ: Lawrence Erlbaum Associates.

Borkowski, J. G., & Day, J. D. (Eds.). (1987). *Cognition in special children: Comparative approaches to retardation, learning disabilities, and giftedness.* Norwood, NJ: Ablex.

Borkowski, J. G., & Muthukrishna, N. (1992). Moving metacognition into the classroom: "Working models" and effective strategy teaching. In M. Pressley, K. R. Harris, & J. T. Guthrie (Eds.), *Promoting academic competence and literacy in school* (pp. 477–501). San Diego, CA: Academic Press.

Borkowski, J. G., Schneider, W., & Pressley, M. (1989). The challenges of teaching good information processing to learning disabled students. *International Journal of Disability, Development and Education, 36*(3), 169–185.

Borkowski, J. G., & Turner, L. A. (1990). Transsituational characteristics of metacognition. In W. Schneider & F. E. Weinert (Eds.), *Interactions among aptitudes, strategies, and knowledge in cognitive performance* (pp. 15–48). Norwood, NJ: Ablex.

Brown, A. L., Bransford, J. D., Ferrara, R. A., & Campione, J. C. (1983). Learning, remembering, and understanding. In P. H. Mussen (Series Ed.) & J. H. Flavell & E. M. Markman (Vol. Eds.), *Handbook of child psychology: Vol. 1. Cognitive development* (pp. 78–168). New York: Wiley.

Brown, A. L., & Campione, J. C. (1986a). Psychological theory and the study of learning disabilities. *American Psychologist, 41*(10), 1059–1068.

Brown, A. L., & Campione, J. C. (1986b). Training for Transfer: Guidelines for promoting flexible use of trained skills. In M. G. Wade (Ed.), *Motor skill acquisition of the mentally retarded* (pp. 257–271). Amsterdam: North Holland.

Brown, A. L., Campione, J. C., & Barclay, C. R. (1979). Training self-checking routines for estimating test readiness: Generalization from list learning to prose recall. *Child Development, 50*, 501–512.

Brown, A. L., Campione, J. C., & Day, J. D. (1981). Learning to learn: On training students to learn from text. *Educational Researcher, 19*, 14–21.

Brown, A. L., Campione, J. C., & Murphy, M. D. (1977). Maintenance and generalization of trained metamnemonic awareness in educable retarded children. *Journal of Experimental Child Psychology, 24*, 191–211.

Butterfield, E. C., & Ferretti, R. P. (1987). Toward a theoretical integration of cognitive hypotheses about intellectual differences among children. In J. G. Borkowski & J. D. Day (Eds.), *Cognition in special children: Approaches to retardation, learning disabilities, and giftedness* (pp. 195–234). Norwood, NJ: Ablex.

Butterfield, E. C., & Nelson, G. D. (1989). Theory and practice of teaching for transfer, *ETR&D, 37*(3), 5–38.

Campione, J., & Brown, A. L. (1978). Toward a theory of intelligence: Contributions from research with retarded children. *Intelligence, 2*, 279–304.

Campione, J. C., Brown, A. L., & Bryant, N. R. (1985). Individual differences in learning and memory. In R. J. Sternberg (Ed.), *Human abilities: An information processing approach* (pp. 392–483). New York: Freeman.

Campione, J. C., Brown, A. L., & Ferrara, R. A. (1982). Mental retardation and intelligence. In R. J. Sternberg (Ed.), *Handbook of human intelligence* (pp. 392–492). Cambridge, England: Cambridge University Press.

Campione, J. C., Brown, A. I., Ferrara, R. A., Jones, R. S., & Steinberg, E. (1985). Breakdowns in flexible use of information: Intelligence-related differences in transfer following equivalent learning performance. *Intelligence, 9*, 297–315.

Carr, M., & Borkowski, J. G. (1989). Attributional retraining and the generalization of reading strategies by underachievers. *Human Learning and Individual Differences, 1*, 201–218.

Cormier, S. M., & Hagman, J. D. (Eds.). (1987). *Transfer of learning: Contemporary research and applications.* San Diego: Academic Press.

Covington, M. V. (1987). Achievement motivation, self-attributions, and exceptionality. In J. Day & J. G. Borkowski (Eds.), *Intelligence and exceptionality: New directions for theory, assessment, and instructional practices* (pp. 173–214). Norwood, NJ: Ablex.

Cullen, J. L. (1985). Children's ability to cope with failure: Implications of a metacognitive approach for the classroom. In D. L. Forrest-Pressley, G. E. MacKinnon, & T. G. Waller (Eds.), *Metacognition, cognition, and human performance* (Vol. 2, pp. 267–300). Orlando, FL: Academic Press.

Day, J. D., & Borkowski, J. G. (1987). The concept of intelligence in diagnosis, theory construction, and educational practice. In J. Day & J. G. Borkowski (Eds.), *Intelligence and exceptionality: New directions for theory, assessment, and instructional practices* (pp. 3–18). Norwood, NJ: Ablex.

Day, J. D., & Hall, L. K. (1988). Intelligence related differences in learning and transfer and enhancement of transfer among mentally retarded persons. *American Journal of Mental Retardation, 93*, 125–137.

Ferrara, R. A., Brown, A. L., & Campione, J. C. (1986). Children's learning and transfer of inductive reasoning rules: Studies of proximal development. *Child Development, 57*, 1087–1099.

Ferretti, R. P., & Butterfield, E. C. (1992). Intelligence-related differences in the learning, maintenance, and transfer of problem-solving strategies. *Intelligence, 16*, 207–223.

Gagne, R. M., & White, R. T. (1978). Memory structures and learning outcomes. *Review of Education Research, 48*, 187–222.

Harris, K. R., & Pressley, M. (1991). The nature of cognitive strategy instruction: Interactive strategy construction. *Exceptional Children, 57*, 392–404.

Jackson, N. E., & Butterfield, E. C. (1986). A conception of giftedness to promote research. In R. Sternberg & J. E. Davidson (Eds.), *Conceptions of giftedness* (pp. 151–181). Cambridge: Cambridge University Press.

Jenkins, J. J. (1979). Four points to remember: A tetrahedral model of memory experiments. In L. S. Cermak & F. I. M. Craik (Eds.), *Levels of processing in human processing* (pp. 429–446). Hillsdale, NJ: Lawrence Erlbaum Associates.

Kavale, K. A., Forness, S. R., & Bender, M. (Eds.). (1987). *Handbook of learning disabilities: Vol. 1. Dimensions and diagnosis.* Boston: Little, Brown.

Lipsky, D. K., & Gartner, A. G. (1989). Building the future. In D. K. Lipsky & A. G. Gartner (Eds.), *Beyond separate education: Quality education for all* (pp. 255–290). Baltimore, MD: Paul H. Brookes.

Lupart, J. L. (1989). An in-depth assessment model for gifted/learning disabled students. *Canadian Journal of Special Education, 6*(1), 1–14.

Lupart, J. L. (1992). The hidden gifted: Current state of knowledge and future research directions. In F. J. Monks & W. A. M. Peters (Eds.), *Talent for the future* (pp. 177–190). The Netherlands: Van Gorcum & Comp.

Miechenbaum, D., & Biemiller, A. (1992). In search of student expertise in the classroom: A metacognitive analysis. In M. Pressley, K. R. Harris, & J. T. Guthrie (Eds.), *Promoting academic competence and literacy in school* (pp. 3–56). San Diego, CA: Academic Press.

Muir-Broaddus, J., & Coyle, T. (1991, April). *Effects of giftedness and achievement on the training and transfer of a strategy for solving analogies.* Paper presented at the biennial meeting of the Society for Research in Child Development, Seattle, WA.

Poplin, M. S. (1988). The reductionist fallacy in learning disabilities: Replicating the past by reducing the present. *Journal of Learning Disabilities, 21*(7), 389–400.

Pressley, M., Harris, K. R., & Guthrie, J. T. (Eds.). (1992). *Promoting academic competence and literacy in school.* San Diego, CA: Academic Press.

Reid, M. K., & Borkowski, J. G. (1987). Causal attributions of hyperactive children: Implications for training strategies and self-control. *Journal of Educational Psychology, 79,* 296–307.

Resnick, L. B. (1987). Constructing knowledge in school. In L. S. Liben (Ed.), *Development and learning: Conflict or congruence?* (pp. 19–50). Hillsdale, NJ: Lawrence Erlbaum Associates.

Richert, E. S. (1991). Rampant problems and promising practices in identification. In N. Colangelo & G. A. Davis (Eds.), *Handbook of gifted education* (pp. 81–96). Boston, MA: Allyn & Bacon.

Rimm, S. B. (1991). Underachievement and superachievement: Flip sides of the same coin. In N. Colangelo & G. A. Davis (Eds.), *Handbook of gifted education* (pp. 328–344). Boston, MA: Allyn & Bacon.

Singley, M. K., & Anderson, J. R. (1989). *The transfer of cognitive skill.* Cambridge, MA: Harvard University Press.

Stainback, W., Stainback, S., & Bunch, G. (1989). Introduction and historical background. In S. Stainback, W. Stainback, & M. Forest (Eds.), *Educating all students in the mainstream of regular education* (pp. 3–26). Baltimore, MD: Paul H. Brookes.

Sternberg, R. J., & Davidson, J. E. (Eds.). (1986). *Conceptions of giftedness.* Cambridge: Cambridge University Press.

Sugden, D. A. (Ed.). (1989). *Cognitive approaches in special education.* London: The Falmer Press.

Sugden, D. A., & Newall, M. (1987). Teaching transfer strategies to children with moderate learning difficulties. *British Journal of Special Education, 14,* 63–67.

Whitman, T. L. (1990). Self-regulation and mental retardation. *American Journal of Mental Retardation, 94*(4), 347–362.

Zimmerman, B. J. (1989). A social cognitive view of self-regulated academic learning. *Journal of Educational Psychology, 81*(3), 329–339.

Zimmerman, B. J., & Schunk, D. H. (Eds.). (1989). *Self-regulated learning and academic achievement: Theory, research, and practice.* New York: Springer-Verlag.

Author Index

Page numbers in *italics* denote complete bibliographical references.

229

Subject Index